Praise for *The Relationship Inventory: A Complete Resource and Guide*

"This is a book that provides all you need to know about measuring perceptions in a relationship. Barrett-Lennard has given us a tour de force of the history and development of The Barrett-Lennard Relationship Inventory which has been internationally recognized for its broad empirical support, strong theoretical development, and practical applications. This work launches the study of the relationship conditions into new territory and provides a significant contribution to the study of human relationships."

Leslie S. Greenberg, Distinguished Research Professor Emeritus, York University, Canada

"Godfrey Barrett-Lennard's Relationship Inventory has had remarkable impact and staying power. This book explains why: a strong conceptual basis, careful cycles of item selection and crafting, alternating with validation studies, and a continuing interest in conceptual elaboration and empirical diversification. This book traces the Inventory's continuing development from its grounding in Carl Rogers's conceptualization of the therapeutic relationship, through a series of revision and validation studies, to application in a variety of clinical and educational settings. There is much history here, but also reviews of current work, copies of Inventory forms adapted for a variety of specific research and clinical situations, and proposals for future research directions."

William B. Stiles, Miami University and Appalachian State University

"This is an indispensable book for all those interested in the therapeutic relationship. Furthermore it covers the author's exciting new work on the idea of the 'contextual self' – the idea that our selves have multiple aspects – an idea gaining momentum in psychology at the present time. Overall it traces the history of the development and use of the Barrett-Lennard Relationship Inventory, surely one of the two or three most widely used instruments for measuring facilitative therapeutic relationship conditions. It provides detailed information on the use of the BLRI, and training exercises based on using it. It also covers its use in other fields such as education, with families, groups and organizations, and medical practice. It is highly recommended for psychotherapy researchers, students of psychotherapy, and researchers in other fields that involve the relationship."

Arthur C. Bohart, PhD, Professor Emeritus, California State University Dominguez Hills

"The Relationship Inventory brings to life the origins of the research on psychotherapy as we know it today, rooted in one of the most enduring common factors of the psychotherapy literature: Therapeutic relationships can facilitate personal growth. It also points to the future of our understanding of who we are as persons in all of life's contexts, increasingly diverse yet embedded in a vast array of (inter-) relationships. The Barrett-Lennard Relationship Inventory family of assessments occupies a unique space from the past to the future and from the diversity within each of us to the interconnections between all of us. The Relationship Inventory provides full access to more than a dozen distinct instruments to measure relationship in nearly any context from the most intimate through the professional to the societal. This book truly is a remarkable resource and a testimony to the enduring process to understand and improve life through both relationships and science. We all can be grateful for it as a contribution."

Jeffrey H. D. Cornelius-White, PsyD, Missouri State University

The Relationship Inventory

A Complete Resource and Guide

Godfrey T. Barrett-Lennard

WILEY Blackwell

This edition first published 2015
© 2015 John Wiley & Sons, Ltd.

Registered Office
John Wiley & Sons, Ltd, The Atrium, Southern Gate, Chichester, West Sussex, PO19 8SQ, UK

Editorial Offices
350 Main Street, Malden, MA 02148-5020, USA
9600 Garsington Road, Oxford, OX4 2DQ, UK
The Atrium, Southern Gate, Chichester, West Sussex, PO19 8SQ, UK

For details of our global editorial offices, for customer services, and for information about how to apply for permission to reuse the copyright material in this book please see our website at www.wiley.com/wiley-blackwell.

The right of Godfrey T. Barrett-Lennard to be identified as the author of this work has been asserted in accordance with the UK Copyright, Designs and Patents Act 1988.

Library of Congress Cataloging-in-Publication Data

Barrett-Lennard, Godfrey T.
    The relationship inventory : a complete resource and guide / Godfrey T. Barrett-Lennard.
        pages   cm
    Includes bibliographical references and index.
    ISBN 978-1-118-78882-0 (pbk.)
 1. Interpersonal relations.   I. Title.
    HM1106.B3727 2015
    302–dc23

                                                            2014021357

A catalogue record for this book is available from the British Library.

Cover image: © David Clapp / Getty Images

Set in 10.5/13pt Sabon by SPi Publisher Services, Pondicherry, India

Printed in Singapore by C.O.S. Printers Pte Ltd

1   2015

Contents

Preface

I always have been interested in journeys of ideas and methods and in continuities over time and changing circumstances. As example, the subtitle "Journey and substance" aptly headed an earlier book (Barrett-Lennard, 1998). One perspective on *this* book is that it is a story unfolding over six decades. In1956, just at the time I was ready to choose a topic for my doctoral research, Carl Rogers circulated one of his *most seminal* papers to colleagues in his laboratory Counselling Centre. It was a formulation that he had approached step-by-step in his writing over ten years, and was a ground-breaking articulation of how therapeutic change happens. I knew at once that I wanted to somehow put this theory to the test and could see that this would require invention of an instrument to measure the indicated qualities of therapist-to-client relationship. Thus was born what I called, simply, the Relationship Inventory. The whole saga of research, thought, and development that followed, and continues to unfold, is largely what this book now presents.

I first conceived of sharing this journey and its products in book form a dozen years ago, but there were other priorities to pursue first – including my most recent volume *The Relationship Paradigm* (2013). I'm retired now from most professional activity and, once able to focus on this present work, it did not take too long. Several main reports over the years, including the monograph flowing from my doctoral research and a long handbook article in the mid-1980s, were repositories of information that I could draw on in writing Chapters 2, 3, and 4. Nothing that I had already written could be used as it stood, apart from many of the research questionnaires gathered together in Appendix 1. Six of the nine chapters were newly written for this work.

The Relationship Inventory came to be called the BLRI by other users, a shorthand name that I finally adopted too. As readers will see, it isn't a single instrument but a "system" or large family of closely inter-related questionnaire forms – and this variety continues with the inclusion of experimental versions presented for the first time in this book. In basic and adapted forms the instrument quite quickly came to be used in diverse contexts and with varied purpose. In addition to study of the therapist–client relationship, relationships between teacher and student, between couples or parents and children, and between member person and group were investigated at an early stage. Supervisory relationships became a focus, third-person observers provided BLRI data in some studies, investigation of nurse–patient empathy has drawn numerous uses, and there have been resourceful endeavors to isolate ways that perceiver characteristics enter into their discrimination of relationship qualities.

Developed but "underused" forms of the BLRI include a multi-relation form to study life relational environments *and* a version to study micro-systems of relationship as a whole (e.g., how couples perceive their "we" and "us"). For investigators who are interested and able to be quite adventurous, there are unused experimental adaptations, for example, to study group-with-group relations in human service and other organizations. Besides illustrating in the chapters many existing and potential lines of research I have ventured to draw attention to entirely new kinds and levels of study that would not have occurred to me earlier in this long-running odyssey.

Each of the chapters in this book begins with a virtual mini-preface about the aim and origins of that part of the story. This makes a long overall preface superfluous, though I will mention two or three more things. First, I have greatly valued and sometimes been nourished over the years by the interest and contacts with other investigators – graduate students in the majority and numbering more than 1,000 in all – who have been in touch with me about their intersecting interests, needs for materials, and sometimes advice. Related to this interest by others, and although the primary 64-item forms of the Inventory have changed little since their revision crafting in 1964, the many adaptations and somewhat shorter forms that followed often have been encouraged or even triggered by the research interests of others. One of the latest of these is an Inventory form (in Appendix 1) that centers specifically on empathy.

All this said, this book does not focus exclusively on the BLRI *or* entirely on research although it maintains an instrument and method focus. One chapter is devoted to the topic of counsellor/facilitator training, using devices that resemble features of the RI but are differently structured for practical ends. Another chapter centers on my Contextual Selves Inventory developed to study the nexus between self-diversity and relationship. A further chapter focuses on forms developed for participant use at the end of experiential group sessions as an aid in self-reviewing and tracking the experienced process. In the final chapter I envision new potentials with applications of the BLRI and reach beyond present instrumentation to suggest an approach to the study of relationship between very large systems of people.

In the context of my own advancing years this book is motivated in part to make available to all interested student, teaching, and research colleagues the full range of information, materials, and ideas that in the natural course of things I cannot indefinitely convey person to person. I am relinquishing individual author control of this material so that it will be as accessible as possible to all who are interested and able to acquire this book for themselves. Good research is demanding but need not be dull and plodding and certainly has not been for me in the region encompassed here. I wish for the reader interest in ideas and materials from this book and excitement in whatever systematic enquiry you undertake.

Godfrey T. Barrett-Lennard
gt_barrett-lennard@iinet.net.au

About the Companion Website

This book is accompanied by a companion website:

www.wiley.com/go/barrett_lennard/therelationshipinventory

The website includes:

- Forms from the book for downloading

Part 1
The Relationship Inventory: Beginning, Fruition, Future

Chapter 1
How Change Happens: The Guidance and Refinement of Theory

Research and practice in a new field can begin in two main ways. In the first the work starts with an existing theory studied in a prior context and imported. In this case the new field is effectively treated as another application of established principles. This could be a theory of how new learning and change in behavior occurs. The theory then also helps to define the forms of practice and process in this field (psychological therapy, for example), since the practice would need to be credibly related to kinds of change predictable by and found within the theory. However, if the practice is itself shaped to accord with the theoretical principles, and its outcomes tested within the same frame of thought, there is a distinct self-confirming risk. In other words, if the theory-based scope and patterning of treatment leads to the targeted changes, this further demonstrates the principles in action but does not test whether the practice is a matching response to the whole complex phenomenon it faces. This 'phenomenon' may include people who are desperately working to cope while feeling divided, torn, alone, or in other mental-emotional agony, yet also with risked hope of finding a way to lift out of this pain and into a path of positive change. In any case, the first-considered kind of helping treatment is exemplified in the influential major approach briefly considered at the beginning of this chapter.

The second broad approach does not rely on a prior theory but begins with careful observation of the unfolding new phenomenon discovered through practice experience; the experience to be examined of working with troubled clients in intensive personal therapy. The close observer of whole recordings of this phenomenon could be expected to discern various distinguishable features of the process, leading perhaps to a landscape view of discriminated elements. This view may reveal regularities across different interviews and client–therapist combinations and go on to show shifts in process during therapy. Close study of subprocesses and their movement may remain a main focus through a range of studies that yield an increasingly differentiated and complete description of the phenomenon. As a result questions then naturally come into view, for example, "How does this descriptively known phenomenon work to produce or enable client change?" "What are the crucial features that mediate its effects?" A theory is then born and begins to guide further research. In contrast to the first approach this method uncovers its principles through examined practice. A major example of it, and the nature of the theory that emerged and came to fruition, occupies the latter part of this chapter. The immediate relevance is that this development triggered the 60-year history, specific instrumentation, and paths of research presented in this book.

Practitioners who draw heavily on B. F. Skinner's work (1953, 1974) exemplify the first approach mentioned above in its application to the field of psychological therapy and related helping practice. The theory grew out of studies of animal and human learning and crystallized in the view that behavior patterns, generally, are shaped by rewards (or their absence) in an operant conditioning paradigm. In essence, people in difficulty had acquired faulty or maladaptive behavior patterns through their environmental history of learning and reinforcement of those patterns. To undo and change these patterns a helper would need to properly understand how they continue to work and to engage with the client to introduce a scheme of rewards that reinforce any appearances of desired alternative patterns and avoid any rewards for the maladaptive ones – so that the former (at least in theory) come to predominate and the latter fall away or are "extinguished."

The Relationship Inventory: A Complete Resource and Guide, First Edition. Godfrey T. Barrett-Lennard.
© 2015 John Wiley & Sons, Ltd. Published 2015 by John Wiley & Sons, Ltd.
Companion site: www.wiley.com/go/barrett_lennard/therelationshipinventory

The process first referred to as "behavior modification" as applied, for example, in institutions for delinquent or wayward youngsters[1] or for people with phobias or compulsions, came to be called behavior therapy in its applications in the clinical field.

In principle the approach is pragmatically appealing. It implies that helpful change is an inevitable and almost automatic process when it arises from an exacting and consistent focus on observable and reinforcing behavior, 'undistracted' by complex mental processes or the inner life of the client. This radical behavior analytic approach based strictly on associative and operant action learning emerged as a mode of helping in the early 1960s, and has continued to be a strong background influence in behavior therapies. Not surprisingly, however, the original or "pure" forms have been largely supplanted. Prominent exponents such as Bandura (1969, 1977), Beck (1976), and Wolpe (1973), while subscribing to experimentally based learning models of change, shifted attention from an exclusive focus on observable behavior to an included emphasis on inner cognitions and to consideration of rewards as social phenomena. In the 1970s the major shift to cognitive-behavioral therapy (CBT) gave room for inner assumptive thought and self-instructive conversations to be seen and treated as having vital relevance in human difficulties, and also for clients to have a greater role in their own change.

CBT practice is now very varied (see O'Donahue & Fisher, 2009) and was becoming more varied by the 1980s (Rimm & Cunningham, 1985). There is a broad zeitgeist, however, that therapists are expert guides, and that the detection of reinforcers and training replacement of maladaptive thought-feeling messages and behaviors remain defining features in accepted mainstream work. Discovery of deeper-lying or "core" cognitive schemas seen as masterminding automatic thought patterns and assumptions also can be a major focus (Riso, Pieter, Stein, & Young, 2007). Indicative chapter titles in O'Donahue and Fisher's (2009) comprehensive edited volume include: "Anger (negative impulse) control," "Cognitive restructuring of the disputing of irrational beliefs," "Differential reinforcement of low-rate behavior," "Contingency management interventions," "Response chaining," "Emotion regulation," "Habit reversal training," "Multimodal behavior therapy," "Self-management," "Shaping," "Stress inoculation training," and "Systematic desensitization."

Alongside the formidable almost surgical language there is significant and growing awareness in CBT circles of the importance of responsive sensitivity and quality of the therapist–client relationship, quite often in terms, or language at least, that borrow from the permeating influence of Carl Rogers' work (see also Chapter 2). The attention to the relationship is largely viewed as necessary for effective communication and problem understanding and as a *pre-condition* for the right choice and effective use of research-based change-inducing techniques. The belief in a reliable, strong research base underpinning CBT is, though, by no means universal ('inside' critique by Follette, Darrow, & Bonow, 2009, p. 58). Bohart and House (2008), for example, examine and deconstruct the evidence base and assumptive paradigm underlying an "empirically supported/validated treatment" approach (exemplified in mainstream CBT), concluding that it is out of keeping with the very complex working of human consciousness and behavior. Certainly, the learning theory based retraining stance and most associated practice as formally described stands in contrast to the second approach exemplified in Carl Rogers' thought and 'person-centered' practice.

Rogers, a practicing psychologist through the 1930s, was knowledgeable regarding the psychotherapies of the time, relatively eclectic in his leaning, and pragmatic in his concern for the practical outcomes of his work with problem children and (in lesser focus) their parents. Exposure to practical ideas associated with the responsive-relational emphasis of Otto Rank and his colleagues (see, e.g., Rank, 1936/1945; Taft, 1933) encouraged and contributed to Rogers' directions, as did his early years of practice experience (Barrett-Lennard, 1998, pp. 6–9; Rogers, 1939). He saw an active potential in people toward developmental growth and change and came to the view that effective therapy hinged on the quality of the relationship between client and therapist in order to release this potential (Rogers, 1942, 1946). Therapeutic change, then, was

---

[1] In such contexts the method may seem to be work at first and then relapse may occur. In the late 1960s a psychologist colleague was responsible for a "token economy" behavioral reconditioning program in an institution for "delinquent" girls in Ontario. At first he was very committed and enthusiastic about this work. Then one day he told me that the girls had mastered the operant reinforcement system and it had dawned on him that they were using it with the staff of the institution to get privileges and rewards that they had not earned – staff who had been unaware that *their behavior* was being shaped by the savvy inmates.

not a matter of directed retraining (though self-discovery learning could be vital) but of providing an environment in which the client's own recuperative tendencies and motivation in the presence of an enabling relationship would bring about integrative shifts leading to growth. These were still broad principles and years of further thoughtful searching was needed for their systematic working out. The existence of bright enquiring graduate students (1940 on) at Ohio State and then the University of Chicago, and Roger's intensive experience as a therapist, alongside focused study of recorded process, flowed into the continuing development of his perspective on the process and outcomes of therapy.

The research began with several years devoted mainly to close descriptive study of the interview conversation over the course of therapy (Raskin, 1949; Barrett-Lennard, 1998, pp. 234–238). This emphasis on process and its regularity of pattern lead on to a significant period where concern centered on establishing the outcomes of this process empirically. Was the therapy, in fact, effective in terms of measurable helpful changes in client functioning and outlook from before to after therapy? Positive results on this level then opened the way to an explanatory focus on just how these valued directions of change come about and, more specifically, what the change-enabling features were in the therapy relationship. Even before systematic attention to this third phase of research, Rogers was reflecting on and periodically articulating therapist attitudes (such as respect, a nondirective stance, and belief in inherent growth forces) that he thought permitted and enabled fruitful process and change in clients. As in these examples, his ideas were at first quite broadly expressed, and it took another decade and more for his view to sharply focus and mature into a distinct theory of change. A new theory may burst into clear view suddenly, but its full meaning hinges on the progression of enquiry and thought that resulted in this emergence – as I am briefly tracing in this instance.[2]

By the mid-a940s Rogers was actively reaching for a general explanatory formulation evidenced in an article he contributed to the first volume of the *American Psychologist* (Rogers, 1946). He began there to use the language of "conditions" of therapist attitude and behavior and proposed six such conditions. These were: that therapists view their clients, first, as self-responsible; and, second, as inherently motivated toward development and health; that they create a warm, permissive, accepting atmosphere; that any limits set on behavior do *not* apply to attitudes and feelings; that they respond with a "deep understanding of the emotionalized attitudes expressed," especially through "sensitive reflection and clarification of the client's attitudes"; and that they abstain from probing, blaming, interpreting, reassuring, or persuading. Moreover, "if these conditions are met" then healing and a growthful process will be reflected within therapy and in an awareness and behavior beyond therapy (Rogers, 1946, pp. 416–417). Although this was a practical formulation compatible in broad direction with the six conditions that he distinguished a decade later, it assembled a diverse mix of ingredients on varied levels. The aspects of "deep understanding" and of a "warm, accepting atmosphere" foreshadow later distinctions in idea though not yet in sharp focus or definition.

The 1946 statement was, however, a systemizing step beyond the vivid account of practice in Rogers' influential 1942 book. Both sources imply a feature that another colleague went on to further elucidate. Raskin (a former student of Rogers) singled out a genuinely nondirective attitude as pivotal in the approach, arguing that it underpinned true acceptance and created the potential for understanding in depth (Raskin, 1948, pp. 105–106). In a further important paper, Rogers spoke with cogent eloquence about the difficulty and importance of entering and holding a mirror to the client's inner feelings and frame of reference, while also checking with the client on the accuracy or otherwise of what showed in this 'mirror.' He pointed out that this is very different from an interpretive focus by an evaluating listener, and then observed that an empathic focus on the experience of the other minimizes possible self-entanglement in the other's feelings (Rogers, 1949). He also found and acknowledged (as did Raskin) that the *client's perception* of the counsellor's response needed to be reckoned with. The whole term "empathic understanding" is mentioned in Rogers' subsequent book (1951, p. 29) although it is not yet defined. This was also the case with the idea of genuineness of response.

---

[2] The outline here and in further paragraphs of this course of development draws on my earlier formulations (Barrett-Lennard, 1998, Chapters 12 and 13; 2007, pp. 26–28).

In a further step, Rogers spoke (1953) of the positive feelings that can naturally arise toward a client sharing his or her innermost consciousness in a sensitive difficult search for deeper connection and wholeness. Respect that ignites into spontaneous warmth, even affection, can be part of the human reality of a deepening helping relationship. As he put it:

> We [now] know that if the therapist holds within himself attitudes of deep respect and full acceptance for the client as he is, and similar attitudes toward the client's potentialities for dealing with himself and his situations; if these attitudes are suffused with a sufficient warmth which transforms them into the most profound type of liking and affection for the core of the person; and if a level of communication is reached so that the client can begin to perceive that the therapist understands the feelings he is experiencing and accepts him at the full depth of that understanding, then we may be sure that the [therapeutic] process is already initiated. (Rogers, 1953, pp. 44–45)

By then, Rogers was on the edge of suggesting that a client's growing regard for self flows in significant part from the therapist's respectful positive regard. Standal, working with Rogers, would have begun his thesis exploration (1954) of positive regard, viewed as a basic human need, in a theoretical contribution that flowed directly into Rogers' further systematic thought on personality development (1959a, pp. 223–226). Standal's study also brought into view the idea of 'conditions of worth,' referring to entrenched beliefs about acceptable and unacceptable personal qualities; beliefs acquired through the highly conditional reactions of others. Thus also the concept that the therapist's positive regard needs to be unconditional to help undo the client's self-devaluing or censoring conditions of worth (Moon, Rice, & Schneider, 2001).

In his mid-1950s 'current view' of client-centered therapy, Rogers gives primary importance to the therapist being "genuine, whole, or congruent in the relationship" (1956, pp. 199–200). If the client is to venture into the reality of self, the therapist needs to be real or transparent in this relation. Therapist acceptance or unconditional positive regard (both terms are used) is a second vital factor, and the therapist's desire and ability to understand with sensitive empathy is the third ingredient of the relationship. By that time, Rogers' sustained pondering and refinement of ideas on the therapist–client relation had moved him, step by incremental step, to a transformative articulation of the conditions for therapeutic change. This bold formulation, published the following year (Rogers, 1957), gave a new level of clarity and force to the cause–effect equation of therapy that was trialed a decade earlier. This theory (Rogers, 1957, 1959a) and its further unfolding and refinement triggered the main instrumentation, research applications, and development of ideas presented in this book.[3]

At the time of the mentioned first stage of empirical study of the client-centered therapy process a typical research procedure was to study and sift what the participants said and implied, and to develop content categories to classify and track the specific observed content of the process over the course of an interview. This also was done interview-by-interview or by fifths (say) of the total transcript and usually in terms of how often particular kinds of client statement or feeling, and/or therapist response, occurred at different stages in the therapy discourse. An interest in outcome, initially in terms of client experience of change, was woven into some of this process-focused research – including the group of studies reported by Rogers and a number of Counseling Center colleagues working with him (Raskin, 1949). Once these and related studies had given a fairly clear picture of the phenomenon of nondirective/client-centered therapy the interest moved, as already noted, to a focus on the impact or outcome effects of this therapy, for example, as reported in Rogers and Dymond (1954). In all, the research became increasingly targeted, with a yield of results and ideas that fed into Rogers' (1957, 1959a) explanatory formulation of how therapeutic change happened – what its 'causal' or mediating ingredients were.

The theory was concise and economical in its basic substance. Its starting point was the general condition that the participants needed to be in "psychological contact." Two other conditions focused on contrasting

---

[3] The development of a fruitful theory generally rests (as in Rogers' case) on a great deal of careful observational study during which investigators discern and reflect on a range of detailed patterns and changes in patterns. A closely considered, partly intuitive and creative emergence of an overall conception may then crystallize. A familiar famous case is Darwin's theory of evolution, presented in his major work *The origin of species* (1872 [1859]).

qualities attributed to the client and the therapist. The client needed to be "vulnerable or anxious" due to the tension of conflict or discrepancy between his or her underlying experience and self-picture – a process state broadly referred to as incongruence. (Such a tension state in clients choosing personal therapy seemed almost self-evident and did not become a direct focus of research.) The therapist, on the other hand, needed to be functioning congruently, at least in the therapy relationship. Two crucial further conditions pivoted on empathic understanding and positive unconditional regard from the therapist. Finally, these qualities needed to be communicated and become apparent to the client. Under these conditions, constructive personal change would occur. The clear form of this unqualified portrayal helped to make it arresting. The idea of sufficiency – that the equation was complete – added force for many readers. The boldness of Rogers' claim that these were the fundamental underlying conditions for healing and growthful change in any psychotherapy stirred and sometimes provoked a wide range of readers. The author was influential and fast becoming famous. Even sceptics could not simply ignore his asserted 'general theory.'

The idea of somehow putting this new and exciting theory to the test immediately attracted me, and how I did this is closely described in the next chapter. My focus from the start was on experienced qualities of the therapist's response – notably as perceived by the client but also as self-perceived by the therapist. Rogers' formulation, though much more conceptually tight than he had advanced before, still needed some refining when it came to developing a measuring instrument and designing systematic research. Client perception of the posited vital qualities of therapist response was not to me a separate condition (like empathy) but an integral aspect of the otherwise stated conditions, including therapist congruence, in their manifestation and influence in therapy. Also, as delineated in the next chapter, the powerful but awkward construct of unconditional positive regard was broken down into two distinct component variables in my work.

If, as in Rogers' theory, the core factors driving a therapeutic process were qualities of *relationship*, would they be confined in process and influence to a psychotherapy context? Rogers and I, almost from the start, considered that any helping/developmental relationship (for example, in teaching and other human services) were contexts in which these qualities may have a vital role and, if confirmed as relevant in these professional situations, why not also in everyday life relationships – of couples and in families, for example? In all, Rogers' formulation, coming out of intensive practice and study as a therapist, was to become a major contributing influence in the human relations domain. First however the focus was on sharpening the theory, developing a way of measuring the component conditions variables, and *empirically testing the conception in the therapy context* that gave birth to that influence – as in the research discussed in the next chapter.

Chapter 2
The Classic Investigation of Carl Rogers' Core Theory

Rogers' bold formulation of the basic conditions for therapeutic change (Rogers, 1957) was an absorbing challenge to me, as soon as I saw it, which was several months before publication. However, just how to put it to the test was not at all clear. For one thing there were no existing instruments to measure the variables of the experienced therapist–client response and relationship. Assuming I was able to develop such an instrument there was the challenge of obtaining all the necessary data from an adequate sample of actual in-therapy clients and their therapists. Additionally, the method and data analysis would need to be done in a way that gave reasonable assurance that an equation linking relationship and change was working in a particular direction, that is, that measured change was resulting (substantially) from the qualities of experienced therapist response. All of this was a very tall order and nearly foundered at the start because of the difficulties in accessing the necessary data. However, Rogers' Counselling Centre was a supportive environment deeply involved in therapy research with a continuing flow of clients and, finally, the way was clear for the study to go ahead. After my dissertation report was complete and I went on to career teaching I was able to get grant support and extend the analysis to include the relationship data from therapists as well as clients and organize a complete report for publication – in Psychological Monographs *(Barrett-Lennard, 1962).*

The monograph report was originally chosen for republication in the 1970s book New directions in client-centred therapy, *edited by Tomlinson and Hart, but then dropped by the publishers as an economy measure (ill-judged, given the burgeoning interest). In any case, that omission adds to the relevance of the account here. This chapter is devoted to the substance of that report. Its retelling is a critical part of the larger story of development and enquiry, which is the focus in this book. Specific knowledge of the beginning and main turning points of this story contribute to critical understanding of what it led on to, as well as to the meaning of measures generated by the Barrett-Lennard Relationship Inventory. Readers interested in the full data analysis and results from the foundation study can write to me requesting it or (better) track down a library copy of my original monograph report, which is long out of print. It has been an extremely interesting exercise for me to come back to this work in a closely studied way after so long, and I hope the reader will sense and share some of the excitement. I think that I have learned to write better and what follows is more readable than the original as well as literally half its length – though still comprehensive in scope.*[1]

When this study began, some 15 years of research analyses of recorded interviews and other data had already been devoted to identifying process features and mapping both the unfolding course and the outcomes of client-centered therapy (Cartwright, 1957; Rogers & Dymond, 1954). There was plenty of room for further study of the orderly characteristics of the therapy process and components of personal change, but that such change did tend to occur was, by then, supported by significant research evidence. Related further work was concerned with sorting out the various dimensions and facets of observed change and advancing the methodology of investigating change (Cartwright, Kirtner, & Fiske, 1963) and

---

[1] The original publishers are being advised that this chapter is based essentially on my *Psychological Monographs* report of 1962.

The Relationship Inventory: A Complete Resource and Guide, First Edition. Godfrey T. Barrett-Lennard.
© 2015 John Wiley & Sons, Ltd. Published 2015 by John Wiley & Sons, Ltd.
Companion site: www.wiley.com/go/barrett_lennard/therelationshipinventory

also with refined inductive and deductive analysis of the interview therapy process (e.g., Braaten, 1961; Vargas, 1954). Then, the watershed theoretical advance by Rogers (1957) opened a new doorway onto the issue of the factors in therapy that brought about change. In tandem with this momentous development another new envisioning occurred that was taken up in subsequent studies. This was Rogers' "process" conception, which provided a fresh differentiation and means of measuring changes in personality functioning during therapy (Rogers, 1958; Rogers, 1959a; Rogers with Gendlin, Kiesler, & Truax, 1967; Walker, Rablen, & Rogers, 1960). These were heady days in the milieu that triggered and fostered this research.

A few earlier studies by client-centered investigators had indirectly provided some empirical evidence about how or "why" change occurs in therapy. In their related studies Fiedler (1950) and Quinn (1950) found that expert therapists of differing theoretical orientations shared capacities for understanding and effective communication (assessed by judges from therapy interview data) to a higher degree than nonexperts. Lipkin (1954) found a positive association between the degree to which clients felt liked by their therapists and their improvement in adjustment (assessed from Thematic Apperception Test (TAT) data). This perceived liking may have helped to release a fruitful change process or been associated with additional factors that directly facilitated therapeutic change. The paucity of previous research focused on explaining change was due partly to: the inherent order in which scientific knowledge tends to develop (studying "causal" relationships is a relatively advanced stage); the difficulty of studying such associations in a process not subject to experimental manipulation; and the result of the previous lack of a systematic theory of the basic conditions producing therapeutic change. Now, however, the time was ripe to begin this level of systematic study.

Rogers' theory (1957) of the 'conditions of therapeutic personality change' at once triggered not one but two independent studies aimed to test its main features. The other study, conducted by Halkides (1958), investigated the theory essentially in the form in which Rogers presented it, except for the addition of a further relationship variable that she felt was implied in his conception. She employed therapy interview data from 20 sound-recorded cases, and extracted short randomly selected conversation units from two interviews in each case. These units were rated by three judges for their degree of unconditional positive regard, empathic understanding, and congruence or genuineness of the therapist (all postulated by Rogers), and also for the degree to which the affective intensity of the therapist's communication matched that of his/her client. The client sample was divided into subgroups of more successful and less successful cases, using a criterion derived from several change and outcome measures. Halkides found significant associations between the criterion of success and all the relationship variables except for affective intensity matching (where the results were ambiguous). Although Halkides' study was not directly followed up or published it encouraged the development and use of broadly similar judge rating scales by Truax and others in the Wisconsin research on psychotherapy with hospitalized schizophrenic patients (see Rogers et al, 1967).

This study is quite distinct from Halkides' work in its methodology and specific theoretical underpinning. It hinged on the view that the *client's experience* of the therapist's response is the immediate locus of therapeutic influence in their relationship. This was a change in emphasis from Rogers' formally stated viewpoint (Rogers, 1957), which proposed that it is first of all necessary that the therapist experience certain things in relation to her/his client (for example, unconditional positive regard) and, second, that s/he communicate these crucial aspects of response to the client. The present investigator's conception took, as its starting point, the presumption that it is what the client experiences that affects him or her directly and would thus be most crucially related to the outcome of therapy.

Viewing the client's experience-based perceptions in the therapy relationship as the direct agent of therapeutic change leads to the further question of what generates those perceptions. The answer conceived at the time was that a client's perceptions result from the interaction of his/her personality characteristics and attributes of the therapist's experience and communication in the relationship. In the hypothetical case of *two clients with identical characteristics*, the differential response of the therapists would be wholly responsible for the different perceptions of the clients and, hence (in theory), for differences in therapy outcome. From this view it was relevant to study and measure the five variables of therapist response, firstly (and most importantly) from the client's frame of reference and, secondly, from the therapist's own standpoint. To do this the 'Relationship Inventory' questionnaire, designed to yield measures of each variable from either client or therapist perceptions, was developed.

Specifically, it was postulated that each of five distinguishable features of the therapist's attitudes and relational response are influential in the process of therapeutic change. These are the therapist's level of regard for the client and (as a separate factor) the extent to which this regard is unconditional or unqualified, and the degree of the therapist's empathic understanding *and* congruence *and* willingness to be known by the client. The resulting questionnaire instrument was administered to client and therapist participants at up to four points during therapy; with principal use being made of the first readings, taken after five therapy interviews. Indices of personal change in the client were also obtained, from independent pretherapy and posttherapy data.

The primary empirical objectives of the study were to determine whether each of the measured qualities of relationship significantly predicted the indices of therapeutic improvement; and whether more experienced and demonstrably competent therapists formed relationships characterized by higher degrees of each relationship dimension than was true of inexperienced therapists. The therapist response variables were formulated as follows.

DEFINITIONS OF THE "THERAPEUTIC" VARIABLES

Two of the variables, the concepts of empathic understanding and congruence of the therapist, essentially corresponded with the meanings given by Rogers (1957, 1959b), although more tightly formulated for the present investigation. Two others, level of regard and unconditionality of regard, represent a division of the concept of unconditional positive regard into what are conceived as being two separate and distinct components. The remaining variable, the therapist's willingness to be known, was original to this study. These are the formal definitions:

EMPATHIC UNDERSTANDING

Degree of empathic understanding is conceived as the extent to which one person is conscious of the immediate and felt awareness of another. Qualitatively it is an active process of desiring to know the full present and changing awareness of another person, of reaching out to receive *their* communication and meaning, and of decoding their words and signs into experienced meaning in the listener that at least matches what is most important to the sharing person at the moment. It is an experiencing of the consciousness "behind" another's outward communication, though with continuous awareness by the listener that this feeling consciousness is originating and proceeding in the other. In particular, empathic understanding includes sensing the immediate affective quality and intensity of the other's experience and where it is pointing (for example, who or what the feeling is directed toward, and/or the person's awareness of the conditions that produce it).

The aspect of the empathic process that involves experiential recognition of perceptions or feelings that the other has directly communicated may be termed empathic recognition. The aspect of sensing or inferring the implied or indirectly expressed content of the other's felt awareness is called empathic inference. In general these two aspects occur together in the empathic process, but their balance will vary from one relationship to another, and from moment to moment in a given relationship.

Maximum empathic understanding of B, by A, requires that A be able to discriminate and permit in his/her awareness all that B gives direct or indirect signs of experiencing. This, in turn, requires that A be open and unthreatened in relation to B. Empathic understanding of B will be limited or reduced if A unconsciously projects feelings of his/her own into the perception of B's experience or in any other way confuses B's experiences with experiences (perhaps similar but not identical) that originate in him/herself.

LEVEL OF REGARD

Regard refers here to the affective aspect of one person's response to another. This may include various qualities and strengths of 'positive' and 'negative' feeling. Positive feelings include respect, liking, appreciation, affection, and any other affirming or warmly favoring response. Conversely, negative feelings include dislike, impatience, contempt, and in general affectively rejecting or drawing-away reactions. Level of regard is the overall tendency of the various affective qualities of response of one person in relation to another (here of A toward B). More specifically, it may be considered the composite "loading" of all the distinguishable feeling reactions of one person toward another, positive and negative, on a single abstract dimension. The lower extreme of this dimension represents maximum predominance and intensity of negative-type feeling, not merely a lack of positive feeling.

UNCONDITIONALITY OF REGARD

In contrast with level of regard this concept is specifically concerned with how little or how much variability there is in one person's affective response to another. It is defined as the degree of constancy of regard felt by one person for another who communicates varied self-experiences to the first. (In a casual or impersonal relationship the concept would have no meaning. Regard might be constant but so shallow and unrelated to the other person that it would not be perceived as a feeling toward him or her.) In particular, the more that A's (a therapist's say) immediate regard for B (a client in this case) varies in response to change in B's feelings toward him/herself or toward A, or the different experiences or attitudes that B is communicating to A, or to differences in A's mood, or any other triggered variation in A's felt response to B, the more conditional (or less unconditional) it is.

CONGRUENCE

The degree to which one person is functionally integrated in the context of his/her relationship with another, such that there is absence of conflict or inconsistency between the first person's total experience, their awareness, and their overt communication, is their congruence in the relationship.[2] The concept is theoretically centered on consistency between total present experience and awareness, which is considered to be the main determinant or condition for congruence between awareness and communication. Absence of inconsistency between awareness and communication is the theoretical criterion for congruence at this level. If a significant perception is not communicated by a person who is functioning congruently, then their overt expression is simply neutral or uninformative with regard to it and does not imply some contrary perception. Thus, the highly congruent individual is completely honest, direct, and sincere in what is conveyed, but s/he does not feel a compulsion to communicate all perceptions, or any need to withhold them for emotionally self-protective reasons.

Direct evidence of lack of congruence includes, for example, inconsistency between what the individual says, and what s/he implies by expression, gestures, or tone of voice. Indications of discomfort, tension, or anxiety are considered to be less direct but equally important evidence of lack of congruence. They imply that the individual is not, at the time, freely open to awareness of some aspects of his or her experience and is, in some degree, incongruent.

In brief, optimum congruence implies wholeness and integration of the complete spectrum of organismic processes in the individual, from physiological to conscious symbolic levels. It implies that the person is psychologically unthreatened and is, therefore, fully open to awareness of what the other person is communicating. And it means that the individual's capacity to discriminate between their own feelings or attitudes, and those of the other person, is maximized.

---

[2]   The meaning of the term "total experience" intended here is conveyed by Rogers' definition of "experience" (Rogers, 1959b, p. 197).

Level of congruence has implications for the other variables already defined. It is conceived to set an upper limit to the degree to which empathic understanding of another is possible, although the individual's immediate interests and purposes will also determine whether s/he uses the potentiality provided by his or her congruence to empathically understand the other. The degree to which an individual can actually respond unconditionally to another is considered a function of their inner security and integration in that context. However, a less congruent individual might give the appearance of being more unconditional in their regard than a person functioning with a high degree of congruence (who acknowledges variability) so that the operational relationship between these two variables may well be a complex one.

WILLINGNESS TO BE KNOWN

This factor was conceived as the degree to which one person is willing to be known as a person, by another, according to the other's desire for this. An openness to be known as a person involves, especially, a readiness to share experiences and perceptions of the self, perceptions of and feelings toward the other, and perceptions of the self–other interaction or relationship (referred to collectively as self-experience). A person who is functioning with a high degree of willingness to be known, in relation to another, is open to awareness of whatever desire the other has to experience and know him as a person, and wants to share self-experience in direct relation to his or her awareness of this desire. The desire may be transient or persistent, specific or general, strong or weak (or vary in other ways), and ideally self-communication is continuously attuned to its present state.

Self-communication under other conditions signifies departure from optimum willingness to be known. These other conditions may include habitual response to certain cues for self-communication, deliberate choice of other conditions of self-communication, or involuntary dependence on self-communication for protection or enhancement of the self. Lack of self-communication under the condition that the other person *is* desiring to receive this (and giving some indication of this desire) signifies a reduced level of willingness to be known. Thus, the individual who is functioning with a low or negative degree of willingness to be known is not stimulated and guided in self-communication by an open awareness of the other's present desire to experience and know them as a person. Relative to this desire s/he may thrust his/her self-experience forward in some way, or hold it back from the other. Both types of response are considered, in principle, to be equally indicative of a lack of positive *willingness* to be known.

Each of the defined relationship variables is conceived to exist on a continuum ranging from some optimum or maximal level to a minimal, or maximally negative, level. They may, in other words, be considered as present in a positive sense, or having a positive value, or as being negated in varying degrees. The theoretical relatedness of the relationship measures is sufficient to expect a moderate degree of positive association between valid measures of them. However, each one is considered to have a significant contributing influence, in its own right, on therapeutic change, so that each one should in theory (over a moderately large and diverse sample of therapy relationships) be associated with change.

INSTRUMENTS AND PROCEDURE

THE RELATIONSHIP INVENTORY

Following is an account of the original development of the instrument to gather the pertinent data and measure relationship over the five variables of therapist response.

Item content: It was planned from the beginning to have separate groups of items for each variable, composed of subgroups of positive and negative expressions of that variable. A number of items from Bown's earlier doctoral work (1954), concerned with giving a broad picture of the therapy relationship as perceived by client or therapist, were selected for possible use. Only a few of these were retained, however, in modified form. Several drafts of items were prepared and revised. The revisions in each case benefited from discussion with and written comment from several staff members of the University of Chicago Counseling Center and associated consultants.

The preparation of items involved constant interaction between theory and operational expression and resulted also in progressive refinement of meaning of the concepts underlying each variable. For some of the variables this process led to the identification of subcategories of meaning. Several such categories were implied in the above definition of unconditionality of regard. A further example was the concept of congruence, which allowed breakdown into the following aspects: (a) direct perception of consistency or inconsistency between two or more of the three levels of primary experience, awareness, and overt communication (for example, in the Relationship Inventory (RI) item, "There are times when I feel that his outward response is quite different from his inner reaction to me") ; (b) an aspect of consistency in the generalized forms of perceived honesty, genuineness, and directness, or their opposites (for example, in the items, "I feel that he is being genuine with me" and "He is playing a role with me"); (c) an aspect of security or insecurity (for example, "He is secure and comfortable in our relationship"); (d) an aspect of self-protective avoidance (for example, "He tries to avoid telling me anything that might upset me"); and (e) a fusing of more than one of these aspects (for example, "He is not at all comfortable [insecurity] but we go on, outwardly ignoring it [inconsistency]"). (In a second variant of this RI form pronouns referring to the therapist were "she" and "her.")

Form: It was intended initially to use a Q-sort form (see Butler & Haigh, 1954; Stephenson, 1953, 1980), but this plan foundered on the problem of obtaining several subscores from a single forced-normal distribution of the items. The multiple-choice questionnaire form, finally chosen, also has the appeal of anchored response categories, relative ease and economy of administration, minimum respondent comparison of answers to related items, and flexibility in regard to refining, eliminating, or adding items.

The specific questionnaire form used made provision from the start for three grades of "yes" and three grades of "no" response identified, as +1, +2, +3 and −1, −2, −3, respectively, by the respondent. This choice was encouraged in part by the similar distinctions used in the California E Scale (Adorno, Frenkel-Brunswik, Levinson, & Sanford, 1950). It was desired in this case to obtain answers that reflected how certain the respondent felt about the item statement being correct or incorrect and also how important it was to him (her) that it was true or false. Concern was with the responding person's feelings about the therapist's response, not merely what s/he observed. These considerations led to identification of the three positive and three negative response categories essentially as follows; "I feel it is probably true" (or untrue), "I feel it is true" (or not true), and "I strongly feel that it is true" (or not true).

The group of items representing each variable was dispersed throughout the Inventory so as to obtain maximum independence of answers. However, to facilitate item identification and scoring, they were arranged so that every fifth item represented the same variable. Positively and negatively worded items occurred in essentially random order. Within this overall framing, in placing specific items the attempt was made to avoid sequences such that a given answer to one item might suggest or encourage a particular answer to the next one.

Content validation: The process by which the RI items were developed seemed to ensure that most of them could be safely regarded as either positive or negative expressions of the variable that they were designed to represent. To eliminate any items for which this was not true, however, a formal content validation procedure was carried out. Directions and definitions of the variables were given to five judges who classified each item as either a positive (+) or negative (−) indicator of the variable in question, and gave a neutral (o) rating to any item that they regarded as irrelevant or ambiguous. (Judges also rated the positive items on a scale of +1 to +5 and the negative items on a scale of −1 to −5, in terms of their strength or importance as positive or negative indicators of the variable. The mean ratings for the items, from the five judges, were used in selecting the two half-samples of items for the split-half reliability assessment to be described shortly.

There was perfect agreement between judges, at the level of classing an item as positive or negative, on all except four items. Three of these items were eliminated the one being retained only having the inconsistency of a neutral rating by one judge. Three consistently rated items were also eliminated, mainly because of duplication of content. Later in the investigation an item analysis was conducted, in connection with revising the RI for further research. The method used was to tabulate and compare the answers given to each item by the "upper" and "lower" half of the sample (N = 40) divided in terms of scores on the variable to which the item belonged. One additional item, which had obviously been interpreted in two different ways by client respondents was eliminated as a result of this procedure. In the final set of 85 items used in the scoring, each variable was represented by 16 to 18 items.

Scoring method: The scoring procedure adopted involves face-value weighting of the numerical answer categories and allows every answer to the items for a given variable to either add or subtract from the resulting score, according to the direction of its theoretical meaning. The specific method reverses the sign of the respondent's answers to the theoretically negative items (giving the answers to positive and negative items the same theoretical direction) and then sums the relevant item scores for each variable. This method yields a possible scoring range of −3n to +3n, where n is the number of items used. (Fuller, later discussion of the scoring rationale appears in Chapter 4.)

Validity of the scales: One aspect of the validity problem is the question of whether the primary data are themselves valid – in the sense that they reflect the respondent's actual experience of his/her therapist rather, for example, than reflecting how s/he thinks the therapist should respond, or what would please the therapist and/or the investigator. Precautions that were taken against any such tendencies included telling subjects, truthfully, that counselors would not see their answers, and seeking to ensure that they understood that the value of the data for research purposes depended on the extent to which it represented their actual perceptions of the relationship. Also, the data were gathered as soon as possible after each client had seen their therapist. In most instances this was directly following a therapy interview, except in the case of posttherapy data where, typically, there was a delay of several days. The investigator gathered most of the data himself and had the strong impression that the participants felt a responsibility to give candid and accurate answers to the Inventory items.

Assuming validity in the sense already discussed makes it meaningful to raise the further question of the extent to which the scales actually measure what they are designed to measure. The preliminary content validation by a group of judges has already been mentioned. As in most research where theoretical variables are given operational form for the first time, further validation on a conceptual level is largely indirect. Having ensured that the elements of information from which the scale is built are content valid, and providing internal empirical features such as the reliability and distribution characteristics of obtained scores are acceptable, the validation process seems essentially to be a matter of discovering meaningful relationships with other variables that are theoretically relevant under the conditions of the investigation.[3]

INDICES OF CHANGE

The participants in this research formed a portion of the sample of clients participating in a large-scale study of personality change associated with therapy (Cartwright et al., 1963). From the change data available two types of measure were chosen. Therapist ratings of client adjustment and change were one primary source. From a number of therapist ratings two specific indices were considered most pertinent. One of these was based on a rating of the client's general adjustment level, made after the first therapy interview and again, independently, at termination of therapy. The ratings were made on an anchored 10-point scale, the two extremes being described as "1. Most extreme maladjustment" and "10. Optimal adjustment (fully-functioning or optimal maturity)." The measure of change was the posttherapy rating minus the rating made after the first interview. This measure has the advantage of being based on independent assessments of the client from the first meeting with the therapist and when the therapy relationship terminates. A disadvantage is that the two assessments are based on very different quantities of 'information,' and fluctuation in standards of judgment over the time spans involved is certainly possible.

---

[3] Further validation evidence not available at the time of this original study is given in the later part of this chapter and in the two chapters that follow.

The other index was a four-point rating of degree of change in the client, made by the therapist at termination of therapy. The item itself is as follows:

How much change in the client as a person has occurred since she/he started counseling?

> not changed
>
> changed very little
>
> somewhat changed
>
> changed a good deal

This item follows immediately after a question of similar form asking, "How much change has there been in the problem(s) that brought the client to therapy?" This is thought to further emphasize that the selected item is enquiring about what the therapist regards as basic personal change. The scale thus lacks specificity as to what is being measured but would seem to have a great deal of power to detect whatever therapists judge to be important in the area of therapeutic personality change. It was presumed, with only four broad categories to discriminate, that the ratings would be technically reliable. Vulnerability to end-of-therapy bias is a possible limitation of the scale.

The selected rating indices appear to possess complementary advantages and, for this reason, were combined to give a single criterion of change. This was done by dichotomizing the data from each index and assigning cases falling in the upper category of change *on both indices* to a "more changed" group and the remaining cases to a "less changed" group. This conservative procedure would seem to yield a stronger, more dependable criterion than either scale in its original form.

A second source of evidence consisted of self-descriptive data provided by the client before and after therapy. Three specific indices were chosen from these data. One index consists of scores on the Q-adjustment scale developed by Dymond (1954). In effect, this method involves reducing the data from Butler and Haigh's self-descriptive Q sort (Butler & Haigh, 1954) to yes-no answers, except for a middle group of items that is disregarded. A score is obtained by counting the number of items answered in a way that clinicians judge a well-adjusted person would answer them.

The two further indices were obtained from Minnesota Multiphasic Personality Inventory (MMPI) data. They consist of scores on the Taylor Manifest Anxiety (MA) scale (Taylor, 1953) and the Depression (D) scale. The D scale had been found to be sensitive to change associated with therapy, in several studies (for example, Barron & Leary, 1955; Gallagher, 1953b; Mozak, 1950). Taylor's scale may be regarded as a measure of symptoms of anxiety or emotional tension (blushing, sweating under tension, nervousness, indigestion, insomnia, etc.) experienced and recognized by the subject. The items in Taylor's scale refer more often and directly to perceived overt actions of the self than the Q-adjustment or D scale items. Gallagher (1953a) found a significant pretherapy to posttherapy decrease in Taylor scores for a group of students in client-centered therapy. These three scales were combined, as later described, to give a single alternative criterion of change.

DATA GATHERING PROCEDURE AND SAMPLE

Except for the adjustment ratings made after the first interview, all of the change data were gathered at pretherapy and/or posttherapy testing points. The relationship data were gathered from clients and from therapists after the first 5 therapy interviews, after 15 and after 25 interviews (for clients still in therapy at those points), and at termination of therapy. After trial administrations, five therapy interviews were judged to be a safe minimum period of association between client and therapist that would provide the participants with a meaningful basis from which to answer the RI items. It also was relatively "early in therapy" for the majority of clients in this research.

The sample of clients in the study consisted of the large majority of those (student and community clients) who started therapy in the Counseling Center on a regular basis during the period in which the sample was being built up. To increase equality of the samples with more expert and less expert therapists the last few additions to the sample were selected on the basis of the experience level of the therapist, the client's sex and/ or their therapist's sex, and whether the therapist already had clients in the project. The total sample consisted of 42 clients, with 21 different therapists. Most clients were in their 20s or 30s (range, 19–45 years; mean, 28.0 years), 60 percent were men, one-third were married, nearly all had some tertiary education, and about half were college graduates. Of the total sample, 30 clients were still in therapy at the 15-interview test-point and 26 continued to at least 25 meetings. The length of therapy ranged from 7 to 96 interviews, with a mean of 33.

EXPERIMENTAL HYPOTHESES

THE UNDERLYING RATIONALE

If each of the five relationship variables plays a part in fostering therapeutic personal change then, in general, the higher the experienced level of each relationship condition *early in therapy* the greater will be the resulting change during therapy. The first reading of these variables, taken after five interviews, implied that the relationship measured at that point could not be merely an outcome of this change. Arguably, the quality of the experienced relationship as therapy progresses will be both a cause and, to some degree, a result of change. If this is true, the qualities of perceived therapist response at termination of therapy should still be associated with the indices of change. However, as the basis for this anticipated posttherapy association differs from the basis on which change is expected to be correlated with the earlier measure of relationship, the specific patterns of association obtained in the two cases are expected to be somewhat different.

Significant associations between the measures of perceived relationship after five interviews and the outcome of therapy would lend support to the concept that change is a consequence of the perceived relationship but would not alone show that this was due to a differential contribution of therapists to the measured relationship. Differences in clients' personalities could, possibly, generate the change-related differences in both the therapists' experience and the clients' perceptions. This ambiguity called for some way of isolating the contribution of therapists to the therapy relationship and outcome.

One approach to achieving the desired control is to identify, by suitable independent means, subsamples of relatively "expert" and "nonexpert" therapists, each having initially matched and equivalent samples of clients. If the more expert therapists foster "better" measured relationships with their clients (particularly from their clients' standpoint) *and* if their clients also improve more than those of the nonexpert therapists, it could be inferred that therapeutic competence is a function of the capacity of therapists to extend the defined qualities of relationship to their clients. Thus, also, the therapists are contributing to the change.

It is expected that there will be cases where client and therapist differ a good deal in their perception of the relationship factors. In general, the therapist's own view of his/her response can be viewed as supplementing that of the client, adding force when they are in agreement and moderating the client's view when they are in disagreement. When both see their relationship in quite positive terms, or both in relatively negative terms, the conditions for therapeutic change would be most favorable and least favorable, respectively. When they disagree the prognosis for change would be more favorable when the client is more positive than the therapist in their respective perceptions of the relationship qualities.

It is thought that experienced 'expert' therapists would tend to express their thoughts, impressions, and feelings in relation to their clients more openly, directly, and unambiguously than nonexperts would – reflecting greater congruence and more developed communication skills in therapy. As a consequence the client's perception of the expert therapist's response is expected be more similar to the therapist's perceptions than in the case of nonexpert therapists.

THE HYPOTHESES FORMALLY STATED

Hypothesis 1. Each of the five relationship variables, as measured from either client or therapist perceptions after five interviews, will be positively correlated with the indices of personal change during the period of therapy. These associations will be stronger when the relationship qualities are measured from client perceptions than when they are measured from therapist perceptions.

Hypothesis 2. (a) Comparison of results for two initially matched groups of clients with relatively expert and nonexpert therapists will show that perceived relationships are better for clients with the expert therapists than they are for the clients with nonexpert therapists. This will hold for each relationship dimension, whether derived from client or therapist perceptions after five interviews. *(b)* The clients who have more expert therapists will, as a group, also show evidence of greater beneficial change from therapy than the group of clients with nonexpert therapists.

Hypothesis 3. When the samples of fifth interview scores for each relationship variable from each of the two sources (clients and therapists) are divided by median splits into "high" and "low" groups, and the cases sorted in terms of their joint classification, the evidence of relative change of the resulting groups will be as follows: the greatest change will occur in cases whose relationship scores from both sources fall in the high category; second in order of change will be clients whose own relationship scores are high but whose therapists' scores are low; in third place will be clients who score low themselves but whose therapists score high; and least change will occur in the group who score low from both sources.

Hypothesis 4. There will be greater agreement between client and therapist perceptions of their relationship, in terms of their scores on each of the five dimensions, in the case of expert therapists and their clients than in the case of nonexpert therapists and their clients – given initially matched groups of clients who have been in therapy for similar periods when the relationship is measured.

RESULTS

INTERNAL CHARACTERISTICS OF THE RELATIONSHIP MEASURES

As the hypothesis testing makes principal use of the fifth interview scores, and as these scores are available for a larger sample than the data from later test points, they were used also in analyses focusing on characteristics of the relationship scales themselves.

Distribution characteristics: Basic distribution characteristics of the data on each scale are given in Table 2.1 for the 40 cases for whom fifth interview data from both clients *and* therapists were available. Mean (and median) scores are given *per item* within each scale, where the same theoretical maximums (+3) and minimums (–3) apply to each item in all scales.

Table 2.1 implies that all the item *means* from both the client and therapist data sample are in the positive scoring range by at least one standard deviation (SD) above the theoretical mean of zero, and some means

Table 2.1 RI scores per item from client and therapist perceptions after five therapy interviews (N = 40)

(/item) Variable	Client score data (/item)			Therapist score data		
	Mean	*Median*	*SD*	*Mean*	*Median*	*SD*
Level of regard (R)	1.82	2.04	.77	2.19	2.25	.56
Emp. understanding (EU)	1.42	1.50	.81	1.37	1.53	.86
Congruence (C)	1.62	1.93	.81	1.82	1.91	.71
Unconditionality (U)	1.47	1.53	.67	1.29	1.23	.92
Willingness to be known (WK)	0.91	1.05	.76	1.41	1.45	.68

Table 2.2 Reliability coefficients of the RI scales, from post-fifth-interview data

Scale	Client data (N = 42)	Therapist data (N = 40)
Level of regard (R)	.93	.93
Empathic understanding (EU)	.86	.96
Congruence (C)	.89	.94
Unconditionality (U)	.82	.92
Willingness to be known (WK)	.82	.88

exceed two SDs above zero. Therapists tended to describe the relationship somewhat more positively than the clients did on the R and WK variables. This implies that within this sample the therapists felt more warmth and appreciation toward their clients than the latter perceived (perhaps because of lowered self-regard) and that, as between clients and therapists, the latter saw themselves as freer to express their own feelings than their clients did. On other variables, inspection of the individual pairs of client and therapist scores showed that 10 clients out of 40 perceived their therapists to be much more unconditional and understanding then the therapists themselves felt that they were. Possibly, therapists had higher standards on these aspects and/or clients' wishful expectation of understanding and acceptance from their therapists influenced their perceptions of the relationship in a positive direction.

Split-half reliabilities: The internal consistency of each scale was assessed by the split-half method. Given the small number of varied items used in each scale, the two half-samples of items were not randomly selected, but were approximately matched in the proportion of positive and negative items and with an eye also to the judges' item-by-item ratings of their theoretical weight or strength. Table 2.2 gives the reliability coefficients of each scale as estimated using the Spearman-Brown formula. These figures are more than satisfactory. They imply, specifically, that theoretically comparable forms of the Inventory, administered at the same time, would yield very similar results. As might be expected, this tended to be even truer in the case of therapists than in the case of clients.

Intercorrelations: Interscale correlations from the client and therapist data showed a very strong association between empathy and congruence in the client data, although the scales are quite distinct in concept and item content. In contrast, unconditionality (U) stood out as most distinct from these and the level of regard (R) scales. The low and insignificant correlation between the U and R scales supported the theoretical and operational separation of these two variables. Even in the therapist RI data U was the lowest of any variable in its average correlation with measures on the other scales. Correlations of client scores with corresponding therapist's scores were low and at best marginally significant.

A possible explanation for the strong empathy–congruence link is that congruent openness to experience is a crucial determinant of a person's potential for empathic understanding, especially when the listener is focused on attuned recognition of the other's felt experience and meaning. If this explanation is valid, lower correlations would be found in nontherapy life relationships under stress – as was found in an early study by Berlin (1960). Using a slightly modified Client form of the RI Berlin asked a group of sorority student women to describe two contrasting relationships with fellow members. Using a sample of 'good' relationships, a correlation of .70 was found between empathic understanding and congruence. For the negatively perceived or 'poor' relationships described by the same group, the correlation was close to zero.

The obtained reliabilities and intercorrelations of the relationship measures, taken together, have indirect bearing on the validity of the scales. The *mean* correlation of the five component scales, in the client data, is .45 as against a mean split-half reliability of .86. Generally, the scales must be measuring different things. Corresponding figures from the therapist data are .65 (mean intercorrelation) and .93 (mean variances .42 and .86), allowing a broadly similar interpretation, though not such as to rule out the possibility of a common factor component.

Although correlations on each scale as measured from the two different vantage points are low, they mostly fall between the 5 percent and 10 percent levels of significance and suggest a muted association.

Assuming therapist actual experience is influencing corresponding client perceptions there is more than one possible reason why this is not more evident in the figures. Potential reporting bias is one of these, since 'error' of this sort could obscure linear trends. A linear model may itself wash out more complex patterns of association. And, it would be unsurprising for client and therapist to "read" the therapist's response rather differently in enough cases to dilute associations.

Scoring levels at different points in therapy: Of the 42 clients in this study, complete data from both clients and therapists at all three in-therapy test points (post-5, -15, and -25 interviews) *and* at termination of therapy, were obtained for 15 cases. Comparison of scores at the different test points, with a progressively reducing sample, showed little overall difference in the quality of the therapy relationship from mean RI scores from client or therapist data. Marked variation did occur in some individual cases, but in general there was no consistent pattern to this variation as a function of time in therapy.

This lack of variation was strikingly apparent in the results from therapist perceptions where closely similar means at the different test points occurred with monotonous regularity. In the results from client perceptions there was one marked exception to the general pattern. The clients tended to see their therapists as increasingly willing to be known as therapy proceeded. Also, these clients ended therapy perceiving a somewhat higher level of regard from their therapists than they had identified at any previous test point.

RESULTS FOR HYPOTHESIS 1

Association of the relationship measures after five interviews with therapy outcome: This was calculated for all the cases (variously 35 or 36) for whom the posttherapy data used in the change indices were ultimately obtained. The two kinds of therapist rating of client functioning were used together as previously noted. Sixteen cases fell in the upper category of change on *both* rating indices and comprised the 'more changed' group. The remaining 19 cases constituted the "less changed" group. The more changed clients ranked much higher on all RI scales except WK (Mann-Whitney U test: .01 significance level) (from Barrett-Lennard, 1962, Table 8). Using the therapist RI, data differences held in the same predicted direction at more moderate levels of significance, with the *strongest* difference on WK (Barrett-Lennard, Table 9). Thus, the *client* RI measures (except on WK) predicted *therapist* judgments of change most strongly, consistent with the *client*'s perception of the relationship being of most direct relevance to therapeutic change.

The alternative evidence of therapy outcome, based on client personality data, produced unanticipated problems. When the Q adjustment, MA and D scale scores were assembled for the 36 available cases it was apparent that (a) the three scales were highly correlated (.8 level, using Kendall's *W)* (b) some *pretherapy* scores on each scale reached a level that left very little room for positive change, and (c) there was a negative correlation between pretherapy standing and amount of positive change, on the scales. The strong correlations invited the decision to combine the three sets of ranked pretherapy data into a single composite measure, and similarly with the three sets of change data. Correlation of the two sets of composite rankings yielded a rho of $-.68$, indicating such a marked decrease in change as pretherapy adjustment increased that pretherapy standing would have to influence the association of change with other factors, including the measured relationship variables.

In light of these problems and the implied marked differences in pretherapy anxiety it was decided to divide the sample in terms of pretherapy adjustment ranking at an arbitrary point, and to compare the two subgroups thus obtained on the pretherapy data. The 'arbitrary point' was to separate the upper and lower half samples, the lower half (nominally more disturbed at the start) ranking 19 through 36 on the composite index. There clearly was room for change in this group in contrast to the initially higher scoring group (who nonetheless changed on the evidence from therapist ratings). In effect, the self-inventory scores for the upper half sample in the present study are not adequately distinguishing their difficulties on entering therapy and indeed on these data could be more like comparison groups who are not seeking therapy (see Dymond, 1954, Tables 2 and 3). In contrast, clients in the "lower" group appear more like the clients in earlier research (Dymond, 1954, Table 3) and evidently enter therapy consciously experiencing considerable anxiety and self-inadequacy, and feeling at least moderately depressed, and they typically change positively in these respects.

Based on the foregoing considerations the correlations between relationship and change in this appropriate half sample were studied. *The correlations obtained were all significant (including WK) to at least the .05 level when the measures of relationship were derived from client perceptions* (Barrett-Lennard, 1962, Table 12). The correlations using therapist-derived measures of relationships were also positive but too low to clearly confirm the association. This small positive association is a trend in the data leaving the possibility of an indirect link between the therapist's self-perceived response and client change as a credible hypothesis.

RESULTS FOR HYPOTHESIS 2

The aim in selecting the more and less expert samples of therapists was to obtain groups who could be expected to differ in their overall therapeutic effectiveness. Therapeutic effectiveness is conceived as the ability to facilitate therapeutic personality change in the setting of professional client–therapist relationships. The best available predictive criterion of this ability was taken to be the experience level and position of therapists in the Counseling Center. The 'less expert' therapists were first year staff interns, and one nonintern research assistant, who had completed a practicum course in client-centered therapy and then been selected for an internship. The more expert group had all *completed at least* the equivalent of a 2-year internship in the Counseling Center and then been appointed to staff counseling positions. These appointments were initially made, in most cases, on the basis of recommendation by a selection committee who had examined evidence (including interview recordings) of the appointee's counseling ability.

Other differences between the two therapist groups were that the more expert therapists were older, averaging 35.4 years compared with 28.4 years for the nonexperts; they had a minimum and mean of 3 and 5.4 years' experience counseling in the Center compared with .5 and 1 year, respectively, for the nonexperts; they had already completed or begun therapy with an average of 45 clients while the corresponding figure for nonexperts was 11; and they had had considerably more personal therapy than the nonexperts. Altogether there were eight therapists in the expert group and seven classified as nonexperts, including more men than women in each instance.

After selection of the two therapist groups the next step was to compare and equate their samples of clients. The theoretical significance of anxiety as a therapy condition (Rogers, 1957, 1959a) led to the choice of the pretherapy Manifest Anxiety and Q adjustment scores as important bases on which to match the two groups of clients. Age has some bearing on attitudes, outlook and, possibly, openness to change and other psycho-social factors. Thus it seemed a worthwhile precaution to match the client groups on age, too. Educational level of clients was included as a matching variable because it would be associated at least with their intellectual sophistication in regard to therapy, and also with their closeness to therapists' intellectual and social levels. To allow for possible differences between men and women in the ways that they tend to perceive and report interpersonal response on the relationship dimensions it was considered advisable to control the proportion of sexes in the two client samples. It may well be relevant, also, whether the therapist is of the same or opposite sex to the client. Client/therapist sex ratios were, therefore, also taken into account in matching the two samples.

Initially, the two samples of therapists had a total of 30 clients in the research sample; 13 with expert therapists (Group 1) and 17 with nonexperts (Group 2). The two client groups were virtually equivalent with regard to age and mean Q adjustment and Taylor MA scores and differed appreciably although not greatly, by groups, on the other sampling characteristics. Close study of the sampling data revealed that it was possible to obtain a high degree of equivalence on all of the sampling variables with a loss of only three client participants, leaving 12 and 15 clients (Barrett-Lennard, 1962, Table 15). Care was taken, in the matching process, to ensure that the selection was "blind" to any knowledge of obtained relationship scores.

Mean RI scale scores were in fact higher for Group 1 therapists in every case, except on WK. These differences reach significance levels in the client data sufficient to reject the null hypothesis with moderate assurance. The perceptions of the therapists, as groups and except on willingness to be known, are all in the same direction as for clients though more uneven in regard to significance levels (Barrett-Lennard, 1962, Tables 16 and 17). Thus, the results support Hypothesis 2a at modest levels of significance, excluding WK. Hypothesis 2b, predicting a positive association between therapist expertness and change was tested using the two-fold index of change from therapist ratings. Nine of the clients with Group 1 therapists fell in the "more changed" category and three in the "less changed" category. Among 14 clients with nonexpert therapists, six were classed as "more changed" and eight as "less changed". Analysis by Fisher's exact probability test revealed that there is less than a 10 percent that a difference as large as this would arise by chance in favor of the experts.

The change index from client self-descriptive data could not be used in a second test of the association between therapist expertness and change since it was not practicable to further subdivide the matched client groups. Length of time in therapy was the one other available possible measure. Therapeutic change is a process over time and, given the same approach to therapy, it is plausible to expect an association between length of therapy and amount of change, especially when prognostic factors such as pretherapy anxiety, are controlled. A study by Standal and van der Veen (1957), employing a sample of 72 clients in the Counseling Center, found a moderately strong correlation ($r = .62$) between log number of therapy interviews and increase in clients' personal integration as rated by their therapists at termination. In a later study, Cartwright, Robertson, Fiske, and Kirtner (1961) confirmed these findings on a different sample of clients, using indices of personal integration based on different therapist rating scales. Thus, notwithstanding limitations, length of therapy was considered a usable basis for discriminating relative change in the two equated client groups.

The two client groups did, in fact, differ significantly and rather strikingly in length of therapy, even when the information was reduced to a two-fold classification of case length (in which subjects were sorted into those above and those below the median of the combined sample). Thus, in terms of both the direct evidence from therapist ratings and the indirect evidence of a wide differential in case length, the prediction that clients who had expert therapists would change more than those who had nonexperts was upheld. *The finding that more expert therapists tended* both *to relate with higher levels of the conditions and that their clients improved more than matched clients in the other group yields crucial further support to the hypothesized therapy conditions-outcome link.*

RESULTS FOR HYPOTHESIS 3

To this point, client- and therapist-derived RI scores have been treated separately in parallel analyses. Both theory and results invited examination of how the combined perceptions of the two participants are associated with therapeutic improvement. Complete relationship data and change data from therapist ratings were obtained for 34 subjects, including 15 in the more clearly improved group separated for use in this analysis. From these data participants were classified as high or low scoring (by median split) on the relationship variables scored from both client and therapist data – yielding four subgroups, as shown in Table 2.3. For each variable, the number of participant subjects in each of the four resulting groups who fell in the more improved category of change (N = 15) were determined and are shown in Table 2.3. The last line of the table shows the theoretically predicted rank order of the subgroups. The previous rows of cells give actual figures.

It is evident from Table 2.3 that the trend of the results is in line with theoretical expectation. Where clients and therapists *both* perceive their relationship in relatively positive terms (H^c/H^t group) clients most often fall in this "more improved" category of change. When the client's score is relatively high and the therapist's score is in the lower half (H^c/L^t) there are somewhat fewer instances of distinct improvement. When relationship scores from both partners are relatively low positively rated improvement is low in frequency. This pattern is most distinct for level of empathic understanding and for the sum of the five scale scores, and next most distinct for congruence. (Among all possible sequences of four numbers there is only a 1 in 24 chance of the exact order 1, 2, 3, 4 occurring at random, which is less than a probability of .05.)

Table 2.3 Obtained and predicted orders of change among groups differing in the way the relationship is jointly perceived by clients and therapists

Combination groups	H^c/H^t	H^c/L^t	L^c/H^t	L^c/L^t
		(Numbers|Orders in bold)		
Level of regard	7|1	4|2	1|4	3|3
Empathic understanding	7|1	4|2	3|3	1|4
Congruence	6|1	4|2.5	4|2.5	1|4
Unconditionality	5|1.5	5|1.5	3|3	2|4
Willingness to be known	7|1	2|3.5	4|2	2|3.5
Sum of (5) scale scores	8|1	4|2	2|3	1|4
Predicted Order	1	2	3	4

Notes: H^c and H^t are high-scoring and L^c and L^t are low-scoring clients and therapists; N = 15 'more changed' clients.

RESULTS FOR HYPOTHESIS 4

Hypothesis 4 also involves joint consideration of client-and therapist-derived relationship scores, in this case to see *how different the scores from these two sources are, as between more and less expert therapists.* To control for differences produced by clients, matched client samples with expert and nonexpert therapists as used in Hypothesis 2 were employed. Discrepancy was measured by simply determining the absolute difference in scores for each client-therapist pair. The resulting discrepancy figures were averaged for the pairs in the expert and in the nonexpert groups.

The results revealed a strikingly large and significant difference in degree of client-therapist discrepancy on the measure of empathic understanding. It would appear that more experienced therapists in this population do, in fact, communicate their understanding much more unambiguously than inexperienced therapists. Possibly, too, the more expert therapist is able to identify and report with greater accuracy than the nonexpert just what understanding of her/his client s/he is actually experiencing. For the remaining variables Hypothesis 4 was not significantly supported statistically, although there were appreciable margins of difference in this sample in the predicted direction for level of regard and congruence (Barrett-Lennard, 1962, Table 26).

The fact that WK did not discriminate was not surprising, given other results. However, it is rather puzzling that the expert therapist appeared not to convey the unconditional regard or acceptance s/he is conscious of feeling any more clearly and unambiguously than the nonexpert therapist. Examination of the original U scores reveals that their distribution was bimodal, particularly for therapist respondents. (For example, in the combined sample used, eight therapists gave scores from 14 to 24, only two gave raw scores in the range 25–35 and seven therapist scores ranged from 36 to 46). This evidence suggests that the answers and scores were influenced by differing response sets. Such an interpretation is also consistent with the fact that the investigator felt, before this evidence came to light, that some U items should be revised (see next chapter) on the grounds that a number of them were too abstract to answer readily from experience in a relationship.

In sum, Hypothesis 4 was partially supported by the results obtained, with empathic understanding standing out as the one factor for which there is a strong and decisive relationship between therapist expertness and the extent to which client and therapist share similar perceptions of the therapist's response. Results are suggestive in favor of the hypothesis for level of regard and congruence, and provide no support at all for the remaining two variables in their present operational form.

IMPLICATIONS AND FURTHER RESEARCH

The findings in support of the first two hypotheses (aside from WK) do not prove that the four defined aspects of therapist response *must* have been direct causes of the identified changes in the client's personality functioning. However, two facts make it plausible to infer that the relationship variables were influential in some way in the generation of this change. Firstly, they largely preceded the change, being measured as soon as the client–therapist relationship could be considered established. Secondly, it was found that the selected more expert therapists – as confirmed by results achieved with their clients – also provided a higher measure of the relationship qualities then less expert therapists did.

Although most of the critical associations between measured relationship and change reached moderate to high levels of significance, in all cases the relationship variables only accounted for a limited portion of the variance of measured change. However, that they account for any significant proportion is a telling result since the perceived therapist response undoubtedly fluctuated during the period of therapy but in the hypothesis-testing was represented by a single reading at one point in time. In addition, the measures both of relationship and of change are estimates not exact indices. The imperfect associations between measured relationship and change could also imply that the theory is not complete.

The findings for Hypotheses 1 and 3 support the presumption that the client's perception of the therapist's response is more directly related to client change then the therapist's actual response as s/he experiences it. This fits the logic that clients are directly influenced by what they experience and process and a therapist's self-experienced response is a step or two removed from this. Seen in this light, the same findings lend broad support to the design and instrumentation of the study. When the contribution of client characteristics to the client's (and therapist's) perceptions of the relationship was controlled, in the testing of Hypothesis 2, direct evidence was obtained that the differential response of therapists was substantially influencing client perceptions and thus had at least an indirect impact on change.

The findings for Hypotheses 1 and 2 suggest that there are "good therapists" and "good clients" – in terms of the former's ability to respond with high levels of the relationship qualities and the letter's capacity to perceive them. The combination of the two would imply an excellent prognosis for therapy. Evidently, there also are poor therapists and poor clients (by the same criteria) who, if paired, would be unlikely to result in any beneficial outcome. A very good client paired with a mediocre therapist may perceive the therapist's response quite positively (and perhaps evoke a more positive response in the therapist partner) and have a productive therapy experience. Likewise, a good therapist working with a "poor" client may ultimately succeed in conveying that he/she genuinely cares and can understand, without judgment or identification, how it feels to be the client, to a degree that is significantly helpful.

In light of the generally positive findings, how are the ambiguous or negative results for the WK factor to be evaluated? It has been seen that under certain conditions, particularly when the same member of the client-therapist pair provides the change data and the relationship data, measured willingness to be known does tend to significantly predict measured change. Some significant associations were found between willingness to be known and change measures, but a viewpoint factor is compatible with these very uneven results (atypical of the other relationship variables), leaving WK of quite doubtful validity.

The WK results also suggest that the nonexpert and expert therapists had somewhat different attitudes or 'policies' toward behaviors that this category refers to. The question of whether it was therapeutically desirable for therapists to have feelings and thoughts of their own openly available to their clients was, at the time, a recent and rather contentious issue in the Counseling Center. The more expert therapists had been trained earlier whereas the nonexperts encountered this issue at a formative stage when this idea was "in the air." Thus, it is possible that theoretically extraneous factors exerted a systematic influence on the results when comparisons were made between the experts and nonexperts.

Given the largely negative results for WK and associated further thought the investigator revised his earlier concept of willingness to be known, to focus on the degree to which the therapist responds openly and personally to the client. Responding or being known as a person clearly is not just a matter of verbal content, such as communicating one's "own feelings" as distinct from "perceptions of the other person's feelings." It does imply an immediacy of response by the therapist, as opposed to putting a distance between his/her immediate experience and what is communicated to the other, for example, because this feels safer and/or maintains an image of how s/he should respond as a therapist (Barrett-Lennard, 1959a, p. 55). In this light, the main essence of WK was understood as an aspect of congruence rather than a separate feature. Thus, it was deemed unnecessary in further work to retain it as a separately measured relationship dimension.

The results obtained for the other four component measures of the Relationship Inventory seem clearly to justify their use in further research. Modification and further refinement of the instrument in light of its closely studied application was called for: most obviously in the case of unconditionality. For these reasons, after completing the early portion of the analysis presented in this report, and drawing on impressions gained in the course of approximately 260 individual administrations of the Inventory to the client and therapist subjects of this research, a preliminary 72-item revision was prepared and used in most immediately following studies.

The results of this research were and are considered to justify serious consideration by therapists of other orientations. Unless improved personality functioning has a radically different meaning at a practical level for therapists of a given alternative school of thought, it would be reasonable to hypothesize that the same qualities of therapist response exercise a decisive influence in their work also. The RI does not contain reference to any particular therapeutic technique, and replication of this study in other psychotherapies would be a challenging further test of the theory on which it is based.

A related avenue of further research, involving deeply disturbed clients and a broader spectrum of therapists, followed hard on the heels of this study. A main aim was to investigate whether the relationship factors are vital to successful therapy with hospitalized psychotic people treated in the context of a large-scale research project by Rogers and his coworkers in the Wisconsin Psychiatric Institute (Rogers, 1961). In preliminary results reported by van der Veen (1961), criteria of therapeutic improvement derived from Rogers' process conception (Rogers, 1958, 1959a; Walker et al., 1960) were significantly associated with total scores from the four retained relationship measures. This held whether the Relationship Inventory data were provided by the clients (schizophrenic patients) or by judges who rated the therapist's response as observers.

Given that the four qualities tapped by the RI are change-enabling ingredients in therapy relationships it plausibly follows that the extent to which they are present in any significant continuing interpersonal relationships (such as that between husband and wife or parent and child) would have an important bearing on the psychological development and functioning of the individuals involved. Early studies with the RI focusing on nontherapy relationships were reported by Berlin (1960), Thornton (1960), and Rosen (1961). These collectively implied that the Inventory-measured qualities discriminated between relationships separately identified as more or less satisfying, adequate, or constructive for the individual.

Although and partly because the findings of the foundation study, as freshly presented in this chapter, gave such promising support to the theory under investigation, follow-up research both inside and outside a psychotherapy context was at once seen as being called for. The chapters that follow illustrate how extensive this work has been and the ways its active promise continues.

CONCLUSION

This study worked to connect 'cause and effect' in the therapy process. Following from Rogers' conditions of therapy conception (1957, 1959a) it focused on the proposition that therapeutic personal change occurs according to the degree that the client experiences positive regard, nonjudging acceptance, empathic understanding, congruence or genuineness, and willingness to be known by and from the therapist. The investigator's Relationship Inventory was developed to measure these qualities and was answered independently by the client and therapist participants in the study. It was conceived that the client's perceptions of the focused variables of therapist's response would be direct, operative influences in the therapy process and that these perceptions would in turn depend on an interaction of client characteristics and the therapists' actual experience in their relation.

Forty-two clients in the Counseling Center of the University of Chicago, and their 21 therapists answered the RI after five therapy interviews. The degree of change in the client during therapy was assessed from a combination of selected therapist rating measures, and from client scores on anxiety- and depression-related self-inventory instruments completed before and after therapy. The principal experimental hypotheses were, in essence: (1) that each relationship factor as measured from either source would significantly predict the indices of change, and that these predictions would be strongest in RI data from the clients' perspectives; and (2) that results for two matched equivalent groups of clients, with relatively "expert" and "nonexpert" therapists would show that cases with experts gave higher scores on each RI measure and also give evidence of greater change than the cases with nonexperts.

A third hypothesis predicted that simultaneous consideration of client and therapist relationship data would show most client change among high scorers from both sources, lesser change in other combinations and least change from low-scoring pairs. Fourthly, it was hypothesized that the RI scale scores obtained from client-therapist pairs would be more divergent for cases with nonexpert therapists than for cases with expert therapists.

Before testing these hypotheses, internal characteristics of the Relationship Inventory measures, including split-half reliabilities and intercorrelations of the five scales, were determined for both client and therapist data. All scales possessed adequate internal reliability and, with possible exception of highly correlated empathy and congruence, each of the five measures proved to be empirically differentiated aspects of the perceived relationship.

Hypotheses 1 and 2 were essentially confirmed throughout, by the results obtained, for four of the measured variables of relationship (but mostly not for WK). The two latter hypotheses were supported clearly on the RI empathy measure. Two features of the study design and results make it plausible to infer that the factors of perceived relationship quality (besides WK) helped to generate the associated change. Firstly, the tapping of relationship quality after five interviews ensured that it was largely a prior condition to client change. Secondly, therapists identified as more competent (on the basis *both* of their experience *and* empirical evidence of results they achieved with their clients) provided higher measures of the four qualities than therapists identified as less competent.

In light of the results for the willingness to be known measure, and the investigator's further thinking, a revision of this concept was advanced. This modified conception, although held to be relevant in a therapy relationship, was afterwards viewed as an aspect of congruence rather than a separate variable in its own right. Further research with the Relationship Inventory (omitting WK) began at once, especially in the investigation of therapy with hospitalized clients identified as schizophrenic. It extended also to application of the theory and instrument to the study of significant "nontherapy" life relationships. A major trajectory of further research followed this first-of-its kind study.

Chapter 3
A Major Revision: Crafting the 64-item RI and Emergent Adaptations

Even before my original study was reported (see Chapter 2) the new Inventory was in demand for further studies and was being revised for wider application. The first amending revisions were prepared at short notice and most of these ran to 72 items for the four retained scales – as in the major Wisconsin study. However, by the time the monograph was in circulation (early 1963) a full data-supported revision was in progress, and was completed in its initial format the following year. While in use from that point on a published full account of the revision and its varied adaptations did not appear until 1978.[1] This chapter retells essential parts of that detailed report, with contemporary relevance in mind. The way the revision was done, and how its adaptations and applications in varied contexts unfolded, help to define the RI still. While the Inventory can be applied without this knowledge it remains relevant for critical understanding and well-informed use of the instrument.

The 1978 report nearly did not see the light of day. The editor of the document journal thought at first that it was redundant in view of Gurman's fine review (1977) at that time. In fact, there is no overlap in purpose and hardly any in content, as Gurman (when I asked him) and I both pointed out. There were no other crises before final acceptance as a "Selected Document in Psychology." Each issue of that publication consisted of informative abstracts, and the full documents had to be individually ordered. In these respects the periodical was experimental and it was discontinued by the mid-1980s. I went on to distribute many hard copies of my report myself, until this eventually became impractical, and am so glad that the document's core content is again accessible to fellow investigators and other interested readers.

This chapter has two main parts. The first part focuses carefully on the aims, theory, and steps involved in revising the Relationship Inventory to produce the basic 64-item forms. The second part is a developmental account of the principal adaptations to the time of my 1978 report. Freshly expressed and in its main forms, the RI samples the perceptions of either participant in a dyadic relationship, relevant to empathic understanding, congruence, and both level and unconditionality of regard. Parallel forms provide for the respondent to focus (1) on the other person's response within their relationship ("other toward self," called "OS" forms) and/or (2) on his or her own response to that other ("myself/me to the other," or "MO" forms). Items are distinctive for each of the four component scales, and answers to them are in a numerical form convenient for summation. The answer codes range (as originally) from +3 ("Yes, I strongly feel that it is true") through four anchored, intermediate levels to −3 ("No, I strongly feel that it is not true"). Half of the items for each scale are negatively worded (e.g., "S/he takes no notice of some things I think or feel"), with signs reversed before summation, since on these items saying "no" counts positively and a "yes" answer is negative for scoring.

As earlier mentioned, the immediate demand for use of the RI in further research prompted a 72-item interim revision, with little change in the selection and wording of items used in the four retained component scales. This version, adapted for special populations in some cases, was used in a variety of additional

---

[1] Barrett-Lennard (1978).

The Relationship Inventory: A Complete Resource and Guide, First Edition. Godfrey T. Barrett-Lennard.
© 2015 John Wiley & Sons, Ltd. Published 2015 by John Wiley & Sons, Ltd.
Companion site: www.wiley.com/go/barrett_lennard/therelationshipinventory

studies, in therapy and nontherapeutic contexts (e.g., Berlin, 1960; Bleecker, 1964; Clark and Culbert, 1965; Emmerling, 1961; Gross and DeRidder, 1966; Hollenbeck, 1961, 1965; Snelbecker, 1967).

PURPOSES OF THE REVISION

Although the 72-item RI forms yielded meaningful results in the studies in which they were applied, several considerations prompted full revision, leading to development of the main 64-item forms:

1. The original RI versions were prepared with the study of client–therapist relationships immediately in view, while application to significant nontherapy relationships lay in the realm of interesting, theoretically consistent potentiality. One main purpose of full-scale revision was to attain forms of expression that the ordinary person could readily respond to in reference to any significant relationship with another person, consistent with maintaining or increasing the usefulness of the instrument in therapy research.
2. Another revision aim was to adequately reflect theoretical refinement of the concepts of unconditionality and congruence, which had occurred since the original development of the RI.
3. Empirical item-analysis applied to samples of RI data had not been employed in preparing previous versions of the Inventory. The content validation by judges, and split-half and test-retest reliability testing, did not indicate how much or consistently in differing samples, *each item* was actually working to produce its scale score. Adjustments could be expected to follow from careful analysis on this level.
4. Samples of 'positively' and 'negatively' expressed items had been represented within each scale of the instrument, though not in equal measure. A further objective of the revision was to achieve a balance, within each of the four scales, of items to which affirmative answers would score in a positive direction and "no" answers in a negative direction and an equal sample of items to which affirmative answers would score in a negative direction and "no" answers would be positive.

In essence, the 64-item revision was directed toward enhancing the item composition, relative to earlier versions, from several standpoints. These included expanding the effective range of application of the instrument, ensuring that unconditionality (and congruence) items were in keeping with definitional refinements, making adjustments suggested by detailed analysis of the extent to which individual items were aligned and in step with their scale scores, and further offsetting certain response bias possibilities (particularly by balancing positively and negatively stated items). Consistent with these aims, finding simpler more experiential or natural language in the case of some more complex or abstract items was desired.

ITEM ANALYSIS AND OTHER FEATURES

THE ITEM ANALYSIS

The item analysis employed data from five sources. *Two* of these were the client and separate therapist returns gathered after five therapy interviews in the author's original study (see Chapter 2). A *third* sample was provided by a group of Auburn University students in an introductory psychology course. Most students selected a member of their immediate family, and the remainder largely chose peer friend relationships. A *fourth* set of data, obtained with MO forms of the RI, was provided by a group of graduate teachers doing further studies at Auburn. Again, the relationships were mostly with friends or members of the respondents' immediate families. The *fifth* sample of data was drawn from a study by Hollenbeck, based on separate father and mother relationship descriptions from students of both sexes at the University of Wisconsin (Hollenbeck, 1961, 1965). From these OS RI data, the son–father group (N = 50) was chosen for the item analysis solely because it contained the widest distribution of scores.

The analysis of item behavior did not lead to automatic inclusion or exclusion of items but was used as an important contributing aid in refining the item samples in accord with all of the subpurposes outlined. It was valuable to be able to systematically study and compare each item's contribution within each sample and across samples. To this end, a time-consuming but informative procedure was devised by the author. The scale scores (from each sample) were first divided at the median, resulting in a higher scoring or "upper" half-sample and a lower-scoring half-sample, each half-sample with its own mean. The difference between these two half-sample means divided by the number of items involved is the *average per item contribution* to this difference. The actual contribution of each item around this mean naturally varied, and was examined one by one. This showed how much each individual item contributed to the overall mean difference.

Scale scores in some samples were more widely dispersed than in other samples. In order to make direct comparisons *across samples* of the degree to which the same item was working to produce its scale score, the effect of these dispersion differences had to be neutralized. This was done in a way that yielded an *average* item mean of unity (1) in the case of each sample. It became evident that some items contributed strongly to its scale in all samples, others packed a punch in some samples but not in others, and a few others had weak weightings in most samples.[2] Examples of the former kind include Item 52, *There are times when I feel that his outward response to me is quite different from the way he feels underneath*, and Item 54, *He understands me* – both of which are preserved in all subsequent 64 item OS forms and given in parallel wording in the MO forms.

The original item 7, which worked well in therapy relationships and in the MO form, but not at all adequately in the son/father or student with friend data, was reworded in more straightforward language. And in a specific example, the congruence item, *He does not try to mislead me about his own thoughts and feelings*, worked unevenly and was changed to the more natural positive form, *He is willing to express whatever is actually in his mind with me including feelings about himself or about me* and, in the MO form to, *I feel comfortable to express whatever is in my mind including any feelings about myself or about him*. (Gender-free language was later substituted.) Added illustration of the outcomes of close item-by-item scrutiny is given below.

ADJUSTING THE NUMBERS OF ITEMS

Previous versions of the RI had been found to possess very adequate statistical reliability (e.g., Barrett-Lennard, 1962; Berzon, 1964; Hollenbeck, 1965; Snelbecker, 1967). With further refinement of the item samples it was assumed that they could be reduced in size somewhat, without loss of reliability and with the practical advantage of a shorter administration time. Balanced against this, item statements need to sample adequately the various facets of each dimension that the Inventory is designed to measure. It was decided to moderately reduce the number of items in each scale from 18 (in the 72-item forms) to 16, of which 8 would be positively worded and 8 negatively expressed. As in previous versions, each item would score on one scale only, resulting in the total of 64 items.

THEORETICAL REFINEMENTS

Unconditionality: As first formulated, this concept focused on the degree of constancy or variability of one person's feeling response toward another person who is communicating self-experience to the first (see Chapter 2). By the time the RI revision was undertaken the former definition was seen as incomplete in that

---

2   The principle was that when each number in a distribution is divided by the mean of that distribution then the mean of the new distribution thus formed reduces (or increases) to unity (+1). The resulting values were a form of *item discrimination index*, in the language used (Barrett-Lennard, 1978). Another whole approach would have been to correlate item results with scale scores, sample by sample, and work from those data. This was far less straightforward to do then than it is now with SPSS and I also felt then that I could keep closer track of how each item was behaving in each scale and sample by the less orthodox method that was employed.

it did not explicitly distinguish *conditional* variation in regard from the broader realm of any variation in attitudinal-feeling response in a relationship.

In the author's revised definition, regard for another is conditional to the extent that it is contingent on varying self-expressive actions, attitudes, or feelings of the other and *is experienced in the form of a response to the person or self of the other*. If differentially positive or negative reactions to particular behaviors carried no message of approval/disapproval, liking/disliking, and so forth, for the self or personhood of the receiving individual then they would not imply conditionality. Put another way, the responding person's regard is conditional to the extent that his/her response implies that the other is more or less pleasing, worthy, valued, trusted, liked, or disliked if s/he manifests certain self-attributes or qualities than if or when s/he manifests others.

In practice, the majority of original items in this category were not at odds with this modified definition, even where the exact language or item analysis results invited some improvement. Other items were changed in light of this modified definition whether or not they held up satisfactorily in terms of the item-analysis data. For example the OS item *His/her general feeling toward me varies considerably* gave adequate results in the item analysis, but was changed to *I don't think that anything I say or do really changes the way s/he feels about me* (parallel wording in the MO form, in both cases). Item 7, previously mentioned, which began (OS form) *Whether I like or dislike myself...* was changed to a more natural language form, *Whether I am feeling happy or unhappy with myself...* and then retained in the unconditionality scale.

Congruence: As implied, features of the "willingness to be known" concept were later treated as an aspect of congruence rather than belonging to a separate variable. The resulting effects on item sampling for the congruence dimension are visible in such items as : *[S/he]___ is willing to express whatever is actually in his/her mind with me, including present feelings about him-/herself or about me* and *[S/he]___ is openly him-/herself in our relationship* (items 44 and 48 respectively in Form OS–64)

From a logical and conceptual standpoint, special problems are involved in the measurement of congruence. The definition of this construct centers on the integrative consistency between a person's inner experience, immediate awareness, and overt communication (see Chapter 2). Experience is assumed to include all contents of immediate arousal and activity of kinds that *could register in conscious awareness* (e.g., not including those physiological processes which, of their nature, lie outside consciousness). Implied is the notion that persons may be more or less 'open to experience' generally or in a given circumstance. Experience that is not expressed might be inferred by the other from indirect verbal and nonverbal cues. The same kind of inferential process is not available to the experiencing person him-/herself, who obviously cannot step outside his/her own awareness and see discrepancy between this awareness and feelings or arousal signs that are not in awareness, at least at the time. (The person may become aware of features of his/her response retrospectively with possible *subsequent* effect on congruence.)

Thus, as between the OS (recipient-perceiver) and MO (self-report) forms of the RI, the evidence respondents provide relevant to congruence differs in principle. Respondents to the OS form are not limited by the self-awareness or explicit messages of the other. In this form, congruence items range from those that call for the respondent's inferential sensing of aspects of the other's underlying experiencing (for example, items 40 *At times I sense that s/he is not aware of what s/he is really feeling with me*, and item 56 *S/he doesn't hide anything from him- or herself that s/he feels with me*) to those that tap more direct observations regarding inferred congruence indicators (for example, item 4 *S/he is comfortable and at ease in our relationship* and item 16 *It makes him/her uneasy when we ask or talk about certain things*). Other items fall in between, and in various ways, tap the extent to which the other person is seen as personally honest, open and in touch with self in the relationship.

In replying to the congruence items in the self-report MO forms of the RI the respondent's report could be expected to provide a fairly good indication of the level of his/her comfort/discomfort with self in the relationship (seen as an indirect indicator of congruence). It should also give a reliable indication of the degree of consistency between his/her awareness and overt communication. Also, the respondent is looking back on his/her processes in the referent relationship and may in some degree discriminate elements that were not in his/her awareness at the moment of interaction. These issues do not fully resolve but mitigate the in-principle problem of self-report of congruence. And, in practice, the scale satisfies the same criteria of internal consistency and reliability as the others do and appears not to have been less effective in predictive studies than other scales in the MO form.

FURTHER STEPS IN COMPLETING THE REVISION

The rigidly parallel wording (just with pronoun changes) of the corresponding items in the "Client" (now, OS) and 'Therapist' (now, MO) RI forms had the intent to maximize equivalence between the two forms. For a significant proportion of items, however, this approach contributed to somewhat forced or unnatural forms of expression in one or other (sometimes both) of these forms. Consistent with other aims, the revision sought to achieve more experiential and natural forms of expression. "Phenomenal equivalence" (or comparability of meaning, intent and significance) rather than equivalence in *semantic form* was the aim. In practice, application of this perspective left nearly half the items (about 30) in exactly or virtually parallel form. The departures from parallel wording were very carefully considered from the standpoint of preserving the same basic intent or meaning, maintaining a similar "strength" of statement (some variations were introduced because parallel wording was judged to leave the item effectively stronger or weaker in the OS or MO form) and achieving the maximum gain from a limited difference in choice or arrangement of words.

Decisions on amendment or retention of items were often influenced by more than one cue. As further instance, the Empathic Understanding item (OS form), which read ponderously *S/he can be deeply and fully aware of my most painful feelings without being distressed or burdened by them him/herself* did not perform well and was changed to read *When I am hurt or upset ___ can recognize my feelings exactly, without becoming upset too* (item 62). At the other extreme, substantial weighting of an item in all or most samples, coupled with straightforward expression, provided confirming evidence for retention of the item, with little or no change. The simply worded empathy item *S/he understands me* (item 54) is a case in point, as is the Regard item *S/he is indifferent to me* (item 17) and the Congruence item *There are times when I feel that ___'s outward response to me is quite different from the way s/he feels underneath* (item 52). The pattern of weightings was often a useful cue, as implied. Strong weightings in the OS form data and weaker weightings in one or both sets of MO form results, for example, was taken to imply that the intent of the item was sound but not well conveyed in the existing MO formulation. In another case, results may indicate that an item pulled its weight strongly in the data from clients and therapists but not in the nontherapy samples, suggesting again that the intent of the item was not a problem but that the language in which it was expressed was unsuitable outside a clinical or client–therapist context.

To further illustrate the item-by-item revision process, attention is again drawn to what is now Congruence item 44. Discrimination index values ranged from .22 (client data) to .99 (son–father data), with a mean of .66 for the five samples. The item began *He does not try to mislead me… .* Those who gave a "no" rating would in effect be saying *Yes he does try to mislead me… .* The revision changes the idea to positive form (ruling out a double negative) and shifts the emphasis to openness or its lack. Also, the OS item beginning *He is willing to…* and MO version *I feel comfortable to…* is an example of the author's meaning of phenomenal rather than exact semantic equivalence. From the responding person's standpoint the issue of open expression may not pivot on "(un)willingness" but on what feels right or manageable in the circumstances.

The personal judgment of the author necessarily played an important part in many details of the revision. In order to guard against avoidable errors or limitations resulting from this individual judgment, after carefully generating a modified sample of items for each scale a draft revision of the Inventory was composed, subjected to further review, and used on a trial basis. Three other investigators closely acquainted with the Inventory and its theoretical foundation, were provided with copies of the draft revision, a statement of the aims and procedures involved and a full set of the item-analysis results. In addition, the draft revision was used in a research pilot study with a group of persons from counselling and mental-health-related professions, who were also invited to provide direct feedback on any aspects of the instrument itself. The feedback and data obtained in these two ways were largely confirmatory but included critical comments and suggestions that were used by the author in the course of a further detailed scrutiny of the instrument, undertaken after an interval of several months. A number of additional adjustments were made and the 64-item revision was finalized and lithographed in mid-1964. Subsequent minimal adjustments to the primary forms were to achieve gender-free phrasing or, occasionally, still better wording of an item.

THE SPREAD OF APPLICATION WITH VARIED ADAPTATIONS

This section carries the further story of RI usage to the mid-1970s, before and after the 64-item revision. Aside from the Wisconsin research and Berlin's mentioned work a cluster of early studies involved adolescent (or even younger) respondents. Moderate changes were made to interim revisions for application with this population. Similar directions, the same answer categories, and the 72-item format were preserved. Item formulations were somewhat simplified where this was deemed necessary for high school age (junior or senior) respondents. The first version of a 'high school' adaptation was prepared by R. E. Bills and the present author, in collaboration, at Auburn University.[3] Its principal uses included Emmerling's (1961) dissertation study, which focused on teacher–pupil relationships, and a thesis by Rosen (1961) concerned with relationships between legally delinquent and 'normal' boys and their parents. Soon afterward, van der Veen made limited further refinements to the HS version and sponsored its initial application in family therapy research (Fike & van der Veen, 1966). This HS (OS) form, with slight adjustment to the directions, was also used in Bleecker's careful dissertation (1964) that focused on the relationship between high school students and their counsellors.

Slightly later research used the regular 64-item forms with adolescent respondents. These included studies by Mason and Blunberg (1969) and Spotts (1965/1966), focusing on teacher-to-student relationships, and by Wiebe (1975) and van der Veen and Novak (1971), who studied parent–child relations. The evidently effective use of the standard form with high school age respondents supports its versatility. However, it seemed premature to draw firm conclusions regarding the form's lower limit of reliable application, in terms of age and educational level. Thompson (1967/1968, 1969), for one, adjusted the 64-item form to make it easier for seventh and eighth grade children, who described their teacher's relational response. A separately prepared version, with simplifying adjustments in wording, was used more widely with children as next described.

THE TEACHER–PUPIL RELATIONSHIP INVENTORY (TPRI)

The TPRI, with the same answer categories and number and arrangement of items as the standard 64-item forms, was prepared by A. L. Scheuer (1969, 1971), with help from this author. Separate 'pupil' and 'teacher' forms of the instrument were adapted and used. The former, based on the 64-item OS RI form was the more distinctive. The setting for his study was a large residential school for emotionally disturbed children. Completed TPRI returns were collected from 169 children (mean age 13.5 years) and their 19 teachers. (Some of the younger and/or lower IQ children probably needed help in completing the Inventory.) Fifty percent of TPRI items were unchanged or virtually identical with the corresponding items in RI Form OS-M–64 (the M stands for male other). The other half of the items, with a few exceptions, are simplified in wording (for example, item 4, *He is comfortable and at ease in our relationship* becomes *He feels at ease with me*). Some simplifying adjustments lengthen the items, for example, item 17, He is indifferent to me becomes, *Most days he doesn't seem to care about me – one way or the other.*

Split-half reliability coefficients were lower than those typically found with the standard OS forms – and were uneven in a different pattern in the version for teachers (Scheuer, 1969, p. 59). The Teacher form of the TPRI is worded for plural others (for example, Item 1 is *I respect them as persons*), and teachers

---

[3] The item content of this 1959/1960 version (while out-of-date in the present context) was preserved in use by R. E. Bills, and reproduced in his book *A system for assessing affectivity* (1975).

answered them in reference to class groups of 7 to 14 pupils. The format and bulk of the item content is similar to the MO form of the "Group" adaptation of the RI, as first prepared by the present author in 1969. The results of this early work were one useful resource in the author's much later preparation of substantially revised 40-item RI forms for students and their teachers (see Chapter 5 and Appendix 1).

GROUP AND "MILIEU" FORMS OF THE RI

Berzon is the first investigator known to have used a group version of the BLRI, adapted from the 72-item interim (OS) revision simply by using plural instead of singular pronouns in reference to the other and adjusting the verbs to correspond. Two pilot studies yielded *total score* test-retest coefficients of .86, for intensive groups and a four session, one-month interval. On being asked, respondents consistently reported no difficulty in use of the plural referent (Berzon, 1962). Substantive results of studies with this form are reported (briefly) in Solomon, Berzon, and Weedman (1968). Desrosiers (1968) was another early user of a similar, self-adapted group version of the RI.

My adaptation of the RI for use in groups resulted in forms OS-G–64 and MO-G–64, which preserved the same item-by-item substantive content as in the regular 64-item version. (Much later, the "group" forms were reduced to 40-item forms, with alterations in wording that follow in substance the alternative 40-item forms for dyadic relationships – see Chapter 5 and Appendix 1.) So far as technical reliability is concerned, I relied first on the 'isomorphism' between the group and the regular dyadic forms. As well, direct evidence has occasionally been provided by other investigators. Abramowitz and Jackson (1974), for example, used a 64-item group form and reported that alpha coefficients in their sample exceeded .75 for each scale, and reached .92 for the sum of the four scale scores. Other applications of group forms occurred in studies by Cooper (1974/1975), Gilmour-Barrett (1973), and Bebout (1971/1972). Cooper's study, in a modified student-instructor context, used the regular OS form of the RI to tap student perspectives and the MO-G–64 form to elicit corresponding instructor perceptions. Gilmour-Barrett used a slightly adapted version of the Teacher form of the TPRI with a large sample of childcare workers, who each answered in reference to the children they worked with. Bebout (1971/1972 and Bebout & Gordon, 1972, pp. 113–114) included a version of the OS group form to obtain the perception of their group's response, by the members of over 150 encounter groups.

"Milieu" (whole group) forms of the RI were successfully used in independent studies by Gross, Curtin, and Moore (1970) and by Wargo and Meek (1970/1971). Wargo consulted me in adapting the OS 64-item form to the milieu context. The referent group consisted of the overall membership of a residential rehabilitation center; where the data were collected from 100 persons of both sexes and varied disability. Some few RI items, including the first which read *People here respect me as a person*, were moderately amended for the milieu context. For Gross and collaborators, the reference milieu consisted of the 13 staff members (psychiatrist to secretary) in a psychiatric hospital ward, concerned with preparing patients for expected discharge. Patients completed the RI (similar to Form OS-G–64), typically, with the words "the staff," "staff members," and "most of the staff" in place of the pronouns "they" and "them." Item 12, for example, read I feel that *most members of the staff are real and genuine with me*. Staff members completed an MO form adaptation, in which Item 12 was: *I feel that I am real and genuine in my relationships with most patients*. Mean differences in the direction of lower patient than staff scores were particularly striking in the case of unconditionality, although the score levels from both sources were low.

OBSERVER/JUDGE FORMS OF THE RI

Observer forms of the RI are designed to be answered by a third party who is either a direct witness to a relationship or has listened to or seen a live recording of its process. In either case, the RI items identify the parties in the relationship distinctively. For example, in a therapy study the first OS form item could become *The therapist respects the client as a person* or *A is personally respecting of _____*. The form is not tied to any one observation position or role. The observer may be someone who knows both parties well and is providing a further perspective on their relationship. Or (with different meaning and purpose) s/he may be observing live or recorded interaction, arranged for the research, between persons seen for the first time. Van der Veen (1970, pp. 220–221) reported an exploratory study in which several judges each rated a sample of therapy relationships from interview recordings. Inter-judge (RI total score) correlations were modest (median inter-judge correlation = .50) although the mean rating from five judges was deemed adequate for further exploratory analyses.

In a very different study by Snelbecker (1967) college student respondents viewed two filmed client interviews with therapists of differing orientation, and the response of each therapist was rated on an observer adaptation of the interim 72-item RI. The scored perceptions of the level of empathy and other RI qualities of the therapists were found to vary significantly, according to observer gender (women gave more positive ratings), whether a film was seen first or second in order (the latter drawing higher scores), and the type of therapy depicted (the Rogers' interview drew higher RI scores). The study suggested complex determinants of naïve observer appraisal with the RI.

An observer does not judge from inside the experience of participants, which the Relationship Inventory in its theory and main forms is specifically designed to do. Thus, an observer form is not a more objective substitute for participant forms, but would have different purposes, for example, to determine how relationship judgments by observers relate to qualities of their own personalities or social attitudes. Another aim might be to contribute to selection for a training program in the helping field. This form also could be useful in studying family relationships, for example, the way other members see the parent couple as a twosome.

FORMS BASED ON FACTOR ANALYSIS OF INTERITEM CORRELATIONS

By the mid-1970s several investigators had generated altered versions of the RI through use of factor analysis applied to data gathered with regular or extended forms of the instrument. The most carefully documented, published work of this nature had been done by Lietaer (1974, 1976), using Dutch language versions of the RI. To the regular 64-item forms Lietaer added 20 items drawn from the original RI (particularly, the Willingness to be Known scale), and 39 items he constructed (including a focus on therapist authority and direction). This 123-item adaptation was applied first in the study of student–parent relationships (Lietaer, 1974), using a sample of 800 college-level men and women students. From these data five oblique factors were extracted, for each of 10 items that were retained in composing 50-item OS and MO forms measuring empathy, positive regard, unconditionality, transparency (made up of Willingness to be Known and Congruence items), and directivity. Of the 50 items, 40 are worded positively. The empathy scale includes 7 out of 8 of the regular 64-item form E + items; and 8 out of 8 of the regular U + items cluster within the unconditionality scale. The positive regard scale is a more varied cluster, but does not include any regular "E," "C," or "U" items.

In a separate study, Lietaer (1976) used the same extended RI with a sample of over 100 client-therapist pairs, representing client-centered and psychoanalytic orientations. His similar treatment of these data resulted in seven factor-based scales, employing 48 items. Five of the scales warranted the same labels as in Study 1, although differing in specific item composition. The additional scales were identified as "Negative Regard" (4 items) and "Incongruity" (8 items, of which 7 are from previous C scales). Lietaer's two factor-based RI forms have just 29 items in common. Notwithstanding the careful conduct of this work, the varied results with different samples and the clustering of items all positive or negative in their wording shows up the directional and limiting influence of factor-analytic methodology when applied to such data.

Related interesting work by Bebout (1971/1972, Bebout & Gordon, 1972) was not all published in detail. Early in the course of a large-scale project on the process and effects of intensive group experience (the "T.I.E. Project"), Bebout (1971/1972) factor-analyzed two sets of data gathered with the OS 64-item RI, using principal components analysis followed by Varimax rotation. One set consisted of the group members' perceptions of the group leader/facilitator's response (N = 287). Set 2 was made up of friend perceptions of member responses in their relationship (N = 261). Each data set yielded four main factors corresponding substantially to the original RI scales. In each data set, five items also loaded on a small factor evidently concerned with perceived imposition/nonimposition and related to Lietaer's directivity factor.

In Set 1 of Bebout's data, the level of regard factor included all except one of the 16 regard (R+ and R−) items; while half of the R− items had insufficient loadings in Set 2. Of the congruence items 13 and 11 respectively loaded on a factor Bebout tentatively labelled "open-genuine." Nine of these items appeared either in the "transparency" *or* "incongruity" factor scales of Lietaer. The majority of items in the empathy and conditionality factors were from the E+ and U+ subgroups; thus resembling Lietaer's corresponding scales. Every adequately loaded item except one on the Regard, Empathy, Open-Genuine, and Unconditionality/Conditionality factors from both sets of data, was from the R, E, C, and U item pool, respectively (of the 64-item RI forms) – indirectly providing further support for the separation of the four scales in the RI. (I am indebted to Dr. Bebout for making available his detailed working record and results, for the factor analyses referred to (see also Chapter 4, p. 45).

This author has not used factor-analytic procedures aimed at further refining the RI. Why? Two observations related to the useful work by Lietaer and Bebout provide a partial answer. Alongside the convergent features and broadly supportive implications there is marked variability (1) in the precise factorial structure emergent from the analyses by these investigators, and (2) in the item composition of the "same" factors. The disadvantages of generating differing scales for different classes of relationship, including the difficulty of pinning down the defining properties and boundaries of any given class, are believed to outweigh any advantage of sharper measurement within a restricted domain. Further, it is doubtful whether improved measurement follows from taking factorial results at face value. For example, the emergence of factors in which all or most items are positively, or else negatively, stated is in keeping with the expectation of potential response bias, which the combination of positive and negative items in the regular RI scales is intended to offset. The evidence is most clearly confirming in this respect in Lietaer's second study, where both positive regard and negative regard factors emerged. Their theoretical and empirical relationship led Lietaer to add a composite positive + negative regard scale. In this author's perspective this composite scale would be much superior as a measure to either component index, and would not be far removed from Level of Regard as normally scored from the RI data.

CONCLUSION

This chapter has focused on the painstaking revision of the original forms of the RI and of its early adaptation for use in schools, and in families with adolescent respondents. Tapping member perceptions of how a whole group (or milieu) responded also required limited modifications, providing for observer-judges to describe a relationship called for another variant, and further adaptations were "in the wings." Although it is now nearly 40 years since the mid-1970s, the 64-item revision and early mushrooming phase of applications is vitally relevant to the whole trajectory that has followed, as unfolded through the next two chapters. The RI had already been or was in use in French, German, Dutch, Japanese, Spanish and Portuguese translations, and a videotaped form using American Sign Language (Ameslan) had been developed. To the mid-1970s more than 100 separate studies using the instrument had been reported or were in progress. Many of these involved careful searching work; a good many others, regrettably, seemed flawed and weak. The intention of this chapter, and of the original publication on which it mainly draws (Barrett-Lennard, 1978), is and was to contribute to well-informed, connected future research. This aim is shared with the next chapter, growing out of a later report that took comprehensive stock of this method and "system" of measures, including accumulated evidence of the reliability, validity and "reach" of the BLRI as an instrument species.

Chapter 4
Mature and Travelling:
The RI "System" in Focus

Here I draw heavily on a report (Barrett-Lennard, 1986) written some 20 years after the main RI revision. In it I suggested that the term "system" may be more indicative than "instrument" to refer to the clearly viewed and distinctive methodology and landscape of applications associated with the Relationship Inventory. The embodied approach does not measure by counting units or judge estimates of interaction, but relies on a crafted gathering of the experience of participants around primary qualities of attitude and response in relationship. It presumes that these qualities can be meaningfully and usefully represented on a scale of quantity, provided the origins, procedures, and main presumptions of such measurement are held in view. The method relies on sampling complementary facets of experiential information that bear in convergent ways on each of the four RI variables; variables that are not like narrow measuring rods but are clusters of relational meaning pointing in a common direction. The respondent participants in a relationship attend to and call on their experience of the other person's or group's response to them OR on their own felt response to the other person or group, OR perhaps to their whole emergent "we" and "us" OR beyond this to their sense of the qualities of a relationship between other persons. A participant might even try her/his hand at predicting the way the other person experiences them in that relation ("my sense of your view of me"). Thus, the idea of a system suited to the many-sided nature of relationship.

This chapter re-examines aspects of theory reflected in each "variable" and delineates the back and forth phasic nature of communication in a relationship – further illuminating the distinctive roles of the OS and MO forms of the Inventory. It also considers how the RI data is best gathered, the principles involved in translating item answers into scales of measurement, and the accumulated evidence of reliability and validity of the resulting measures. The developments and applications of the instrument in its mid-life, and of relevance thereafter, are explored, along with illustration of some research frontiers. This chapter provides a vital further base for Chapter 5, which carries the BLRI story to the burgeoning present.

THE THEORETICAL STRUCTURE OF THE BLRI REVIEWED

As documented, the 'therapeutic conditions' Rogers advanced were more tightly defined in the process of developing the Inventory, and some of these definitions were further amended in revising it (see Chapter 3). Almost two decades later, it became time to examine them again, as discussed in the following sections.

Level of regard has been modified the least of any RI variable since disentangling it from the operationally awkward concept of unconditional positive regard (Barrett-Lennard, 1959a, 1959b, 1962). Broadly, it centers on the feeling aspect of one person's total response to another, conceived on a single continuum extending from a positive to a negative extreme. It is an axis of response in a relationship as presently experienced, perceived, or (sometimes) observed. 'Presently' refers to what is ongoing or current not a momentary state of affairs. The relevant elements are 'positive' feelings and affective attitudes, and 'negative' feelings and attitudes toward the other, on the part of the person whose regard is being considered. Otherwise expressed, level of regard is the composite "loading" of the distinguishable feeling reactions of one person toward another, positive and/or negative, on a dimension that exists in a conceptual space that contains these various feeling elements.

Level of regard does not, however, gather and include all possible aspects of feeling response in a relationship. On the positive side, it is concerned in various ways with warmth, liking/caring, and "being drawn toward," all in the context of responsive feelings for the other as another self broadly like oneself. It does not encompass very passionate and intimate feelings (as of romantic love), or generalized qualities of personality. On the negative side, feelings of extreme aversion (except for contempt), hatred, or anger to the point of rage, are not encompassed. No item points to possible feelings of fear of the other. As it is, the RI taps quite deeply into subjective inner experience and can be emotionally demanding; *and* the very lowest ranges of the regard scale are rarely used. Following are illustrative Regard items from the principal OS RI form. Rather than including pronouns for the Other, the pronoun space is left blank in most forms – see examples below – and the instructions invite the respondent to enter or imagine the name of the Other in each item.

Positive Items
1. _____ respects me as a person.
25. _____ cares for me.
37. _____ is friendly and warm toward me.
57. _____ is truly interested in *me*.

Negative Items
9. _____ is impatient with me.
21. _____ finds me rather dull and uninteresting.
45. _____ doesn't like me for myself.
53. _____ shows contempt for me.

Empathic understanding is conceived as a pivotal though not by itself sufficient relationship condition in therapy and in other developmental or nutrient relationships. If it is viewed as *the* critical condition, the evidence may tend to be self-confirming, partly because of its vital contribution, and also because higher levels of empathy tend to accompany relatively high levels of regard and congruence and would seldom be associated with strongly conditional attitudes. This view is consistent at least with a large quantity of correlation evidence and with the theoretical underpinnings of the RI from the time of its first development. The definition of empathy that follows, while essentially in keeping with the author's earlier envisioning (Chapter 2), has been somewhat rearranged, in order to more sharply expose the nature and qualities of the process.

Empathic understanding is a personal awareness of the other in their immediate feelings and meaning through actively receptive experiential engagement. It includes taking in the other's live words and other signs to gain a matching inner sense of their feeling and meaning. This human recognition of the focus and essence of *the other's* felt awareness includes (especially in therapy) a continuity of following attention and attunement. A depth of empathic engagement permits an accurate experiential grasp of that which has immediate priority or centrality for the other. The process can go further, beyond "experiential grasp," to a kind of entry into and resonation to features of the other's inner consciousness. Effectively, the deeply empathizing person sees, at least in glimpses, through the other's eyes, shares the person's struggle, pulses with their sensed feeling, knows as from within almost how it is to be the other at some special or critical moment in their journey. This lived knowing, however, proceeds or happens within a frame of clear awareness of which the touchstone is the moving consciousness of the *other* person.

Illustrative items from a main 64-item form of the RI (Barrett-Lennard, 1964, 1978) are listed below. The + and – signs confirm an item's positive or negative wording.

(+) 2. _____ *wants* to understand how I see and feel things.
(–) 26. _____ thinks I feel a certain way because that's the way s/he feels.
(+) 30. _____ realizes what I mean even when I have difficulty saying it.
(–) 38. _____ takes no notice of some things I think or feel.
(–) 58. _____ response to me is usually so fixed and automatic that I don't get through to him/her.
(+) 62. When I am hurt or upset _____ can recognize my feelings exactly without becoming upset him/herself.

Unconditionality of regard was discussed in updated meaning in Chapter 3, though a further point remains to be mentioned. Respondent *expectations* of how others, or particular categories of other persons, will respond to him or her in a face-to-face relationship must play a part in answers to the RI especially in cases of limited contact between the parties to a relationship. The role of expectancy in RI data, and the potential of a virtually unused "conditional" form of the RI (e.g., *S/he would respect me as a person*) justify later attention in their own right.

Examples of positively worded (first two listed) and negatively worded (latter two) unconditionality items from the 64-item OS form of the RI are:

39. How much s/he likes or dislikes me is not altered by anything that I tell him (her) about myself. (*Or*, in simpler version:
39. No matter what I say about myself, _____ likes or dislikes me just the same.').
59. I don't think that anything I say or do really changes the way s/he feels toward me.
27. S/he accepts certain things about me, and there other things s/he does not like in me.
55. Sometimes I am more worthwhile in his/her eyes than I am at other times.

Congruence has from the start been considered a foundation variable on which each of the other conditions measured by the RI partially depends (see Chapter 2, p. 12). The original definition still applies in its thrust though not in every detail, as discussed in Chapter 3. One cannot be open without also being genuine or 'authentic' and the simpler language of openness covers most of what is implied. Each person in a relationship is of course contributing to the other's response and clients voluntarily in therapy are in general not intentionally hiding. They are trying to share their real experience and are assisted in this by helper open-availability to a depth of meeting; meeting the other in an unimpeded collaborative spirit of enquiry into their life of feeling, meaning, and relationships. The 16 scale items capture differing facets of congruence/incongruence as a process. As previously noted, the wording in the OS and MO forms varies in exact language in the interests of achieving phenomenal equivalence between message meanings given and received. Table 4.1 shows a small further sample of statements as framed for both positions.

Table 4.1 A further sample of congruence statements as framed for both OS and MO positions

Further OS items	*Corresponding MO items*
12. I feel that she is real and genuine with me.	12. I feel that I'm genuinely myself with him.
20. I feel that what she says nearly always expresses exactly what she is feelingand thinking as she says it.	20. When I speak to him I nearly always can say freely what I'm thinking or feeling at that moment.
40. At times I sense that she is not aware of what she is really feeling with me.	40. At times I don't know, or don't realize until later, what my feelings are with him.
64. I believe that she has feelings she does not tell me about that are causing difficulty in our relationship.	64. I feel there are things we don't talk about that are causing difficulty in our relationship.

PHASES IN DIALOGUE EXCHANGE LINKING TO THE MAIN INVENTORY FORMS

By the early 1980s, and focusing first on empathy, different stages of the process in dialogical exchanges were distinguished (Barrett-Lennard, 1981). Essentially, the advance involved distinguishing a sequence and potentially repeating cycle (in therapy) of distinct steps or phases in the total interactive process of empathy. For the crucially linked but "semiautonomous" phases to occur in sequence one party (at least) in the relationship is self-expressive in some way and the other party (at least for the time being) is closely listening. As conceptually framed, the crucial first phase of empathy may then occur in the listener. If or when this listener communicatively expresses or signals his/her empathic response this comprises a mediating second phase of "expressed empathy." The receiving person's sense and perception of the degree to which the listener is attuned and actually "with" him or her in immediate personal understanding is the third phase of "received empathy" (ibid.). Expressed more fully the distinctions follow.

Phase 1 empathy may range *from* a resonation that is distinctly and precisely attuned to the essence of the other's experience *to* a contrasting extreme of having no awareness or sense of the other's feeling and/ or of quite misperceiving their messages and whole frame of reference. But even when empathy in this phase is high this quality of experiential knowing might not be expressed to the other; and, if expressed, it might or might not be "heard." Alternatively, even when there is very little Phase 1 empathy, it is possible that highly polished communicative skills used in the second phase, *or* the thirst of the receiving person for understanding, may yield amplified "readings" for Phase 3 empathy.

As in the case of Phase 1 empathy Regard, in the first instance, is an experiential process occurring in the regarding person. A given level of inwardly felt regard may not be closely matched and reflected in the regarding person's communication, and typically there is some slippage in the other's reading of the signals that are present. Likewise, an unconditional or conditional quality of regard has reference in the first place to a quality or pattern of responsive/reactive experience in the regarding person. So too with congruence, which in definition is concerned with the relative presence or absence of free flow between the listener's primary arousal of inner feeling response and their accompanying awareness, and of consistency or otherwise between self-presentation and conscious awareness. Thus, one may speak not just of Phase 1 empathy, but also of Phase 1 of all of the relational conditions reflected in the first person (MO) form of the RI.

When a helper or other engaged respondent is seeking to give as faithful an account as possible, under adequate conditions of administration, of his or her own experienced way of being with and toward the other person(s), the RI in MO form is tapping relationship conditions of therapy at their source. I do not mean to imply that this is the whole or most ultimate source but that it is a starting point or first stage of responsive process that is crucial for any further authentic steps in the empathy and conditions cycle.

Phase 2, the level of communicative verbal expressions and nonverbal signs is also a basic, potentially recurring, stage in the flow of the interactive-relational process applicable not only to empathy but to each RI theory-based variable. This phase is not represented directly in the generally used forms of the inventory, which are answered by participants in the relationship. However, third-person observer or judge forms, variably used in a number of studies, could be tailored to tap the degree to which the therapist is seen by the observer to be manifesting the relational conditions. The normal scoring method would yield indices of Phase 2 empathy, congruence, regard, and unconditionality. The precise guidelines for respondent observers would be crucial, as well as the nature and degree of their exposure to the client-therapist (or other) interaction. Given adequate selection and exposure, no coaching-type training in responding to the RI would be called for.

Phase 3 is the sphere of received empathy and, with the other three scale qualities, corresponds directly to the other-to-self (OS) form of the RI (Barrett-Lennard, 1976, 1981, 1993). The client's perceptions will be mediated by the Phase 2 level of process, as discussed, in interaction with role-related expectancies and personal qualities of functioning and outlook of the client. S/he is apprehending through his/her own eyes, information is not taken in like a closed package and simply unwrapped. His/her perceptions derive significantly but indirectly, with processing on the way, from the Phase 1 level of therapist experience and behavior.

Whether or not the phases of the therapy relationship conditions in action – given some further dilution in the course of measurement of the necessary but not cog-like connection revealed in theoretical analysis – will be significantly correlated in a given sample (especially in the case, of Phase 1 and Phase 3 empathy), is not certain. From the standpoint advanced, however, the overall trend of associations in data from client-therapist (C-T) pairs, on any of the four RI scales, should be positive, presuming generally able therapists and significant relational experience (a few interviews at least) in the particular C-T pairs, before the RI data are gathered.[1]

Measures from the OS form of the RI (based on the perceptions of clients) should be most strongly related to client change, as argued. This proposition is clearly in keeping with evidence from numerous studies (e.g., reported by Gurman, 1977). However, unless the more indirect and thus more weakly outcome-related Phase 1 process step (measured by the MO form) is contributing through Phase 2 to the Phase 3 level, a strengthening of the process-outcome link from step to step would not be expected to occur. In therapy, level of empathy derived from the client's experience of the therapist tends to be strongly linked to outcome (see Kurtz & Grummon, 1972; Gurman, 1977; and Chapter 5). Empathy-relevant signs and signals visibly conveyed by the therapist are a partial but critical determinant of the "concentrated" client-perception measure, although less fully in step with client outcome. The same basic reasoning applies to the other RI variables. A focus on the careful usage and technical soundness of the instrument itself follows.

GATHERING, SCORING, AND USING RI DATA: PRACTICE AND RATIONALE

ADMINISTERING THE INVENTORY

It is vitally important that clients, therapists, and/or other respondents have a clear understanding of the task (largely conveyed by the instructions on the RI forms), and receive carefully considerate explanations of why they are being called on to respond to the questionnaire, who will have access to their returns and, in general, how or with what attitude and care this rather demanding-to-give and sensitive information will be treated. There is virtually no intentionally hidden meaning in the RI. Taken item-by-item, the statements that participants are called on to consider, in reference to a particular relationship, are mostly transparent and personally revealing. It is important that respondents be as open as they can be to their experience, in responding to the instrument, and either encouraged in or not distracted from motivation to faithfully record what they experience. Any condition that would stimulate or encourage interest in slanting answers to give a more (or less) favorable picture from the respondent's standpoint would reduce the integrity of the primary data and all further steps in its treatment and interpretation.

In general, then, at least three conditions (or groups of conditions) seem essential to ensuring adequate administration and data gathering for research purposes with the RI: (1) a felt attitude of informed confidence and trust by responding individuals in the person(s) requesting and gathering the relationship data and in the (broad) purpose for which it is being obtained; (2) data-gathering arrangements such that other parties to the relationships being described do not handle the questionnaire returns at any stage and would not be consulted during the answering process; and (3) avoidance of mass administration of the inventory in settings directly associated in the respondents' experience with formal examinations, quizzes, and other performance contexts or with quite impersonal or superficial interactions.

---

[1] One study I have identified, using full-length forms of the 64-item RI, separately answered by (experienced) therapists, by observers *and* by clients, was reported by La Crosse (1977). Observers proved to be much more conservative than clients in their ratings (with therapists falling between) of empathy and the other RI variables, The significant correlations in scores from the differing vantage points were between those from observer and client data – effectively, from adjacent Phases 2 and 3.

As noted, in my original research with the RI five interviews in therapy were judged and chosen to provide a "safe minimum" amount of contact between client and therapist in order for participants to respond to the full range of items in the RI on the basis of experience in, and with specific reference to, this relationship (Barrett-Lennard, 1962, p. 8). In counselling and therapy research by other investigators, the RI data have been gathered earlier, not infrequently, after only one or two interviews or, in analogue studies, after 30, 20, 15, or even 10 minutes of contact or observation (Alvarado, 1976/1977; Brauer, 1979/1980; Brown, 1981; Brown & Calia, 1968; Feldstein, 1982; Fretz, Corn, Tuemmler, & Bellet, 1979; Goldfarb, 1978; Murphy & Strong, 1972, McKitrick & Gelso, 1978; Melchior, 1981; Seay & Altekruse, 1979). Such "early" data gathering may not vitiate the usefulness of the RI but yields results with fundamentally different meanings to those obtained after several full therapy interviews or longer, or within the context of life relationships with significant others. After such short exposure effects that are less about the other and more about the perceiver would be of foremost influence.

It is possible for subjects to answer the RI in conditional form (e.g., *S/he would respect me as a person*) to describe the way they expect a relationship to be, with a fictional or real other that they had not met but were given some brief personal picture of. Answers to the RI in this case would be almost wholly a matter of expectancy; and variability among respondents presented with the same "portrait" would reflect their personal characteristics and ways they read relationships. This is often a direct interest in analogue studies where the RI data is gathered after a very brief, prestructured interaction (see, e.g., McKitrick and Gelso, 1978). Even after a single interview in therapy, situation-related expectancy and subject characteristics are expected to substantially influence the perceptions of responding participants. As therapy continued, recurring instances of distinctive and relationship-relevant responses by the listener-helper naturally would tend to play an increasing part in the client's (or therapist's own) perceptions. In person-centered and related therapies, this increase may be quite rapid. And, even where transference was being cultivated, the therapist would gradually, or in periodic sudden shifts, stand out more in his or her own person and less in terms of "projected" characteristics.

In summary, on the issue of how soon RI data are gathered, unless research interest is centered on individual or group differences in response to a "standard" relationship stimulus, or in some way is focused on respondent characteristics rather than the engagement itself, it is essential that there be substantial experience in the relationship in focus (or adequate observation in the case of observer RI usage). Only under this condition could subjects reliably be responding to the specific relationship; carefully discriminating from experience that speaks to OS form items, or, to the statements in MO or observer forms. My current judgment is that, in general, at least three full interviews in actual therapy or help-intended relationships are necessary to provide the experience from which the forming identity of that specific relationship can be dependably revealed via the RI.[2]

SCORING RATIONALE AND PROCEDURE

The well-documented reliability of the RI scales (Gurman, 1977, Table 1) plus the validity evidence reviewed shortly, support treating the RI answer codes (+3, +2, +1, −1, −2, and −3) as an interval scale, and continuing the main scoring method used from the beginning. From the start, the item answer system was seen literally as providing for "three grades of 'yes' and three grades of 'no' response" (Chapter 2), for which the numerical symbols used were convenient codes with their own logic and usefulness in scoring. However (given direct use of the number codes as measures), an issue that arose at the beginning, and which might

---

[2] This is not to negate the potential importance and impact of the initial interview in therapy, which in my observation may constitute the complete or main part of the entry phase of therapy (Barrett-Lennard, 1998, Chapter 7). However, more experience than is usually possible in a 1-hour initial contact is needed to furnish the store of experiential events and impressions indigenous to a particular relationship that the RI (in most applications) assumes and calls upon.

occur to the reader, is the existence and justification for what amounts to a 2-point difference between +1 and −1 answers:

Arguably, there is an implicit, although unused, "equally true and untrue" middle category, for which one logical answer code would be "0," in the +3 to −3 scheme. Several drawbacks were seen to adding this further choice. The result would no longer be a differentiated yes/no system. Periodic respondent use of a zero option also would mean, effectively, that scale scores arose from a variable number and selection of numerically contributing items. In addition, such a category could very easily be used for the 'wrong' reasons; perhaps to avoid recording a reluctant (but real) "yes" or "no" perception or, simply, to dispose of the task more easily on items that were tougher to answer. Finally, the 2-point numerical difference between +1 and −1 seems in keeping with a discontinuous gap between even a qualified 'yes' and 'no.' As indicated, the answer codes have proven quite satisfactory to take and use literally as a measuring scale (given the sign reversal in answers to the negatively worded items).[3] These considerations, as well as the fact the procedure works well in terms of psychometric indicators, converge in supportive accord with the six-step item scale form in prevailing use.

The score sheet for hand scoring all 64-item RI forms is reproduced in Appendix 1. It reflects and details the standard scoring method, and also can be drawn on in preparing and setting up machine-scoring programs. In the hand-scoring form, the item numbers are arranged in four columns, one column for each scale, with provision for answers to the negatively stated items to be recorded in a separate grouping for subsequent sign reversal. Entries taken directly from an actual protocol illustrate the scoring procedure. Most often, the majority of answers to positively worded items involves some grade of Yes and are, therefore, numerically positive. The majority of answers to negatively items are some grade of "no" that, with the sign reversal, count in a positive direction. Sometimes the *subtotals* for positively and negatively worded items differ in sign, and total scores for different scales can vary widely. Since relationships are emergent products of two (or more) unique individuals, and that they arise in a wide variety of surrounding attitudinal conditions, they are expected to be diverse in their profiles. And, it would be surprising, not expected, if each of the four RI scales happened to have the same distribution characteristics.

Scale scores generated from individual respondents tend to be in the upper half of the theoretical range of −48 to +48, for 16 items (or −3 to +3 per item). A sprinkling of negative scores within a given sample is not unusual, nor is it thought to be rare even in data from client–therapist relationships. There is no absolute meaning to the zero point in the theoretical range, and particular scoring values have only broad and approximate meaning (see below), This said, a below zero score implies that a respondent is mostly answering "no" to positively worded items and/or "yes" to negative ones, and does suggest that the relationship is significantly lacking or weak on the aspect in focus. Average scores in samples tend to be higher for Level of Regard than for other scales; and usually are lowest on the Unconditionality scale.

THE ISSUE OF NORMS: PROBLEMS AND AN APPROACH

Official norms for the RI, from which any particular score could be ascribed a percentile or decile value (for example, that it falls in the upper 10 percent of obtained population scores), do not exist. Although not ruled out in principle, the task in practice is particularly complex in the case of the RI. Nor are such norms needed for research. There is of course a range of 64-item (and shorter) variants (see Appendix 1), and the most-used forms have been applied in a wide diversity of therapy and life relationships. The same norms could not apply across this spectrum. Variation of origin also limits direct comparison. As mentioned, RI data have been gathered after a few minutes of highly structured, systematically varied contact

---

3 I do not mean to imply that it would be plausible to think that each point contributed by item A toward its scale score regularly had the identical theoretical or practical significance as each point for item B, or item C, D, and so on, or that there was literal equality in each given instance to the difference between, say, a +3 and +2 answer and a −1 and −2 answer. Treating the data as if such presumptions are sound demonstrates, however, that fine-grained variability or 'error' must tend to cancel out, and at the least, that scale scores (in adequately constituted arrays and comparisons) approach linear measurement.

(in analogue studies), after first interviews, following several (or many) hours of experience in intensive therapy, and from couples and others in life relationships. The RI form, subclass or context and duration of the relationship, and the role or position of respondents in the relation, would need to be the same or distinctly similar in order to accumulate and organize data in any meaningful normative form (in diverse samples even the factor structure would vary, as earlier discussed). The task of establishing empirically based norms for psychotherapy relationships alone is formidable.

In light of all these issues, one suggestion is to utilize a three-fold approach to assembling comparison data and working standards – avoiding slippage into a prescriptive-evaluational stance. One 'prong' of this approach would be to organize means and variance data (the latter perhaps in terms of z score equivalents) from available therapy studies reporting such data from 64-item OS RI forms. Selection criteria would include regular scoring, carefully conducted and monitored data gathered after at least three therapy interviews (but without mixing in post-therapy RI data), and clearly described samples of actual clients and professional therapists. A composite profile from sources having relevant ingredients in common might be useful, taken in conjunction with the two further component features of approach.

The second component would involve gathering data systematically from the clientele (and from their therapists, if possible) of a particular treatment center or setting, in order to build up a local data pool, which would cumulate to give current RI scale specifications for that context. This would provide comparison data for further work and programs in the same setting, and make it possible to view scores and scoring levels meaningfully against the arrays from reported data, selected and organized as suggested above. If the therapist and/or treatment program evaluation was one main purpose of this exercise, sophisticated consideration would need to be given to the populations of clients involved in the samples compared – bearing in mind (1) that better-functioning clients are likely to perceive their therapists more positively on the RI variables (Barrett-Lennard, 1962) and (2) that clients who are quite impoverished in extent and quality of life relationships may gain from more modest in-therapy levels of received empathy, and other conditions than the levels required by clients whose interpersonal life environments are generally favorable (Barrett-Lennard, 1978; Holland, 1976).

The third kind of entry to establishing comparison standards – suggested as a complementary or alternative to the two above – is to consider different scoring levels or zones based on the ways that subjects must be replying to the items in order to give rise to these scores. The likely meaning of below-zero scores has been mentioned. Any scale score can be linked to an average response to the constituent items. By the standard scoring method (with a scale range of –48 to +48) a scale score of 40 or above would require a mean response of at least 2.5 (produced, say, by +3 and +2 answers on all positive items and –3 and –2 on all negatively worded ones). This degree of consistency and strength of 'positive' response would seem about as high as one could plausibly expect in any relationship context, in terms of honest, discriminating perception. In practice, scores above 40 occur but are rare, except on the level of regard scale – where distributions tend to be negatively skewed and whose 'ceiling' may be lower than optimal for some life relationships.

A score of 32, found or not uncommon within most samples, represents an average item score of 2 (after conversion of answers to negatively framed items). Such a case would necessarily include a sprinkling of 3s in a positive direction, and inevitably some 1s. Few, if any, item answers would weigh in a negative direction. Thus, this score on the face of it would imply clear affirmation that the referent person was experienced as very substantially empathic or congruent, and so on. A similar analysis applied to a score of 24 suggests that this level achieved, say, on at least three of the variables and averaged over all four, would tend to be minimal in fruitful helping relationships. On the other hand, scores of 16 – resulting conceivably from answers of "probably yes" (+1) and "probably no" (–1) to every item, and otherwise stemming from a mix of responses carrying positive and negative weight – would be expected to represent a less than adequate level in therapy relationships.

A thorough combing of relevant, existing reports – including selected doctoral dissertations – could provide some (perhaps most) of the necessary data for the illustrated focus on client-generated RI measures in therapy. Another basic area in which reported research does provide very extensive information has to do with reliability and validity of the RI scales, especially in respect to the principal OS and MO forms applied in two-person helping relationships.

RELIABILITY AND VALIDITY: ISSUES AND EVIDENCE

Reliability is centrally concerned with whether a measuring system yields the same result whenever it is appropriately applied to something that has itself remained constant from one occasion of measurement to another. As such constancy cannot be taken for granted (and actual variation would reduce apparent reliability) a complementary method can be applied when a measure involves adding numerous nonidentical bits of information. In this case, if one subset of bits yields approximately the same result at the same time as another similarly representative subset, metric consistency is well on the way to being established. Further, if each bit of information used in a particular scale regularly contributes in the expected direction the resulting homogeneity of elements makes for measurement constancy. Of course, if one subset of elements yields exactly the same result as another, or if various bits correlate perfectly with the whole, component information is duplicating itself and parts of it are redundant as they stand.

The first checks on reliability of the RI, centered on split-half analysis applied to the data from Clients and Therapists, as outlined in Chapter 2 (p. 18). The reliability of all coefficients exceeded .80, and across the four retained scales mean reliabilities exceeded .85 in the client data and over .9 from the therapist returns. The later item-analysis reported in Chapter 3 was oriented toward increasing the conceptual homogeneity of items in some scales and, on the balance of probability, would have increased not diminished their reliability.

The review by Gurman (1977) still includes the principal *published accumulation* of internal and test-retest reliability of RI scales, based on data from a range of contexts. Fifteen respondent samples from the work of 12 investigators or collaborating pairs generated the data for *internal reliability assessment using split-half and alpha coefficient methods*. Results from differing RI revisions, from several groups additional to the therapy-relationship majority, and from naturalistic and analogue studies, are included together in Gurman's summary. Separate reliabilities for all four of the primary scale variables are presented. The means of coefficients cumulated by Gurman are for regard .91, empathy .84, unconditionality .74, and congruence .88. Only one of the 50 coefficients listed is below .67, 60 percent were .87 or above.

The *test-retest reliabilities* listed (Gurman, 1977, Table 1) are based on ten samples, yielding 45 scale and total score coefficients, which range from .61 to .95. There is more evenness across the four scales than in the case of internal consistency, with *means* of coefficients varying only from .80 (for unconditionality) to .85 (for congruence). The extremes in test-retest intervals were 12 days and 12 months. Overall, especially in view of the heterogeneity of sources, test-retest intervals, and specific RI forms, the levels and consistency of obtained reliability are striking. It seems safe to say that, given sound administration/data-collection procedures, a very adequate level of technical reliability of primary forms of the RI is well-established.

The issue of *validation*, in all its ramifications, is exceedingly complex in psychosocial measurement. It hinges on clarity of concept and definition of what is intended to be measured, on the meaningfulness of viewing the construct involved as varying on a high to low continuum or category sequence, and on congruence between this construct and the variable produced in operation by a particular measuring scheme. The various types of validity often distinguished – content, concurrent or predictive, 'factorial,' construct, and so on – involve alternate/complementary strategies or levels of entry in dealing with these basic issues. There are firm grounds to claim that, providing the instrument is understood and applied appropriately, its scales may be presumed and treated as valid. Bases for this conclusion, some already mentioned, are in summary as follows:

1. In the original development of the instrument, and in subsequent revisions, much care was taken in the item sampling of each of the defined interpersonal variables. In practice, the total endeavor to do justice to the theory, in producing the RI scales, led to further refinement and sharpening of the constructs themselves. Direct checks on the effectiveness of the operational translations initially included consistency of appraisal of the items by judges, as spelled out in Chapter 2. In preparing the 64-item revision, each of three relevantly experienced colleagues were asked to review and comment on the draft selection and wording of items, given detailed item analysis information and up-to-date definitions of the four scale variables. Feedback from these appraisals was used in finalizing the exact sampling and form of the items. These steps have contributed to, and effectively provide, evidence of content validity.

2. The RI is deemed metrically sound (1) judging from the nature and described principles of its structure, (2) given the reported item analysis and data used in its refinement (Chapter 3), and (3) in view of the extensive evidence of high internal reliability and stability of measurement already referred to. These features and the careful theoretical grounding establish potential for valid measurement.

3. The positive results of a range of independent predictive studies concerned with association between the RI-assessed relationship conditions and outcome in actual therapy or help-intended situations cumulate to form extensive evidence of (predictive) construct validation. From his searching review of research in this sphere, Gurman (1977, p. 523, italics in original) concluded that "it is clear from the findings presented . . . *that there exists substantial, if not overwhelming evidence in support of the hypothesized relationship between patient-perceived therapeutic conditions and outcome in individual psychotherapy and counseling.*" The evidence is most clear-cut in respect to the OS (or Client) forms but more limited in regard to the lesser-used MO (Therapist) form measures. However, in light of the perspective advanced in this chapter, the typically much lower outcome predictive power of the MO form scales is entirely consistent with and expected from conceptual process analysis and is not evidence of invalidity.

4. The many studies in contexts other than therapy, which have examined *cogently predicted intersection of RI measures* with other relational and behavioral parameters, or with effects of change-intended experience, include examples in the marriage and family sphere, in education, supervision, and other areas. The first such investigation was by B. M. Thornton (1960), using data from marriage partners, each of whom completed both early OS and MO RI forms on their relationship. Either partner's perception of the other's response (OS RI scale and total scores) were very strongly correlated with the classical measure of marital adjustment – unlike the RI in content or scope – developed by Burgess and Cottrell (1939). Thornton's other findings, from joint consideration of husband and wife data, were also as predicted from theory.

Quick and Jacob (1973) found that scores on each of the RI scales, from perceptions of the husbands or the wives of the other's response, were significantly lower where either or both partners were seeking counselling than for couples not evidencing distress. Further, the RI differences held up even where the influence of a correlated Marriage Role conflict Questionnaire (MRQ) was partialed out, but the MRQ difference did not survive partialing out the RI contribution. The investigators concluded that the RI process dimensions evidently were more basic in marital disturbances than the behavioral role conflict components. Wampler and Powell (1982) collated mean score data for each RI scale as reported by a number of investigators, for their samples of distressed and/or nondistressed couples. For three scales, the means without exception are much higher for the assorted, nondistressed groups. For unconditionality, the pattern is not totally consistent, although the overall separation is strongly in the same direction.

A variety of other studies focusing on intervention (helping/communication-learning) strategies with groups of couples, have used the RI as a measure of change. The evidence is that the most used scales (empathy, regard, and congruence) are as a rule especially sensitive to effects that have been assessed in other ways or carefully predicted from theory (Epstein & Jackson, 1978; Wampler & Sprenkle, 1980; Wells, Figurel, & McNamee, 1975; VanSteenwegan, 1979, 1982; see also Wampler & Powell, 1982, pp. 141–142).

In the educational arena, there has been an emphasis (in studies of variable quality) on the relation of teacher regard, empathy, and the other conditions to variously focused and assessed qualities of learning, gains in academic achievement, and/or other development. I see no basis for positing a direct relationship between the relational process conditions and gains in academic achievement. However, a study by Griffin (1977/1978) concerned with reading improvement yielded a pattern of results implying that the level of the RI measured conditions affected the learner's attitude toward reading, *and that this attitude* was associated with reading achievement gain. (No direct correlational link was found between the measured conditions and reading gain.) In research by Hall (1972/1973) with younger-than-usual subjects (fourth graders) and a simplified form of the RI, pupils who were above the sample median in RI-measured quality of relationship with their teacher scored significantly higher on later measures of reading achievement and self-esteem, and lower on anxiety, than those below the median. Other investigations with direct or indirect relevance in the present context, include those by Mason and Blumberg (1969), Libby (1974/1975), and Smetko (1982/1983).

5. Varied studies, using quasi-experimental designs, have predicted *effects on RI-measured relationship quality* of actuarial and other factors (e.g., particular individual or group characteristics, or training and other intervention procedures). The more well-conceived and managed work of this broad kind, involving uncontrived data or well-crafted analogue situations and using the full RI, has usually upheld hypotheses in regard to factors that should convincingly influence relationship quality. Examples of early work include Emmerling's (1961/1962) study, in which students of more "open" teachers – who felt a responsibility for difficulties and remedial action in relation to their student's work – saw these teachers in a significantly more positive light, on all RI scales, than the pupils with teachers portrayed as more closed and externalizing of issues; and research by Cahoon (1962), who found experiencing levels (Gendlin Experiencing Scale) and open-mindedness (Rokeach Dogmatism Scale) of practicum counsellors were significantly related to client-perceived relationship quality. Tosi (1970) also used the RI and Rokeach scale with results similar to Cahoon's.

Other research to the mid-1980s of related theme includes: Churukian's (1970/1971) study, centering on interpersonal need compatibility between supervising and student teachers, with effect on their relationship; the work reported by Abramowitz and Abramowitz (1974), concerned with the relation of client "psychological mindedness" to relationship quality and outcome in group therapy (see also Gurman, 1977, pp. 529–530); Brauer's investigation (1979/1980) focusing on therapy relationship effects of high and low self-concept on the part of deaf students, and their relative perception of deaf and hearing interviewers; and a study, by Junek, Burra, and Leichner (1979) using a "half-length" observer adaptation of the RI applied with novel effectiveness to study effects on interview quality of a carefully portrayed practice-training seminar for psychiatric residents. Generally, the results of these studies supported investigator predictions, with indirect positive bearing on validity of measurement.

6. The results of *factorial studies* based on item intercorrelations have yielded primary factors essentially reflecting the theoretically based variables – as discussed in detail in Chapter 3. Results of the studies involved included Walker and Little's early finding (1969) of three factors, in which unconditionally, a composite of empathy and congruence, and level of regard, are principally reflected, Lietaer's work (1974, 1976) with an expanded RI OS form used in two contexts that wound up with a factor structures identified with major components of the primary RI variables, and Bebout's work (1971/1972), in which a large majority of items fell in factor groupings in line with the RI item-scale structure. (See also Ganley's factor study (1989) mentioned on p. ???).

In his 1977 summary, from evidence to that point, Gurman concluded (p. 513): "On the basis of the existing data deriving from properly conducted factor-analytic studies, it appears that the RI is tapping dimensions that are quite consistent with Barrett-Lennard's original work on the Inventory." Two later factor-analytic studies in England by D. Cramer, using large student samples of closest friend relationships yielded broadly similar results. The prerevision Client R1 form (less the willingness to be known items) was used in the first study (Cramer's 1986a), while the second study (1986b) was based on the 64-item RI *extended by addition of items concerned with advice giving*. In both cases the four primary factors (plus a factor of advice giving in Study 2) corresponded to the four RI scales. In Study 2, 15 of the 16 Regard items loaded on the same factor (as was also true in Bebout's data), with varied attrition of items loading on the other factors. From his later study, using the regular OS RI without the U items (further discussed in Chapter 5), Ganley (1989) concluded that the three-factor solution "robustly replicates the original subscale structure reported by Barrett-Lennard" (Ganley, p. 113). Given that an intentional diversity of items represents each variable, and the quite varied contexts and differing factor-analytic methodology used in these studies, the striking degree of commonality in outcomes is deemed to reflect favorably on the integrity of the instrument's basic structure.

7. The reputation and usage of the Relationship Inventory in hundreds of doctoral dissertations and other theses and in major programmatic studies (see Chapter 5) while not in itself constituting formal evidence of validity, reflects positive appraisal by other investigators for whom much is riding on the feasibility and integrity of their own work or research that they are supervising. This situation has been evolving without fanfare for over half a century – counting work documented in Chapter 5. Usage has become more diversified within counselling and therapy research and extends to wide application in other human service contexts and significant personal life relationships.

Overall, the validation evidence is perhaps as unequivocal as one could expect in the presumptuous sphere of measuring complex attitudinal-relationship variables. This is not to imply, however, that the instrument should not be tested in new ways or amended in any circumstance. Indeed, one kind of active development involves the formation and use of fresh adaptations, which necessarily introduce changes at least in detail – as further discussed below and in later chapters.

NEW AND UNDERUSED APPLICATIONS OF THE BLRI

What follows explores some aspects of new and underused applications of the RI, (an area further taken up in Chapter 5) and it is not intended to infringe on the inventiveness of the reader. My focus here is on features opened up by the late 1980s, and gives more attention to potentialities than specific method or plans. Some of these new developments have been followed up in later work and there is much unrealized promise that may interest the reader.

LIFE RELATIONAL ENVIRONMENT: HELPING RELATIONSHIP BASELINE?

The Inventory has been adapted in this case to tap not just one but many relationships that represent the respondent's experienced interpersonal world over three principal domains: family relationships, voluntary friend-relationships, and work/public life relations. Thus, it is designed to appraise the main areas and axes of the participant's world of lived interpersonal relationships – effectively, their 'relational life space.' 'Experimental Form OS-S-42' of this instrument was first used in a thesis study by Holland, in 1976. Given the demand of the task (most respondents rated 7 or 8 relationships on the single composite form) the number of items was reduced to 42. Following a trial pilot study, Holland used a larger student sample (N = 56) for his main data. Additional information on family composition and activity, and the kinds and degree of respondent contact with other people, was used in the validity check of the new form. Overall, there was strong preliminary evidence that this adaptation achieved what is was designed to do, that it was highly reliable (split-half measure) and that it's other measurement characteristics approached those of the regular RI forms. Its application also generated ideas and implications for refinement (see Chapter 5).

One potential of this life relationship space form is that it offers an empirical grip on whether or how clients entering therapy differ in their (experienced) interpersonal environments from control samples not entering therapy, or from themselves after therapy. An implied assumption of conditions theory is that in therapeutic/helping contexts higher levels of the therapy conditions exist in the client–therapist relationship than in any other currently active relationships in the client's life. Also, as noted, even in client/person-centered therapies the qualities tapped by the RI do not account for most of the variance in outcome. Do differences among clients in the quality of their relationships outside therapy play a part in this? Is it the absolute received level of empathy (or congruence, etc.) in therapy which is most important, or is the degree to which this level exceeds the client's own baseline experience more critical? Used with clients this new form could shed valuable empirical light on such issues.

FAMILY RELATIONSHIPS AND CHANGE

Versions of the RI received widely varied application, from 1960 on, to family relationships. Boettcher (1977), Carter (1981/1982), Epstein and Jackson (1978), Griffin (1967/1968), Quick and Jacob (1973), Thornton (1960), VanSteenwegen (1982), and Wampler and Sprenkle (1980) all focused on couples, and there was some spirited advocacy of the RI from the family context (Wampler & Powell, 1982; also Ganley, 1989). Early studies by Hollenbeck (1965), Lietaer (1974), and Van der Veen and Novak (1971) centered on parent–child relations. Other investigators, including Gomes (1981) and Luber and Wells (1977) tapped into more than one class of family relationship. For Gomes' thesis study (GTBL supervision), we adapted the mentioned OS-S-42 version for application solely to family relations. This version allowed for the response of family twosomes as well as single others. An example from a child's position is the instruction to describe the response of "your mother and father in the way they generally respond to you when they are involved together as a pair. In this case, you need to think of the two people as one 'you' or 'they' in the way they respond to 'me' when they also are occupied with each other."

An additional form used in Gomes' study (1981) yields any family member's perception of the whole (nuclear) family system. (Sample items are "We (the members of my family) respect one another" (R+); "We may understand each other's words but we don't see and take in each other's feelings" (E–); "We are openly ourselves, as we really are, in the family" (C+); and "Sometimes we judge each other as more worthwhile than we do at other times" (U–). Another emergent form allowed for a third person to describe the relationship system as they perceive it. Called the dyad-observer form (Form DO–64), representative items read "They respect one another" (R+); "Each nearly always knows what the other means" (E+); "It makes them uneasy to bring up or talk about certain things" (C–); "They are openly themselves with one another" (C+); and "They want the other to be a particular sort of person" (U–).

A more general adaptation similar to the whole family form is answered by participants in any dyadic relationship to describe their 'We' system as one unit. The instructions acknowledge that "one member or partner would not give the same picture as another one and that either/any person's view could change." Respondents are advised to think of actual situations and the atmosphere of feeling and attitude in their everyday worlds together (see Appendix 1, pp. 108-110). Following is a sample of the wording of the 64 items, three from the empathy group and one each from the other scales: "We each look at what the other does from our own individual point of view"; "We realize each other's meaning, even when something is hard to say or find words for"; "We often don't realize (at the time) how sensitive or touchy the other one is about things that are said or done"; "We like and enjoy one another"; "Either of us can be 'up' or 'down' in our mood without it changing the other one's attitude toward us"; and "Sometimes one or other of us is not at all comfortable but we go on, outwardly ignoring it" These and other possible arrangements of relationship system forms of the RI have interesting potential for promising new lines of research in the family process field.

CLASSROOM AND CHILD–ADULT RELATIONSHIPS

A number of mentioned studies used the RI in educational research, focusing on teacher–student or staff relationships. Younger children (e.g., mid-primary) are seldom heard from directly in respect to qualities of relationship that nurture or awaken their curiosity and desire to engage and learn. Even at high school level students seldom are invited to candidly portray the way they experience their teachers' interpersonal response and attitudes. Working beliefs and arrangements regarding the promotion of learning have little anchorage in empirical study of the impact on learners of their teacher's perceived empathy, warmth, and openness.

The Teacher–Pupil Relationship Inventory (TPRI), first developed in the late 1960s (see Chapter 3), was finally revised and reduced to 40 items, with school children of about 10 to 14 years old – including grades 5 through 9 – especially in mind. A small group of congruence and unconditionality items help to illustrate the language (but see Appendix 1, pp. 124-125): "What he is thinking or feeling shows out in the open" (C+); "If I say something I'm ashamed of, he still treats me the same" (U+); "He keeps quiet about what he really thinks and feels inside" (C–); and "I feel he is always judging us as 'good' or 'bad' (or, dumb or smart)" (U–). School administrators and teachers may feel uncomfortably exposed or awkward on other grounds about having children answer such questions about their teachers. Where teachers and schools feel secure enough to let this happen, it would seem extremely important to treat the children's responses with sensitive and genuine consideration for everyone involved. (One expression of such consideration would be to offer group feedback, to the teachers, in a form that invites exploration and discovery.) There is a vast reservoir of awareness and discrimination among children to which pertinent RI studies could give very illuminating access and expression, helping to open to founded view phenomena that may switch a learning relationship on or off.

I use the term "meta-perception" to encompass *predictions by one party of the other party's view* of their relationship. The focus might be on the way A thinks or senses that B experiences A in their relationship (*or* on the way that A thinks that B views his/her own response to A). Further possibilities include the way that A (wife and mother, say) thinks her husband sees his attitudes and response to a third person (their child, say). Using the RI to tap meta-perceptions need only involve adjusting the instructions in regular OS or MO forms. In an early instance the members of a residential 'therapeutic counseling/experiential learning' workshop nominated outside partners to twice answer the regular OS 64-item RI on the members' relational response to them. The forms were completed prior to the workshop and about one month after it ended and returned directly to the investigator (Barrett-Lennard, 1967, 1998, p. 296). The workshop members themselves were asked at the *beginning* and again at the *end* of the *two-week workshop* how they believed that each of their nominated outside partners would perceive and describe them. Having no contact with their partners during the workshop they drew on the same pool of experience-in-relationship. However, in the pre/post comparisons the most interesting trend was a marked convergence in the member and partner scores, reflecting shifts that suggested greater member openness and sensitivity after the workshop, in processing their *prior* experiences.

The degree to which A correctly anticipates B's perception of A's relational response is akin to empathy. A significant pool of experience in their relationship would give rise to at least a broad sense of B's perspective. In usage, A and B answer the same OS RI form, except for an adjustment to the instructions for A. This adjustment indicates clearly that A's task is to answer as he or she thinks B will answer, that is, in a way that reflects his/her closest sense of how *B construes* and *views* A's attitudes and response in their relationship. Kagan (1968) conducted an early study of this kind, finding that field instructor-supervisors (of social work students) were more accurate in predicting how the student would see their response than the student was in predicting their instructor's view. Both partners, as might be expected, became more accurate in their predictions (more aware of the other's relational perceptions) over a three-month period of supervisory association.

These examples only begin to illustrate potentially salient comparisons and patterns. It may well be the case that predictions are usually more on target with respect to regard or congruence than to empathy (or perhaps even to unconditionality). Thus, there may be different profiles of accuracy of prediction among the RI variables that have distinctive implications and meaning. The largely untapped potentials of meta-perception applications of the RI appear to me to have special salience in the twin spheres of interpersonal learning and relationship change. Marital and family therapy research is one very promising setting for their application.

CONCLUSION

This chapter began with careful commentary on the theoretical structure and item content of the RI and worked to illuminate the phasic nature of communication – especially between client and therapist – and how these phases tie in with the distinctive roles of the OS and MO RI forms. It has offered practical advice on how (and when) to administer and use the Inventory, and has addressed the scoring rationale and issue of norms in detail. This chapter is where the accumulated evidence of reliability and (especially) of validity of the RI scale measures is closely reviewed and summed up. Further research applications (up the mid-1980s) have been explored, some of these including adaptations used in the vital areas of family and teacher–student relationships. "Meta-perception" (predictive) applications and potential were considered. All this work complements and extends the foundation of the next chapter (Chapter 5), which fast forwards to the 'pregnant' present.

Chapter 5
The BLRI Story Extended: Later Work and Looking Ahead

When I "return" from other projects to focus on the Relationship Inventory it can surprise me still that the most-sustained and perhaps best-known strand in my professional journey pivots on a questionnaire instrument. I have occasionally overheard someone else refer to this device as "The Barrett-Lennard," which is most strange to my ears since to me my name refers to my living self! Yet the BLRI, a name I adopted from its use by others, is not a frozen entity and does connect with lived meanings, my own and meanings of others, over a broad area. It does not directly estimate trust between people but hones in on equally subtle qualities that the person answering the questionnaire may not discriminate even though his or her own perceptions provide the entire data for the resulting measures. Each of the four scales rests on a theoretical definition, further refined and with many added connotations in my own thought over the lifetime of the instrument. I do not think or mean to imply that the scale measures capture the whole nature of those underlying qualities. The measures clearly are not the actual phenomena to which they refer but useful quantitative estimates of their presence.

This chapter builds on those before it to bring the story and usage of the methodology fully up-to-date and suggest further directions. It illustrates continued and new foci of research and further instrument development. Some of the further studies have used new adaptations of the Inventory. Several dozen studies, at least, have employed translations of the RI. I hope to encourage readers to consider promising, though little used, adaptations of the instrument and will refer to investigation of interesting problems not so far directly addressed. The later part of this chapter articulates directly with the Appendix 1 and the full spectrum of present forms of the instrument it contains. This includes a couple of experimental versions only available in draft and intriguingly distinct in their potential from the familiar RI.

Expressed in one short phrase the BLRI taps "perceptions in a relationship." A perceptual emphasis has always characterized client/person-centered thought, it also characterized the fertile thought of pioneers in the Gestalt movement in research and understanding (e.g., Koffka, 1935) and is reflected in the work of phenomenologists and others who stress that people mostly respond to reality as they experience it, not as it may be viewed from the outside or "objectively." A person's field of perception is influenced by a variety of factors, internal and external. The therapy relationship is a case in point. A therapist's response to a client can be examined by an observer in carefully systematic vein. But for the client it is her/his own experience and perception, however acquired and influenced, that s/he goes by. This way of thinking has been fundamental to my approach to measuring qualities of relationship – in therapy and a spectrum of other life contexts – as already implied. Even in the occasional use of an "observer" RI form, it is not behavior as such that respondents identify but qualities and patterns of attitude and feeling in relation perceived in the target persons.

The Relationship Inventory: A Complete Resource and Guide, First Edition. Godfrey T. Barrett-Lennard.
© 2015 John Wiley & Sons, Ltd. Published 2015 by John Wiley & Sons, Ltd.
Companion site: www.wiley.com/go/barrett_lennard/therelationshipinventory

REFLECTIONS ON THEORY AND THE INTERRELATION OF CONDITIONS

The theory and particular interpersonal axes on which the RI is based was radically new in the helping field at the time of its original formulation in 1956/1957, and thus new in the research it immediately led to (Chapter 2). My work has focused on the "core" attitudinal or relationship conditions, as they are variously called. It has not focused directly on "psychological contact," which is implied in the other conditions, especially, empathic understanding and positive unconditional regard. Nor have I focused on the broad quality of client personality, namely 'client incongruence,' that Rogers also posited as a condition of therapy (see below). Not that I think being 'out of sync' and in troubled conflict inside isn't relevant to a person's readiness and motivation for therapy, but it belongs in another category separate from qualities of relationship found in the therapist–client encounter.

Movement from relative incongruence to greater congruence or integration was viewed by Rogers as being at the core of healing change in therapy, especially as spelled out in his fullest statement of theory (1959a) – this work already available prepublication when the 1957 paper came out. Such change also is implicit in the preceding research on therapy outcome (Rogers & Dymond, 1954). However, the casting of client incongruence and its expressions *as a prerequisite condition of therapy* never did become a focus of research. Nor (at that time) did the broad further condition that the therapy partners "are in psychological contact" draw direct study. It essentially meant that the parties are aware of one another and that the posited context for change is a relationship. Prouty (1994) finally brought this aspect into focus in the development of "pretherapy" for interpersonally disabled clients who were virtually disconnected from relational engagement. As for the specific conditions of therapist response, these needed to be 'communicated' (in Rogers' 1957 formulation) although before long he stressed that the client's perception was the crucial factor. He also acknowledged that although the conditions were first described as if they were all-or-none elements they also could be viewed as existing in varying degree over a wide range (Rogers, 1959a). He was, I believe, influenced in this by the fact that such measurement was already occurring by this author and Halkides (1958).

More has and can be said about each construct embodied in the RI. Its development took account, for example, of a number of distinct facets of empathic response. In current expression complementing my previous definition, these include desiring to know *the other's* perspective and becoming genuinely absorbed in connecting with their experienced world; moving close in experiential recognition and understanding without being overtaken by triggered *self*-experience that could cloud the listener's perception of what is immediately alive in the other's experience; sensing below the surface of awkward or searching attempted expression to reach the other's felt meaning, and thus also responding freshly to their distinctive experience *now*; visibly acknowledging their living feeling, including their hurt, confusion, or felt despair when present; and, responding not only to limited parts of the other's meaning but, somehow, to the whole sum or core of it. The RI items still seem to me to tap into these facets and thus connect with most of the domain of my concept of empathic understanding (Barrett-Lennard, 1993, 2003, pp. 34–50).

Specifically, in reference to the phasic model discussed in Chapter 4, the initial phase of empathic arousal or 'resonation' by the listener requires and occurs in response to expressive sharing or action by the other person. Put another way it depends, in the moment of its occurrence, on an attentive openness by the listener to signals from another who is expressively with them in person or 'present' to them at a distance. An empathic response in the listener might occur in response to vivid *recorded portrayals* of an expressive-experiencing other – although the whole interactive sequence cannot happen. In everyday situations where substantial Phase 1 empathy occurs, the listener may or may not convey his/her immediate empathic recognition and understanding. Even in therapy a client may be tentatively feeling their way and only gradually reach a deeper level of self and relational sharing that interacts with and contributes to an enhancement of empathic response by the listener. If the empathy cycle flows through to include Phase 3 received empathy, and assuming also sustained active attention by the listener (as in therapy), the empathy cycle can be repeated – and there may be an extended sequence of repetitions. This phasic conception can be extended (Chapter 4) to the other three conditions variables, especially in therapy conversations.

Since respectful interest and a genuine and unjudging quality of response would seem necessary for higher levels of empathy it would be surprising, and even suggest that something was amiss in measuring these qualities, if there was zero correlation of the other RI measures with empathy. In fact, although reported scale intercorrelations vary considerably between samples they are almost all positive. In his compilation from a number of studies Gurman (1977, p. 511) found mean correlations of .62, .53, and .28 between empathy, on the one hand, and on the other congruence, regard, and unconditionality, respectively, from the original "client" and later OS RI data. Broader discussions of empathy than my own include the excellent first and last chapters, by the editors, in the volume *Empathy reconsidered* (Bohart & Greenberg, 1997). My own chapter in that book looks at *client* empathy and its potential recovery or increase through therapy.

RI-measured level of regard and unconditionality of regard emerged as only lightly correlated variables in virtually every study reporting their association. This evidence and the origins of UPR as a conjunction of ideas that began with a focus on positive regard (see, e.g., Moon et al., 2001) affirm to me that breakdown of the construct was justified conceptually and is supported empirically. The notion of conditional regard is itself a fairly straightforward idea. Unconditionality implies that the experiencing self of the other is neither praised nor condemned for its particular feeling, belief, attitude, or consciousness at any given time. By itself, unconditionality implies neither a high nor a low level of *positive regard* – either in my theory or as seen in research. High unconditionality without liking or positive regard could be perceived as indifference or even as a generalized (nonselective) rejection of the other. To contribute to a healing, or a freeing and growthful process, unconditionality would in theory need to be coupled with at least a moderate ambience of positive regard. Most of us are conditional or judgmental toward ourselves, at least at times or in some areas (c/f Rogers' (1959a) concept of "conditions of worth"). A conditional response from others may tend to perpetuate or reinforce 'self-conditionality.'

Searching later examinations of UPR and unconditionality include contributions by Bozarth (1998, pp. 83–88), Freire (2001), Iberg (2001), Lietaer (1984), Purton (1998), and Wilkins (2000). Lietaer emphasizes the centrality, for unconditional regard, of true openness and receptivity on the therapist's part. The unconditionally responsive therapist, he implies, is very actively engaged with the other. Expressed personally, it "means *that I keep on valuing the deeper core of the person*" (p. 47). In other words, "it has nothing to do with indifference but rather points to a deep involvement with and belief in the other" (Lietaer, p. 48). Lietaer sees expression of this quality as having a certain directional influence. This paradox appears to be accentuated in passages under the heading of "confrontation and unconditionality" (pp. 54–57). Bozarth (1998, p. 77 and pp. 84–87), while clearly respecting his colleague's scholarly acumen and raising of issues, saw intended confrontation or guidance of clients into a more experiential focus as being at odds with a deeply respectful unconditional quality of regard. The hypothesis that this quality permits the undoing of acquired rejection of parts of the self seemed incompatible with steering the client into particular kinds of process. The distinctive explorations by other colleagues, including those mentioned, point to a construct that remains alive and pivotal in theory and in practice.

Rogers' emphases both on therapist congruence and unconditional acceptance, especially if the former *is interpreted* simply as being genuinely oneself and the latter as being impartially receptive to the point of conveying no value direction, makes for a certain tension among principles. Genuineness is not an adequate synonym for congruence though there is some overlap (see, e.g., Hough, 2001). Nor, for that matter, is consistency between underlying experience, awareness and expression any longer a sufficient definition of congruence, given the dynamic complexity (Hough) and multisided nature of the human self (Barrett-Lennard, 2013, pp. 14–21, 30, 53). The natural pluralism of self implies a situational variability in degree and expression of congruence in different modalities of self (see Chapter 7), though research is yet to directly address this issue. The BLRI measure reflects congruence as experienced in one relationship at a time, without *necessary* generalization to other relationships, and thus is not compromised by current thinking on self-diversity. Study of dyadic relationships in which one person's level of congruence is perceived by different others (tapped by the OS RI), and may vary in self-perception (MO RI), could shed further light on the potential variability of manifest congruence.

In more recent years several colleagues, among them Bozarth (1998), Greenberg and Geller (2001), Hough (2001, as mentioned), Lietaer (1993, 2001), and Seeman (2001), have published thoughtfully enquiring analyses of the meaning and process aspects of congruence. Among these, all of which include original elements of perspective, Seeman's is perhaps the most distinctive. He examined congruence from a human systems perspective, which posits complex interrelatedness among elements and subsystems throughout the organism and carried through to engagement with others. When natural connections are all open and communication is flowing freely within and among the subsystems, from physiological levels through the regions of consciousness and to relations with others, the whole can be said to be functioning congruently. Accounts by other authors embody variations in language and emphasis in describing congruence, with a shared core of meaning relating to wholeness, free inner flow and openness or transparency. I do not see any contradiction with the thought on which the RI is based but some enrichment of it.[1] I will turn now to further studies already completed or ongoing and later address potential and adventurous work.

LATER STUDIES AND ANALYSES

IN THE THERAPY DOMAIN

The ambitious US National Institute of Mental Health Collaborative Research Program on treatment of depression included interpersonal therapy (IPT) and cognitive-behavior therapy (CBT) and more conventional clinical management Exhaustive analyses of the many-sided outcome data showed that clients improved under the varied regimes, particularly including CBT and IPT – with IPT having some advantage with more severely depressed patients (Elkin et al., 1989). Outcome differences, however, were "generally not predicted" by type of treatment but *were linked to quality of the therapist-to-patient relation* (Blatt, Quinla, Zuroff, & Pilkonis, 1996, p. 169). Thus, these authors' conclusion that it seems "more productive to explore dimensions of the interpersonal relationship established between patient and therapist … that affect therapeutic change than to continue to look for differences among different types of therapeutic intervention" (Blatt et al., p. 170).

A later report (Zuroff & Blatt, 2006) focuses more closely still on the BLRI data, using here a composite measure from the R, E and C scales. This carefully argued report is based on elaborate and sophisticated analyses from the large sample (total resultant N = 191). Data-intensive composite outcome measures administered at several points were used. The BLRI data gathered after the *first two* of 16 interviews was found to predict relatively rapid decline in assessed maladjustment among clients in all the treatment conditions. "A positive early therapeutic relationship also predicted better adjustment throughout the 18-month follow-up as well as development of greater enhanced adaptive capacities" (ibid.) even when a wide range of client characteristics were controlled. Thus, the conclusion that across varied types of treatment "the therapeutic relationship contributes directly to positive therapeutic outcome" (Zuroff & Blatt, p. 130). Most therapists in the study had three or more clients. A further analysis by Zuroff, Blatt, Kelly, Leybman, and Wampbold (2010) from the same data pool confirmed that the higher therapy conditions for some therapists than for others (between therapist differences) played a big part in predicting improvement. So, the therapist effect was a crucial factor.

Using the empathy scale only of the OS RI, Barkham and Shapiro (1986) focused on two groups of clients differing in the extent and circumstance of their involvement in counselling. The first group of 12 had volunteered for at least a one-hour counselling session whereas members of the second group of 12 had been in therapy (with one of the same six counsellors) for three sessions or more when the data were gathered. *Clients* (but not their therapists) in the ongoing group perceived substantially higher levels of counsellor empathy than the 1-hour clients did. The result is unsurprising, suggesting that it takes time for the percep-

---

[1] Arguably, species complexity has a role in unity of functioning. The more adaptive and less preprogrammed an organism is, the greater the potential for incongruence. Learned patterns can be at odds with each other and with those that are more inherent. Features of personality and behaviour can develop in ways that are not only diverse (mostly a strength) but at odds with each other. The potential for incongruence is part of the price we humans pay for the complex diversity of our make up, including our differentiated awareness of self and of other and the intricate interweaving of these and other foci of experience.

tion of counsellor empathy to build up. However, RI data gathered at the *end* of therapy as, for example, in Salvio, Beutler, Wood, and Engle's (1992) ambitious study, can partly reflect effects of therapy itself (discussed in Chapters 2 and 3). If these investigators had chosen to include analysis of relationship and alliance data all gathered early in therapy, the results would have had different added meaning. Lafferty, Beutler, and Crago (1989) also gathered OS RI data at the end of therapy. For their analysis, therapists were divided into 'more and less effective groups' based on client outcomes. The more effective therapist group received higher mean scores on all RI scales, reaching strong significance on the E (empathy) scale. One can reasonably conclude that by termination, at least, the therapists of more successful clients were perceived as more empathic.

Later studies also have often singled out the component empathy scale of the RI. Myers (1995) reported closely on the experience of five clients who each worked (for 20+ interviews) *in turn* with the same two therapists. The data included transcribed interviews, therapist narratives, the RI E scale, and a relationship Q-sort. Intensive qualitative analysis was both central and illuminating in regard to listening and empathy. The RI and Q-sort data also implied individuality in the working and deepening of empathy over the course of each relationship. Other investigators that have used the RI in varied recent therapy-relevant studies, just to measure empathy, include Fuertes et al. (2007), Hart (2005/2006), Marci, Ham, Moran, and Orr (2007) and Messina et al. (2013). Fuertes et al. (2007) found significant correlations between RI empathy and both Gelso's 'real relationship' measure and the Working Alliance Inventory, as well as with outcome. (Some association between the RI E and WAI scales is usually found but it tends to be weak, in keeping with joint relevance but distinctiveness of each measure.)

In a distinctive study, Messina and her colleagues (2013) used a sample of volunteer "clients," each client was interviewed by three variously qualified listeners. Continuous recording of skin conductance for both participants was obtained for each pair. Interestingly, a significant correlation was found between client-perceived empathy and the index of physiological concordance – tying in with the idea of mirror neuron involvement in empathic engagement. Marci et al. (2007) also studied physiological correlates of perceived empathy, using the RI E scale and distinguishing segments of high versus low concordance in skin conductance. Significant association between these two very different aspects of arousal and response was again found. (This work has an early precursor, in Berlin's 1960 study.) Hart (2005/2006) was interested in the possible relation between "secure" versus "insecure" attachment style and the perception of empathy, finding in an analogue study that students manifesting a secure attachment style perceived the therapist in a recorded interview excerpt as more empathic than those with an insecure attachment style.

Withers and Wantz (1993) reported a study that examined types of personal belief system that could affect perceptions of therapist response. The data were provided by 270 students recruited from various academic areas, who watched (in small groups) the recorded interview of Carl Rogers with "Gloria" (descriptive commentaries in Farber, Brink, & Raskin, 1996, pp. 57–73). The students were called on to imagine themselves in a session with Rogers responding as he did with Gloria, and to rate the qualities of his response on the OS–64 RI. This large sample of participants had also completed the cognitive personality Belief Systems Test (Gore, 1985), each student was then sorted into one of the four systems of belief outlook. Scores on all four RI scales varied significantly across the belief groupings of the participants. Generally, Systems 1 (concrete in thinking and fixed in attitude) and 2 (wary and mistrustful) people gave the lowest RI scores. System 3 members (interpersonally sensitive and support-seeking) perceived the therapist most positively, closely followed by the System 4 group (more open, self-directing, and stress tolerant). The last group was also characterized as having been most unconditionally accepted by their families.

In a UK study by Weston (2011) RI Form OS–40 (slightly adapted) was answered by samples of clients on their therapists (321 clients in all, with 27 therapists). This study looked (as a familiar overall aim) at whether the therapist-client relationship, as scored from client-perceptions, predicted outcome. The research was of a kind to focus on "therapy in the real world," thus without close tracking or control, for example, of the kind and severity of presenting problems, length of therapy, or just when during therapy the client completed the RI. Careful subsequent analysis to curtail these limitations showed that, controlling for initial level of depression, the measured relationship qualities predicted depression outcome, with a small- to medium-effect size. Clients who perceived their therapist as offering greater levels of congruent empathy and unconditional and positive regard had lower depression scores at the end of their counselling, whatever their starting level of measured depression (86 clients, 16 therapists). The results were seen to have broadly affirmed, over a large and "unwieldy" sample, that client-based RI measures of therapist congruence, empathy, regard, and unconditionality had a moderate influence in reducing assessed depression, anxiety, and level of distress.

Outcome-related data is sometimes obtained from use of the RI by itself as, for example, in results from participants in the early residential Australian workshops focusing on experiential learning in small groups. An MO (myself-to-other) form of the RI was answered just before and shortly after the initial workshop in the series, in reference to the "last client" to enter a therapy/helping relationship with the respondent. Postworkshop, the directions were to answer for the same relationship as remembered before the workshop began. It was thought that participants would afterwards admit further data into their awareness and/or set different personal standards for themselves, and the RI measures were examined for decrease or increase. Congruence scores diminished for 26 of the 32 members, increasing for six only, a result with very low chance probability. Almost the same proportion also diminished on the unconditionality scale, and empathy scores tended to fall as well. Whatever the exact meaning, participants wound up with a more modest view of their previous helping relationship response.

The RI was used in another way in a further workshop to check for possible changes in predictive accuracy. Intending members nominated a current client and/or other person in close contact with them. These 'observers' were called on before the workshop, and again a little time after it, to complete the OS RI on the member's response to them, and mail their returns directly to the investigator. Workshop members answered the same RI form, but *for the way they expected their observer to perceive them,* doing this after arrival at the workshop and again a few weeks later. Complete before and after returns from 23 member-observer pairs revealed that members anticipated their observers' perceptions of them more accurately following the workshop than beforehand. Replication would be needed for any firm conclusions, but the work is indicative of meaningful predictive uses of the RI (see Barrett-Lennard, 1998, pp. 294–298 for a fuller picture).

IN COUPLES, FAMILIES, AND FRIENDSHIPS

Vansteenwegen's (1979) action study of couple therapy examined change in qualities of couples' relationships as measured by Lietaer's revision of the RI. Greater overall shifts in experienced relationship occurred in the treated group than in a control sample. The changes in perception of the partner's response were significant across all scales (VanSteenwegen, 1979, Table 1). At a two-year follow-up point, the *direction* of all of these changes was sustained (VanSteenwegen, 1982, Table 2).

Relationship change as a measure of outcome was studied in another context by Verwaaijen (1990). She too used a translated modification of the 40-item RI though not with couples, but to assess relationships between behaviorally troubled adolescent respondents and their parents before and after therapy. These data were studied in relation to coded features of therapist behavior, with results supportive of a quite active role with these (evidently "difficult") clients on the part of therapists (e.g., to enhance commitment).

Boettchner (1977) used a measure of "interspousal empathy" adapted directly from the BLRI, which was administered to husbands and wives before and after marriage counselling. Analyses of the data variously supported the relevance of the empathy variable. Much later and outside a counselling context, Cramer and Jowett (2010) also focused on empathy in couple relationships (N = 149). Perceived empathy of the partner, as measured using the positively worded items only for this scale (64-item RI), was positively associated with relationship satisfaction and inversely linked to indices of depression and conflict. This pattern did not occur in the case of another index of "accurate empathy."

A short course (4 weeks/8 hours) of highly structured "empathy training" with couples was studied for its effects by Hines and Hummel (1988). Judge-rated empathic ability (JEA), perceived spousal empathy (OS RI empathy scale), and marital satisfaction (Locke-Wallace test) were examined. JEA ratings increased for trained groups as against controls, but there was no appreciable change in RI empathy or marital satisfaction. The brief training affected trained performance but did not appear to help participants become more empathic persons with their spouses. In a more ambitious work using the whole RI, Wampler and Sprenkle (1980) examined effects of the Minnesota Couple Communication Program. Expected change was studied, both in RI relationship quality and in "open" versus "closed" communication style (a focus of the learning program). Early communication style gains in two differently sequenced groups fell away by the follow-up point. However, the experienced quality of relationship rose and held (except in a control group), with significant pre- to follow-up-differences on RI scales. *Thus, change toward the more open behavioral style did not persist but enhanced relationships evidently did* (Wampler & Sprenkle, p. 581). The crucial comparisons were made for people who stayed with the project for the whole 33 weeks, implying both motivation and time for relationship quality to develop.

Ranney (1995) called on 160 young women to describe their "current primary adult relationship" on the E and C scales of the OS RI. The sample included 59 women reporting childhood sexual abuse. Significantly lower received empathy and congruence scores were found in returns from the formerly abused group than for the others.[2] Within this group, E and/or C scores also varied with age at the time of (first) abuse, and with the way authority figures had originally responded to disclosure of this abuse. Since self-development is seen to occur through formative relationships the fact that the abusive and other behaviors evidently affected later experience of or even capacity for empathic engagement confirms expectation.

During final checking of this chapter, McNeill (2014) completed a long-running multipart doctoral study centered on the relation between quality of couples' perceived empathy and the extent of their individual difficulty in recognizing, processing, and expressing emotion involved in the condition known as alexithymia. RI measures of empathy, both received from (OS form) and extended to the other (MO form) were obtained from 170 community couples, plus the data needed to assess alexithymia and additional variables. Higher levels of assessed alexithymia in husbands and wives were associated with lower received and extended levels of empathy. Moreover, as *differences* between partners' degree of assessed alexithymia increased there were exponential decreases in both spouses' empathy (MO and OS). This was regardless of which spouse manifested the higher alexithymia. The more detailed findings of this research could further inform relationship counselling of couples where qualities and differences associated with alexithymia are present.

In Gomes' earlier study (1981), mentioned in Chapter 4, three levels of relationship were tapped: each family member's perception of the individual response to them of each other member; their experience of the ways *pairs* of others responded to them (parents jointly and parent-child combinations, in two-child families); and their perception of the relational quality and feeling in the family as a whole – using an early family-specific version of the general "We" form (see DW–64 in Appendix 1). Gomes found that relationships were more homogeneous in one-child families than in the two-child case, where mothers were experienced as responding more positively than fathers *and* the whole-family 'We' was more distinct from other relations (Gomes, pp. 63–70). His results are of unknown generality and, in any case, invite further research building on the theory of multiple levels of relation (Barrett-Lennard, 1984, pp. 238–240; 2003, pp. 77–92).

Following Wampler and Powell's advocacy (1982) of the BLRI, Ganley (1989) administered the OS RI without the U items to 345 women (ages 25–40, ≥2 years married), who answered in reference to their spouse. The data were used for an investigation of factor structure based on inter-item correlations: In all, 47 of the 48 items were found to load above the criterion of .30 on factors directly reflective of the original subscales containing the same items. Thus, as mentioned earlier, the author concluded that the three-factor solution replicates the original subscale structure of the BLRI (Ganley, p. 113) and went on to suggest a number of applications in family systems and related research. (It is not clear to me why Ganley omitted the U component. Its basic role in the underlying theory, later item improvements and results from other studies, all point to retaining this component in family research.)

---

[2] Such evidently reduced capacity links to this author's idea of studying the recovery of empathy as a potentially significant aspect of *client change* in therapy (Barrett-Lennard, 1997).

The influential relation of teachers to students remains a fertile area for research use of the BLRI. The early studies by Emmerling (1961) and by Scheuer (1969, 1971) were mentioned in Chapter 3. Due partly to limitations in quality of some of the pertinent further work in this area the field remains wide open for careful and inventive inquiry. To this end, up-to-date 40-item 'student' and 'teacher' forms of the RI are available, designed for high school age children. A simpler OS Child form is also available for use in studying formative relationships generally in the world of younger children (forms in Appendix 1).

The study of supervisory relationships, especially in education and therapy, is a related focus of application of the RI. Cline's inquiry into the "confirming behaviour of school executives" (1970) remains an interesting example. About 700 teachers completed the OS form on the relational response of their principals. The principals answered the same Inventory for the way *they expected their staff to perceive them*, and also provided self-descriptions via the California Psychological Inventory. From the CPI personality results, respondents and their schools were grouped in quartiles. The best-functioning principals (CPI data) fell in the top quartile (Q_1), the least well-functioning fell in Q_4. The teacher RI data revealed that Q_4 principals received significantly lower scores than the Q_1 group on *unconditionality* (Cline, p. 32) – viewed by Cline as a key element in confirming behavior. Prediction by Q_4 principals of how teachers experienced them also were of generally lower accuracy than predictions from the Q_1 principals. Cline pictured the school as a self-balancing field system and considered that his evidence broadly supported "the idea that each school faculty represents a nuclear unit with perhaps a reflected personality of its own" (Cline, p. 30).

In a later illustration (Jaeger, 1989), 362 teachers from a large sample of elementary schools also answered the OS RI on their school principals and described the organizational climate of their school on a multifactor questionnaire instrument. Each RI scale moderately but significantly predicted factors such as intellectual climate, achievement standards, and organizational effectiveness (Jaeger, pp. 171–185). Level of Regard was singled out as the strongest predictor among the individual scales (Jaeger, pp. 186 ff.). The results broadly affirmed the importance of the principal–teacher relationship in contributing to the climate and teacher-viewed effectiveness of the schools studied. Spence (1988/1989) chose to focus close-in on feedback dialogue with teachers informed by supervisor observation of their teaching. The RI tapped teacher-perception of relationship quality in the supervision process. Teacher satisfaction appeared to hinge mainly on this relationship quality, while relationship quality *and* task achievement both fed into supervisor appraisal. Spence's full dissertation report includes a careful account of the supervision style and a useful range of quite specific results.

A related area of research that the RI can help to illuminate is the function of peers in group supervision. Byrne (1983) explored reciprocal peer supervision in a practically oriented study of therapy training. Six graduate students were taped during three individual sessions with their faculty supervisor and three with their peer partner, these sessions were then content analyzed. 'Client focus' and 'self-focus' emerged as broad primary categories. More 'teaching' from faculty (linked to client focus), and more support from peers, were both expected and received. Scores on the OS–64 RI scales were "in the positive range for both faculty and peer supervisors, with peers scoring higher on all dimensions" (Byrne, abstract). Handley (1982) found that supervisors' BLRI ratings *of their own response to trainees* on three of the scales were significantly related to trainee intuitive tendency reflected in their self-descriptions on the Myers-Briggs Indicator (based on Jungian theory). Dettlaff (2005) examined students' and their supervisors' personality characteristics also using the Myers-Briggs Indicator. If dyad members were matched in respect to extrovert or introvert tendency *or* in respect to sensing versus intuition then total scores on the BLRI (whether from student or supervisor perceptions) were significantly higher than they were from unmatched dyads.

IN NURSING, MEDICAL PRACTICE, AND OTHER HEALTH CARE CONTEXTS

Many studies of nurse–patient relationships and communication have made research use of the BLRI. This work has mostly singled out nurse empathy, as experienced by patients, as the interpersonal quality of primary interest. There needs to have been appreciable contact and communication in nurse–patient (as in any other) relationships if the results are to be regarded as based on experience in the particular relationship and having distinctive reference to it. In a busy hospital situation with medical issues tending to dominate and nurses moving from patient to patient, attention to *personal* support needs may be cursory even where nurses are quite capable of attentive personal listening and empathic response. In addition, there can be a marked lack of modelling and encouragement in this direction by nursing instructors, as was evidently in the case for a sizable proportion of the nurses in Persuad's (2002) survey of recently graduated nurses in Ontario.

For Persaud's study, 106 nursing graduates answered Form OS-G–64 of the RI (worded for the perceived response of a plural or group other – see Appendix 1 for the current GS-40 form) in reference to their teaching faculty. These data were considered to reflect the quality of caring in the teacher-to-student association as observed and felt by the students in training for a caring/helping profession. Other less structured data and feedback also were gathered. The most specific and interesting results were documented under the heading "Serendipitous findings" (Persuad, 2002). Scored in the usual way, the theoretical midpoint of zero (possible range −48 to +48) on each RI scale was conservatively chosen as the cut-off point to discriminate between low and inadequate perceived relational response and potentially adequate response. A large minority of RI protocols scored in the negative range. This was true of nearly half (48) of the respondents on the empathy scale and interpreted by the investigator as implying that the nursing faculty, in their relations with students, "was deficient in empathy" (Persuad, abstract).

Soldwisch (1990) had also investigated nurse caring with RI data gathered from 32 nursing students in a study of the expected association between level of caring and ego stage development. The MO–64 RI was slightly adjusted to refer to "your present relationship with patients" (e.g., item 2. *I want to understand how the patient sees things*). Boyd's 160-item Self-Description Questionnaire provided the data to calculate stages of ego development. The investigator concluded that caring in nursing, especially the aspects of nurse empathy and congruence, were strongly related to a nurse's psychosocial development. The fact that both kinds of linked data originated in nurse perceptions had its counterpart in a study by O'Conner (1989). In her work the central interest was an expected and confirmed strong association between relationship measures from the hospital patients and their satisfaction with their care tapped by a different questionnaire instrument (this common source made discovering the link more likely). In this case respondents answered the OS–64 RI slightly modified to refer to their nurse carers as a group (e.g., *The nurses respect me a person*). As in the next-mentioned study a good many patients couldn't handle the whole questionnaire,[3] although O'Connor still retained a broad sample of 262 participants.

Hospital patients who could manage it similarly rated their nurses' *response* on the RI E items in a study by Madrid (1993). The empathy scores were expected to be contingent on nurse personality type, as derived from a personality inventory based on Jungian theory, but no such associations were found. The study was done carefully within its framing, but at least two problems were identified. Although patient perceptions of nurse empathy may be crucial, the respondents were sick people (some critically) answering the empathy items from quite limited relational contact over a short period (a good many who were approached declined to participate). In addition, close analysis of the personality instrument data suggested marginal reliability and raised questions about item-scale coherence and structure. I mention the study partly to illustrate how early choices in a research plan can limit outcomes, notwithstanding immense and capable effort afterwards.

There also has been a gradual movement in medical training and practice toward more concern with the physician–patient relationship discussed, for example, by Simmons, Roberge, Kenrick, and Richards (1995) – coupled with advocacy of use of the BLRI in this context. Hornblow, Kidson, and Jones (1977) had already used the empathy scale of the RI (OS and MO forms) with medical students, but only in the context of attempted validation of the Hogan Empathy Scale designed to measure empathy as a trait. A recent study in Taiwan (Chu & Tseng, 2013), used the OS RI empathy scale in Chinese translation for the patient-perceived doctor's response in a sample of 144 hip and knee replacement surgery patients. Patients scoring

---

[3] The investigator emphasized particular confusion with "The negatively worded LOPSS [satisfaction scale] items [which] presented an apparent cognitive barrier to participation in the study, particularly for the elderly" (O'Connor, 1989, p. 114).

above the median in empathy from their doctor had a better understanding of information relating to their operation than did the other half sample. Low empathy implies a lack of awareness by the doctor of the patient's experience and frame of reference as they face major surgery and its aftermath.

IN GROUPS, ORGANIZATIONS, AND LEADERSHIP PROCESS

Marques-Teixeira, Pires de Carvalho, Moreira, and Pinho (1996) translated and used the 40-item OS RI in Portugal, with members of five kinds of small group: an actual therapy (psychodrama) group, a group of psychotherapy trainees, a religious group, a group of close friends, and a team of workers. Each group member answered the Inventory on the perceived response of other individual members, after the groups were well established (367 returns in all). A distinctive "group" effect was conceived to involve the emergence of a group whole from the interplay of members, a whole that then itself is an influence on the group's interior process. Sophisticated analyses of the RI data revealed highly significant differences between the groups on three scales with a marginal difference for congruence. A qualitative difference was found, notably in respect to empathy levels, according to whether or not a facilitator was present and contributing to group intensity. This level of empathic communication evidently had special bearing on the clear emergence of a *group* effect. The research is almost unique among RI studies in the diversity of the groups involved and in the joint attention to systemic process and personal relationship qualities.

Two varieties of possible leader–member influence, one kind concerned with member-to-leader identification and the other with member *self-ideal* congruence, were the focus of two studies by Cooper (1969, 1973). In each case the RI congruence scale was answered by group members on their trainer/facilitators, early in the life of the groups. In study 1, 12 T-groups, participated. It was found that when the trainer was seen as attractive participants tended to identify with him/her and become more like the trainer in attitude and behavior as assessed; when the facilitator was perceived as congruent (RI measure) participants changed toward increased personal congruence (movement of self-concept toward self-ideal) (Cooper, 1969). In the second study (Cooper, 1973), with fresh T-groups, trainer attractiveness was the degree of convergence between member self-ideals and their perception of the trainer, using a custom-designed inventory. Congruence was assessed as before. Change in this case was based on later estimations by fellow employees. Results were essentially consistent with the previous findings.

Leadership was the focus in a study by Kramer (1997) involving 106 hospital employees who reported to 26 different managers. The participants completed the 40-item OS RI minus the U scale in reference to their manager, and answered other instruments including the Leadership Practices Inventory (LPI, by Kouzes & Posner, 1993). The study centered on whether the RI scores predicted the measured leadership qualities. All correlations between RI variables and five LPI scales – concerned with the degree to which leaders challenge, inspire, enable, model, and encourage their team members – were highly significant. The concordance of results is suggestive but perhaps not surprising given the relational nature and transparency of most items, answered by the same respondents bringing their overall attitudes to the ratings task.

IN FRIENDSHIPS

One-to-one friendship relations are understudied – generally, and in terms of research that has made use of the BLRI. Cramer is one investigator who has actively pursued work in this area. The relation of self-esteem and the facilitative quality of friendships (measured by the RI, in a regular or shortened form) has been a main axis of this work. Having established such a link in his initial studies (1985, 1987, 1989), especially in the case of women, Cramer went on to employ sophisticated statistical procedures in an effort identify the presumed causal influence of relationship quality on self-esteem. An illustrative report of this work (Cramer, 1994) used relationship and self-esteem data gathered twice, with a 15-week interval. In the analysis employed, unconditionality stood out in predictively affecting self-esteem (as did the combined score for the four RI variables) (Cramer, 1994, Table 2). My own ideas about causation have evolved (Barrett-Lennard, 2013, pp. 55–65) and I now fully expect reciprocal (or more complex) influence processes in the region of Cramer's research. In this way our starting points may differ, but I see his careful work as a complement and encouragement to further inquiry in this vital region. (A fuller summary of Cramer's studies with the RI appears in Barrett-Lennard, 1998, pp. 315–316.)

IN WHOLE RELATIONSHIP ENVIRONMENTS

Studies where respondents describe a span of life relationships or report their experience of an interpersonal milieu, is another understudied area, although it does include a few early examples of interesting work (e.g., by Gross, Curtin, & Moore 1970, and Wargo & Meek, 1970/1971) already mentioned in Chapter 3 (p. 32). The results of the Wargo and Meek study evidently had informative value for the setting's program. I conceived the idea, in the mid-70s, of an even wider, basically redesigned, form of the RI that would tap relationship quality over the whole spectrum of the respondent's experienced interpersonal world. Specifically, a profile of measures from up to 10 or 11 experienced relationships across the person's family, friendship, and vocational life can be tapped in one form. The new version (then 42 items, now 40) was initially tested in Holland's (1976), validity study on a sample of upper high school and university students (see Chapter 4, p. 46). Reliability estimates were adequate or better for each RI scale. From the *separate validation data*, it was evident that some subjects lived in a much more connected and supportive family/friendship environment than did others, and they were sorted into three criterion groups. Average RI scores were all higher for the top support group than the bottom one. Higher overall RI scores were also found, as expected, for family and friendship relations than for vocational relationships.

While preparing the new form, I shared my draft work with another investigator, who proceeded with his own related study (Sundaram, 1977), using a working adaptation of only 24 items. Forty-nine, first year tertiary college students, men and women, rated the response of individual family members, friends, teachers, and additional significant others, for a total of *up to* 20 relationships. This was done twice, with an interval of 5 months. Sundaram was interested, much as Cramer was later, in the bearing of facilitativeness of life relationships on personal well-being. He deduced adjustment levels from another instrument, and hypothesized that the general quality of relationships would correlate with *change* in adjustment from test to retest (Sundaram, pp. 34–39). Careful (step-wise multiple regression and path) analyses were used in an effort to establish causality, with a model of reciprocal causal interaction between relationship and adjustment being the best fit to the data (Sundaram, pp. 49–52). (This reciprocity is very much in accord with my own present thinking.)

I was not able at the time to follow these studies up but my new form received occasional use by other investigators, notably including Townsend (1988). She used *total score means across all relationships* as an index of a person's experienced facilitative environment. This correlated strongly with measures of loneliness (inverse relation) and of interpersonal self-efficacy (Townsend, Table 4). Further results suggested that actual self-disclosure with partners was partly a function of overall experienced facilitation. Much more recently, after revision of the instrument and further student research, added refinements were made and Form OS-LR-40 (see Appendix 1, pp. 132-139) is waiting for new uses.

USES IN TRANSLATION

The BLRI has been used over time in varied translations in a broad range of studies. In most cases I provided guideline suggestions to non-English colleagues about how to go about making a reliable translation (see Appendix 1, end section). These colleagues include investigators working in Arabic, Chinese, Dutch, French, German, Greek, Italian, Japanese, Korean, Malaysian, Polish, Portuguese, Slovak, Spanish, Swedish, and Turkish. My records also indicate usage in American Sign Language and possible translation in further languages. Some of the translations are in my files, but I do not have the linguistic fluency to check or edit them myself. However, interested readers working in other languages might well be able to locate the original translators, or their reports, from the listing of these colleagues given in the final section of Appendix 1 (p. 159).

As example, there have been several Spanish language translations including a published Chile-based version by Celis (1999). Celis's report centers on the RI itself, describes the instrument and presents a complete translation of Form OS–64. In a differing translated application, the empathy scale only, arranged in observer form, was used in a dissertation study by Rodríguez Irizarry (1993) in Puerto Rico. Research participants used this version in rating four videotaped interviews designed as nondirective or directive or as affective versus nonaffective. Interaction effects were not found in this observer context, but empathy scores were significantly higher for the nondirective and more feeling centered affective interviews. Other Spanish translations have originated in Spain, Mexico, and the United States, and there has been more than one translation in some languages.

WHERE TO NEXT? UNDEREXPLORED AND ADVENTUROUS REGIONS

In therapy research one suggested focus mentioned in Chapter 4 and that still (evidently) has not been pursued, would be to obtain baseline measures of client-experienced interpersonal life quality outside therapy (using RI Form OS-LR–40, see pp. 132-139). and to compare these with measures from the client's view of the therapist's response (regular OS form). Such data would make possible a new kind of test of conditions theory: if experienced empathic understanding and the other RI-measured qualities have a crucial role in enabling change, their experienced presence in the client–therapist relationship surely must be at a more consistent or higher level than in other current relationships in the client's life. If this were not so in instances of successful therapy, then complex interactions are occurring and/or there is weakness in the theory. Another issue is that of whether, over the course of a productive therapy experience, relations with significant others become experienced as generally more positive. And if life relations do improve, is a narrowed "gap" (if found) between crucial qualities in the therapist–client relation and close life relationships linked to voluntary termination of therapy?

Depression, anxiety, and other manifestations of personal-emotional stress and conflict can play havoc with a person's effective capacity for empathic contact with others, this tending to increase emotional isolation in a potentially self-reinforcing pattern. The way clients relate to their underlying experience (perhaps with little self-empathy) and their connection with the inner experience of other persons, both fall in the domain of empathy. I have explored these twin aspects and their interconnection elsewhere (Barrett-Lennard, 1997), and see a number of possibilities for research. For example, does empathic attunement in significant life relationships become a more significant priority and source of meaning to clients, through therapy? And is it demonstrable that individuals' empathic sensitivity, as experienced by significant others, tends to increase over therapy? On the second issue, clients might, for example, be asked to nominate individuals toward and from whom they feel understanding. These 'understood' persons would then be invited to describe the client's response to them (OS RI) in empathy-relevant ways, both before and after therapy, to test for change. As an added feature, if the client's own view of his/her understanding of these persons (MO RI) was also obtained, client empathy seen from the "outside and inside" vantage points should be more congruent afterwards than before – presuming therapy had been effective in helping the client become more open to experience.

Another potential usage of the RI is to call forth the respondent's view of an *ideal or desired relationship* – with a therapist, a partner, a child, a teacher, a close-knit community or group (by a member), or in another category of relationship. The underlying theory implies that the more the better: the more positive the experienced relationship on each RI variable the more facilitating (or healing) and growthful in quality it is. But this would not be the view of therapists of all persuasions, and one would not expect it to be consistently the case among all classes of relationship and in all communities or cultures. The nature of personal ideals on the unconditionality dimension may be particularly variable. Personal congruence in respect to the transparency component is not likely to be equally valued in all therapies. Since Rogers (1975) wrote his article "Empathic: An unappreciated way of being," everyday language has continued to evolve and some notion of empathy is common in the lexicon of our time – as is regard, warmth, caring, and their synonyms.

Granted that these qualities are, on the basis of evidence, arguably axial in therapy and relevant for constructive relationships generally, whether they literally are comprehensive or "sufficient" conditions for therapeutic change is not proven in research or entirely credible in idea. Good therapists have learned much from experience and are not merely implementing a preconception or formula. Conditions theory cannot convincingly represent the *entire* foundation and orbit of their response to clients, and such an idea is not tested in the research that supports their importance. Moreover, the immediate relationship between therapists and clients always takes place in a larger context. Therapy and personal–relational helping relationships broadly depend in turn on supporting conditions in the societal and institutional frameworks that make such resources possible and valued, and the relevant features of this larger context call for close examination even in therapy research (Chapter 9).

Another potential realm of inquiry, adventurous in a different way, is the study of relations within the self. This would involve application of an intriguing so-far-unused experimental "self-with-self" RI adaptation. It is not uncommon for people to feel that they have a relationship with themselves and to experience selective liking or dislike toward particular actions or patterns of the self. I see the human self as normally complex and multisided and have developed the Contextual Selves Inventory presented in Chapter 7 to study this plurality of being. A self-to-self version of the BLRI would be a means to assess relational-attitudinal quality within the self and might greatly enrich the notion of inner conflict and its positive counterpart. A working version of RI Form S-S-40 appears in Appendix 1, and I invite the reader to try it out personally and consider its use in research (see Chapter 9 for fuller discussion of this new form).

THE SPECTRUM OF BL RELATIONSHIP INVENTORIES

Nearly all forms and adaptations of the BLRI have been previously mentioned. I will briefly refer to the whole spectrum again, in a way that ties in with the inclusion of *current forms* in Appendix 1. The original 5-scale Client and Therapist version is closely described in Chapter 2, and the temporary 4-scale (mostly 72-item) forms that immediately followed are mentioned in the subsequent chapter. All current forms, however, stem from the 64-item revision crafted in 1964 (see Chapter 3). These include the 40-item variants and the even shorter new form centered on the empathy measure (Appendix 1, pp. 150-154). The first adaptations of the 1964 version were the Teacher-Pupil RI (adapted with Scheuer (1969) and no longer current) and the group OS-G–64 form (now replaced by GS–40 – in Appendix 1, pp. 141-142). The slightly adjusted group "milieu" version is not current but could readily be revived. Observer/judge versions (e.g., *The therapist respects the client as a person*) also came into the picture quite early and remain available in fresh 40 item forms (see Chapter 9 and Appendix 1).

The long-running general OS–64 and MO–64 forms are now complemented by the alternate 40-item version, prepared initially for use in survey-type studies by other investigators. The structure and rationale of these two variants are identical. The shorter form essentially reduces the number of items from 16 to 10 in each scale – mainly by omitting some item statements, merging others, and (in two or three cases) reversing the positive/negative wording of an item to maintain a balance between the two kinds. Further inspection of item-by-item data also contributed to the choice of items to "sacrifice" or modify. The generally high reliabilities with 64-item versions could be a little lower with the reduced item sample, although evidence to date suggests that there has been little if any change in this respect. Because the 64-item forms have been long-used and tested, they are deemed preferable when suited to the kind of relationship studied and when their length is not a problem. However, the more compact 40-item version has practical advantages, and other current forms are either adapted directly from its item content or have common origins in the longer forms and underlying concepts.

I have mentioned the "relational life-space" RI, now more simply named the Life Relationships (or LR) form. This generates a representative profile of one's lived world of varied relationships and is the most time consuming of the BLRI forms, although it is held to 40 items that are virtually identical with those in the basic OS–40 form. Respondents need to be prepared for up to a full hour exercise *in the live presence of the person gathering these data*. A participant might require assistance in understanding all features of the task spelled out in the Directions section and clearly identifying the relationships they will describe on the Answer form (see Appendix 1, pp. 131-139). Typically, each participant would select at least seven or eight relationships to describe. Resulting scores can of course be searched into in different ways according to the purposes of the investigator and applicable statistics. Besides their examination as whole profiles of scores, average levels within each of the three subspheres (family, work and "public" life) may be pertinent to compare. Combining the results across all relationships to get an overall view of the person's experienced relationship environment (in respect to regard or empathy, say) has already been done at least once (Townsend, 1988). As mentioned earlier, the results could provide theoretically meaningful comparison with therapy relationship data for the same persons or studied in relation to the subcultural identity or other circumstance of participants. It may also find use with some clients in therapy.

Teacher-student RI forms now also run to 40 items, with their own score form (in Appendix 1). These are designed for use with in-school students, potentially down to grades six or seven – depending partly on reading and comprehension standards. The form for students has reference to an individual teacher. For simplicity of wording, items use gender pronouns to refer to the teacher – making for two variants. The version for teachers is a modified myself-to-others (MO) group form on which the teacher describes his/her response to a collective of students. The items run in parallel to those in the student form but with distinctive wording. In framing them I was minded to use "natural language" and to formulate the negatively worded items so as not to invite any automatic response and make it easier for teachers to enter some degree of 'yes' where that was their real attitude. It obviously is a sensitive matter to obtain these data from students or teachers, and respondents need to have confidence that their answers and scores will not be made known to other staff or students within the school or, in most cases, to parents. (For a teacher to be given information, on request, about overall results from his/her students s/he would need at least to understand something of the underlying theory and measurement limitations.)

The BLRI does not have to be used as an on-paper questionnaire. A computer-administered (and scored) version of the whole OS–64 form was successfully used years ago in a thesis study under my supervision (Watts, 1989). It would run only on an IBM-type computer of that era, however. I finally gave up on attempts to convert it from the original floppy disk to work on my Macintosh and it would now require fresh programming, presumably for Windows systems. Watts developed this computer version so that each item was clearly presented on the screen by itself and an answer given and confirmed before going on to the next item. Thirty couples were recruited and each partner provided the full range of data, which included the usual on-paper version as well as the new computer (C) version of the RI, identical in item content and answer categories. Half of the participants answered the C version first and the other half began with the on-paper form. There were no appreciable differences in mean scores as between the two forms and other analyses pointed to psychometric equivalence.

Some carry-over memory by participants of previous answers to the same items was of course possible, since all of the data were gathered in a single session. Although some participants did not have (in the late 1980s) any hands-on experience with computers, their preference ratings pointed to predominant favoring of the computer administered version – also seen as somewhat more friendly, interesting, and simple to answer. It was also more novel at the time. Thus, well-designed (and closely-monitored) computer administration of the RI is an acceptable alternative. Some other investigators have used online answering systems and I expect any computer program-savvy investigator could develop and test a version for full computer administration and scoring.

My review of studies indicates that a good many investigators have chosen to focus on empathy and some have left out the other RI variables and scales altogether. When approached in advance about this intention, I always have recommended that each empathy item be separated from the next by at least one other unlike item. The empathy statements are mostly transparent and some of them are similar in form.

My concern has been to avoid the possibility of a consistency response bias. Some respondents might actively seek to give a consistent picture or avoid seeming to contradict themselves, with the effect that answers to some items would be influenced by answers given to other items. The arrangement of statements in the whole RI intentionally minimizes this possibility (Chapter 2). I have now arranged a new form that includes a strong complement of 12 empathy items separated, however, by a mix of items from the other scales. Rather than make a random selection, four selected items (in both positive and negative wording) from each of the further three scales are included. These *could also be* used to provide a broad approximation to the other measures, single or combined (see form OS–E+ and its score sheet, in Appendix 1, pp. 149-153). I strongly believe that this new form would be a better (safer) choice than simply to use an original set of empathy items on their own.

CONCLUSION

This chapter has presented a broad sample of the later studies in which the BLRI has been used, and has looked ahead to meaningful further potentials – some to consolidate previous work and others that will break new ground. It is not my intent to try to anticipate all potential kinds of application of the Inventory, although I will revisit this issue within the wider compass of thought conveyed in Chapter 9. Foundations of this expanded view were advanced in an earlier book (Barrett-Lennard, 2005). There I proposed that the realization of a helping relationship broadly in the Rogerian tradition depends in turn on supporting conditions in the institutional and larger societal frameworks that make such applications possible. Further, if the scope of our practice and research is expanded to the further levels envisioned in Chapter 9 and anticipated in my most recent book (*The relationship paradigm*, 2013), it is evident that principles extending beyond classical conditions theory are required. These would enlarge the scope of inquiry, although the RI in its main forms and numerous present and possible adaptations would remain a pertinent cluster of resources. This book is the first context in which the instrument is being made freely available out of formal copyright and in the substantial range of forms presented in full in Appendix 1. Another appendix includes very broadly related but differently purposed and quite distinctive forms that are the central topics of the next three chapters.

Chapter 6
Training Applications: Exercises in Facilitation

I used to conduct a course in counselling at Murdoch that emphasized a person-centered process. The participants were selected fourth-year undergraduate psychology students who were able to include applied studies in their final year. The students were not in a position to meet with actual clients, but enrolment was kept to about 15, who could work intensively and learn from each other. Our activity included structured exercises along with the topically focused course meetings and a low structure group experience. The full BLRI had been used in relationship development contexts, mainly with couples, and the whole instrument can also be a resource in beginning training. However, at the time I was looking for a highly focused, significantly involving, and reality-based application. The arrangement of mini-group triads of listener, speaker/'client,' and a participant observer came to mind. The way that I structured it and the improvisation of short BLRI-related rating forms to draw corresponding observations from each of the three interview-engaged participants had all the interest of a promising discovery. The format I will describe also found some application in groups conducted with graduate student trainees early in full therapy practicum contexts.

Preparation for these workshop-style exercises included careful construction of plans "on paper," which were then presented and discussed in live communication with the participants. An easy acknowledgement that the situation can at first feel a little artificial, as people feel their way into it, and a personal-facilitative style of communication in advancing and conducting the exercise, are vital to it working as an authentic and valuable experience. The way the plan is conveyed to participants, although it is meant to spell out its structure clearly and offer specific pointers in regard to the process, can have a thoughtful invitational quality rather than being directly instructive in style. As overall facilitator-guide I keep track of the time and movement of the groups through each of three "rounds" of the exercise (use a timer of some description). First, however, I will speak briefly of an approach to using the whole BLRI in a training context.

USE OF THE WHOLE BLRI EARLY IN COUNSELLOR TRAINING

The OS–40 RI form, with modified instructions, would be my choice when using the full BLRI as an aid in training. When an exercise with this aid is being initiated, clearly a crucial feature is the way that the course leader engages with the trainee participants, who need to feel secure and interested in being involved in such a hands-on learning exercise. Qualities such as being easy but assured, genuine, and perceptive are important in the exercise leader. A more specific basic aspect is to frame the exercise appropriately, sensitively, and clearly. Each person would be provided with a BLRI form, ready for use, and the task then described. An example of how to communicate what everyone is being asked to do , follows:

Take some moments to think of any issue on your mind that you might like to discuss with a trusted friend or counsellor … Imagine yourself, in this case, not with a friend but with such a counsellor … Try to picture yourself actually sitting with and facing that person. They are not a complete stranger; you have begun to know each other … Answer the Inventory to describe his or her response to you *in the way you would most wish it to be* … Remember this is

The Relationship Inventory: A Complete Resource and Guide, First Edition. Godfrey T. Barrett-Lennard.
© 2015 John Wiley & Sons, Ltd. Published 2015 by John Wiley & Sons, Ltd.
Companion site: www.wiley.com/go/barrett_lennard/therelationshipinventory

not an ongoing personal or life relationship but is a situation of one resourceful human being engaging with and responding helpfully to another who has an issue that concerns or troubles them. Picture this counsellor's desired attitude and way of relating and responding to you, as you answer the Relationship Inventory questionnaire.

Some people will visualize and imagine themselves in this situation more readily than do others, and there may well be some further inquiry and discussion before they all turn to answering the RI. *After completion* each person would receive a scoring sheet on which to self-tabulate and score their answers for the four component RI scales. Taking one scale at a time, everyone's scores would be listed for open discussion and exploration of their meaning. Naturally, the scores will vary – on congruence, for example. Someone might wish their counsellor to be completely open and transparent (as well as warm and perceptive, etc.) about their own reactions, resulting in a very high congruence score. Quite possibly someone else would especially want the counsellor to be focused on listening, helpfully drawing them out, and judiciously offering suggestions and possibilities to consider, and this emphasis and general expectations about helping professionals could lead to a somewhat lower congruence score. There might be more variation still in answers and scores on the unconditionality scale.

At best the whole process becomes quite engaging and leads to further development of the participant's awareness of the meaning in practice of empathic understanding, congruence, and the other qualities built into the RI, and further consideration of the philosophy or values underlying the instrument. It is important for each person to feel "received" in their own reactions and opinion as well as taking in each other's contributed ideas and understandings. This consideration and process of discussion could also be an illustration of how facilitation works. In a second suggested exercise the participants would be invited to envision themselves in the counsellor's position. After an introductory explanation they would be provided with the MO–40 (myself-to-the other) form of the RI. The exercise could be explained approximately as follows:

This time, imagine yourself positioned as a counsellor engaging with a client who is concerned, possibly quite anxious and/or confused about him- or herself, perhaps hurting or frustrated in a relationship, and struggling to cope and manage whatever it is that is troubling them. They need to feel that it is not only safe to openly share whatever is disturbing them but that you are capable of understanding their feelings and dilemma – what it is like for them inside. Desirably, they will come away from meeting with you feeling a bit less strained, easier about sharing their difficult feelings, and with increased hope or sense of being able to move through and beyond what is oppressing them. There you are, in your mind, with such a client in need and looking to you for assistance. Stand back a little and please answer the Relationship Inventory to picture the way *you would most like to respond and be as a counsellor-helper* in this situation.

As in the first exercise, each person would be given another score form on which to tabulate their answers and calculate scores on each of the RI scales. The course leader's task and challenge would be to enable beneficial comparison, joint exploration, and furthered awareness of response qualities and processes at work in a helping relationship. The overall process can be seen as involving a special use of the self on the helper's part, which feeds into and finds expression in the emergent relationship with the client. As in a dream state, where the presence of another can be intensely real, some participants may actually feel an imagined presence they are responding to. For others their thinking brain may well engage without any visualization of being in that situation. In either case the participant is extrapolating from experience and understandings they already have. These are not static and, thus, are most likely to alter through the whole engagement of the exercise. The immediate engagement and interaction in triad groups, next considered, has the potential for still greater impact.

LEARNING FROM INTERVIEWS IN TRIADS WITH BLRI-DERIVED PARTICIPANT RATINGS

One way to form the mini-groups of three is by lots (and thus minimize the effect of prior relationships). Prepare a pack of cards with a letter on the underside; A, B, and C (the letters used depends on how may mini-groups you require; A, B, and C will produce three mini-groups, if you require three members for each group then prepare three cards with each letter). Hand out the cards and those with the same letter form a mini-group.

Normally, as practitioners, we don't choose our clients and never know quite what is to come, which further justifies the chance selection. If the number of participants is not divisible by three, one group could have two observers or a group may only include two people (unless the course leader chooses to participate, as I usually do in this circumstance). If a group of two is not avoidable, each of these two would fill out their part of the form in the usual way and then distance themselves a little to try to represent in discussion how an observer (or perhaps a professional expert) might have viewed the process, as well as the ways they perceive it themselves.

The three complete exercises presented below each take, with explanation and ending discussion, one-and-a-half to two hours and thus require separate course meeting sessions – unless included, say, in an all-day workshop-style context. Most of the text below is taken from outlines I have prepared in advance and draw on in the exercise sessions. As formulated, the order is important. The first exercise focusses on empathic listening, the second highlights the aspect of congruence, and the third is concerned with regard and unconditionality. *They are framed as for direct communication by the course or workshop leader to the trainee participants.*

EXERCISE 1: FOCUSING ON EMPATHIC LISTENING

Here are guidelines and suggestions regarding each role in the triad groups, expressed as they might be spoken, thus to give a live sense of the communication:

1. *The listener:* Listen as receptively and acutely as you can, with the aim of tuning in to where the speaker is coming from in their felt meanings. The first feeling might be a reaction to the immediate situation, which could seem a bit artificial to start with. Don't ignore expressed or clearly implied reactions to the immediate context as well as responding to felt concerns that the speaker brings with them and wants to share and explore. Some of you might find that you are more comfortable being a listener than you are at sharing and talking about yourself. If this happens to be true, that is, if you feel anxious when the spotlight is on your own personal self it might be helpful to speak of this to your listener when your turn comes. My further suggestions are:

   • As the listener, in this exercise, let go if you can of any conscious concern to produce change in the other person's thinking or feeling. Try 'simply' to really tune in and let their experience and meanings come alive in you. Let yourself follow the other without trying to lead, and allow yourself to become absorbed in whatever they are sharing and exploring.

   • If you ask questions I urge you to use them very sparingly, not just to fill an awkward silence, not just to get information about the person's situation, but only to be more in touch with them in their immediate felt experience and meanings, how they construe their situation, what their immediate point of search or struggle is, for example.

   • If you lose track of what the speaker is expressing, simply acknowledge this as your difficulty or lapse of attention, along with your wish to understand their feelings and meaning. The speaker can then go on with awareness of where you are in response to them.

   • Sensitive reflection of what you are hearing or understanding can let the other know where you are with them. This might be expressed somewhat tentatively as your present sense of their felt meaning. If you are on target the other person is likely to go further (with a little relief at being understood so far) about the same issue or a connecting concern. If your 'reflection' is off-target they have a chance to correct you or make themselves clearer. Helpful reflections don't just parrot what the other has said but convey a degree of inner empathy or experienced recognition of their immediate feeling and meaning.

2. *The sharing speaker*: you need to choose an issue that's on your mind, to share and explore. It should be something real that concerns and matters to you though not a huge problem (or else a circumscribed part of a larger problem) so that you can draw back from and leave the exploration after a fairly short time. The more you can "own" and be directly expressive of whatever it is you share (e.g., using I/me language), the more chance the listener will have to connect with you in what you are experiencing.

Try to arrange the order in your mini-group in such a way that the next role you take after being the speaker is that of observer – rather than so soon being put on the spot as the listener.

3. *The observer's task*: this is to attend perceptively both to the speaker and to the listener and how the latter is responding. After the mini-interview and *before* the observer shares his/her impressions, each person needs to fill in the relevant section of the rating form. That only takes a couple of minutes and then the observer would have 7 or 8 minutes, say, to offer his/her impressions and for the discussion that this leads into. Effectively, the observer is another listener who can focus on the exchange between the other two with no pressure to respond while the interview is going on. Afterwards s/he seeks to provide honest useful feedback. The listener's main focus is on listening to understand and, through this understanding, to facilitate the other's sharing exploration. S/he is not directly communicating a separate viewpoint on the speaker's issue. Observer feedback, on the other hand, does reflect the observer's own perspective. It might point, for example, to something we see as observer that the responding listener didn't visibly pick up on, or to an aspect of the way they expressed themselves, or to some quality of process in the interchange. It is a focused impression conveyed directly from a closely but quietly attending witness to the interchange. Here are further suggestions to the observer:

- In your feedback, try for an attitude of personal ownership of your observations and perceptions – you are not sitting in objective judgment of the listener.

- Your attentiveness to the speaker–listener process is not at odds with being sensitive to the listener when they receive your feedback. However, you don't need to beat about the bush. You are all in the same position as learners, and perceptive feedback from peers can be especially valuable, and is generally welcomed.

- Helpful observer feedback is not of course a point-scoring exercise but involves sharing your own sense of the listening engagement you witnessed in a way that draws attention to particular process elements, qualities, and possibilities.

- Desirably, you would not be trying to convince the listener of anything but you may want to bring some things to their attention that you had the chance to notice as you looked on and listened without any pressure to respond. Your message may imply that you would *like* to have responded differently somewhere had you been in the listener's position.

- At the same time, the feedback message, to be of value, needs to be clear, straightforward, given without apology, and in straightforward language.

- Hopefully your feedback will involve minimal second guessing but will refer to tangible features of what you saw and how it struck you.

The above suggestions are not exhaustive. When you are on the receiving end of observer feedback, after you have been the listener doing your best, some difference in emphasis or a further helpful feature might occur to you. When you are observing, I suggest that you have a pencil and paper handy, so that you could jot down things that you notice as the interview is going on – just enough to jog your memory in giving feedback. Each of you will have a turn listening to one sharing classmate while being observed by another who subsequently gives you their impressions: Does any further query or suggestion come to your mind about how you would like this process to work? Do you feel nervous – or eager to get on with it?

For the exercise leader/facilitator: Suggested final checks and advice are:

- Ensure that everyone knows who their triad partners are, and that each person has a copy of the one page questionnaire form [in Appendix 2].

- Emphasize the need for participants to each fill in their own section of the form *before* any feedback discussion, so that their ratings are independent. Suggest they need not be protectively over generous in the ratings, or they won't mean much and could suggest that there was little room for improvement.

- Unless otherwise arranged, everyone would keep their own filled-in questionnaires for later reference. *The form provides an opportunity for the* **listener** *to copy the completed observer and speaker ratings next to her/his own.* Each person thus will wind up with a record of three complementary perspectives on his/her listening response in the focused-practice session.

- Regarding time limits, observers are in the best position to keep time and to help bring each interview to an end after whatever time is set to start with – maybe 15 minutes. If we allow 15 minutes, and up to 10 minutes for the ratings and feedback discussion that follows, then the second speaker would start about 25 minutes after the first and, in theory, the whole exercise would take 75 minutes once the interviews begin. In practice, it could run a bit longer, and a time and place (if subgroups separate) needs arranging for everyone to get back together as a total group for some debriefing before the whole session ends.

As author and facilitator of this exercise, I have tended to look in unobtrusively (and provide time reminders *if* required) on the various mini-groups in action and have moved around unobtrusively and remained on call throughout. My final words, before the groups begin, have generally been to invite any further queries and also acknowledge that I know this is a challenging experience, though typically an interesting one. I might imply that, along with everyone doing their serious best, this is a constrained learning exercise and shining instances of empathic listening and following may be too much to expect all at once.

When the described process is complete and members of the mini-groups reassemble in a single group this provides another context for reflection, sharing, and appraisal. It is also an opportunity to feedback impressions and ideas to the overall leader-facilitator. This debriefing phase might also be assisted by facilitator queries, prompted partly by his/her own interest. To give possible examples: "Was anything that happened unexpected or surprising to you?," "Which of the three roles were you most or least comfortable with?," "Can you say what you personally take away from this experience (perhaps questions as well as conclusions)?," and "Would you have wished for longer or shorter interviews or any other change in the structure?" After the debriefing discussion the session presumably would end with some reference to "next time." Presuming this will include the next described exercise, it could be natural to mention that it will give particular attention to the aspect (say) of congruence and provide further practice opportunity with newly arranged partners. Follow-up readings might be suggested.[1]

EXERCISE 2: FOCUS ON LISTENER-HELPER CONGRUENCE

Following the same structure as the first time, participants are first sorted by ballot into fresh mini-groups. The rotation of roles would be the same and time arrangements (with possible adjustment in detail, stemming from feedback on the first exercise) would be similar. Each person would have a fresh rating form with items corresponding to the emphasis on congruence (available in Appendix 2). Empathic response would of course remain highly relevant, but the aspect of congruence would be brought into focus in the group's preparation and in the rating form, observer feedback, and other discussion. The outline, given next, is again based on notes prepared by the author as a guide to his oral communication with the participants in conducting this exercise.

In almost any relationship, either party (if they stop to think about it) might experience the other person as *either* easily and comfortably themselves (terms like authentic, real, open, up front, and genuine come to

---

[1] Tolan's book on person-centered counselling skills (2003, with later reprints) is one of the potentially helpful resources (chapters 4 and 5 focus directly on congruence in concept and practice). Reference sources on listening and empathy might also include the chapters in Part I of *Steps on a mindful journey* (Barrett-Lennard, 2003).

mind) OR as presenting a somewhat contrived quality, or being guarded, controlled, not spontaneous. It's hard to be open and freely expressive of oneself with someone else who is guarded, or who gives us the impression of having a hidden agenda, or who seems to be performing as opposed to responding, or appears to be distracted by other thoughts. We are, of course, seeing the other through our own eyes in perceiving them in any of these ways. Our perception is also influenced by the immediate context and by any prior interplay with the other person.

Relationships are not merely interactive exchanges between fixed parties. They develop their own life and qualities, which are not just a mirror of either individual. If the qualities of another person do tend to hold across many differing situations this can feed into our perception of them. However, I believe that most behavioral and feeling qualities are more or less situational: context plays a big part. (If context were not important would a vulnerable client, guarded in other relationships, ever open up to a therapist?)

I suspect that most of us, in some situations, try hard to *be* a certain way. We mask some reactions, accentuate others, and risk giving the impression of being artificial. If we are holding part of our experience at bay, subtle signs may "leak out" that we are anxious, worried, or uncertain or possibly impatient or angry. Denied or unnoticed feelings seem to be commonplace. Which of us hasn't had reactions that we became aware of afterwards? Such experiences fit the idea of *in*congruence.

If *you* (as the client) are to see *me* (as the therapist) as authentic, real, and focused as a helping person – a person you can trust with your vulnerable or troubled self – then my special learning and skill need to have become part of me, ideally, the 'true me' that comes forth in a therapy/helping context. I said 'ideally'; in practice, we can approach this open way of being in relation with our clients. It is its *direction* that might start early in our training experience, and then continue almost indefinitely. It's a form of growth, a growth in which we become more congruent with our clients and perhaps generally.

Professional therapy, however skilled, begins and continues as a form of human encounter. I think of it as a specialized use of the self. It can be said that the therapy relationship begins with what each person brings out in the other and how these expressions then trigger further elements in the complex interactive process and experience of the participants. Any relationship acquires its own life, a third invisible presence, one might say.

Back to congruence: would one expect empathy and congruence to be significantly related, within a helping relationship? Why/why not? (Congruence implies being open to one's own experience. Empathy depends on being open to and perceptive of the other person's experience. In research on the therapy relationship measures of empathy and congruence tend to be the most highly correlated of the therapy conditions.)

How far is it possible to go with *trying* to be congruent without tripping up? This is almost like trying to be spontaneous, which is paradoxical. However, there are a few other things that can be done toward enhancing one's level or quality of congruence, if not generally then at least in the in the context of a therapy or helping relationship. Here are some possible steps:

• Ask yourself (outside the interview situation and not too critically, perhaps even kindly) "Am I/was I anxious or on edge in some way, in this context?" It would be surprising if your answer were "No, not in the least." Perhaps you would then ask, for example: "Am I wanting to give *the impression* of professional or interpersonal competence and uncertain whether I can do this?"; "Am I very conscious that there could be a great deal at stake for a troubled client person who has taken the plunge to seek help, and I *desperately want and "need" to really help them*?"; "Am I entering this situation "programmed" with a strongly preconceived image of how I *should* be, and the results I *should* get?"; "Do I feel as if my *self*-image is in some way on trial here?" Of course, you are consciously trying to do your best and you have some ideas about how to be helpful. But if you are to be undistracted, fully present, and available with all of your concerned, knowledgeable, and outreaching compassionate empathic self, then *conscious self-prescription in the immediate encounter with the other* can defeat your purpose.

• Another kind of self-observation is for developing therapists is to listen back to their own therapy or practice tapes, which can be both confronting and sometimes valuable in evoking awareness of incongruence (among other effects). Conducive supervisor and/or peer feedback can further this awareness in tape-listening and other sessions.

- Most of us have issues that are sensitive and less than fully 'resolved.' We all are vulnerable in some measure, including those who gravitate to the personal helping field. Close involvement with clients and the issues they are a struggling with may easily arouse uncomfortable awareness and anxiety in sensitive trainee therapists. One way of dealing with such disturbance is to confront and work on such issues with a trusted supervisor for whom this working through is not a role conflict. (Sometimes, it would be a role conflict.) *In many contexts intensive training and development groups are a built in recourse in which all trainees take part.* Going into therapy oneself can be a significant further option. All such contexts, with facilitator-therapists of high skill and integrity, can be valuable or even crucial component experiences in becoming more congruent as a therapist.

As in the case of the first exercise, after the practice interviews end and members of the mini-groups reassemble in a single group another level of reflection, sharing, and appraisal opens up. People who were in different mini-groups with one or two fresh partners have added experience to reflect on and selectively share in the whole group. Again this phase might also be assisted by facilitator queries, both overlapping and different from the first time. Some comparison of the two occasions may occur spontaneously. The substance of facilitator queries suggested before (such as what members are freshly thinking about or take away from the experience) may still be relevant. Further possibilities might include: "How if at all did your awareness that the session was highlighting the aspect of congruence affect you as observer or listener?" and/or "Did you feel less or more self-conscious as responding listener then you did last time?" Reference to 'next time,' at the end of the debriefing discussion, could anticipate special attention to a further aspect of relationship within a similar structure of interviews and appraisal.

EXERCISE 3: FOCUS ON POSITIVE AND UNCONDITIONAL REGARD

Unconditional positive regard (UPR) is a powerful though complex concept, as discussed in previous chapters. Many papers by Rogers and others, and a book of articles by Bozarth and Wilkins (2001) have been devoted to exploring its meaning in theory and practice. The outline given here includes a brief picture of the theory and leans toward distinguishing the twin aspects of level of regard and unconditional response, represented as separate scales in the BLRI. This exercise follows the same structure as before, with re-composition of the mini-groups and the same rotation of roles. Each person would have a fresh rating form with distinctive items corresponding to the present focus (available in Appendix 2). Empathy and congruence remain highly relevant, but the aspects of regardful warmth and nonjudgmental responsiveness to diverse attitudes and self-experience are now highlighted and reflected in the rating form. The following outline is approximately as prepared prior to introducing the exercise to participants.

- Given that the concept or image of ourselves that each of us has develops in large part through relationships then its 'shape' is or has been influenced by qualities of relationships with significant others. We may in theory assimilate or 'introject' self-standards and develop what Rogers called 'conditions of worth.' If our most formative relationships have been quite highly prescriptive we are probably programmed for inner conflict at some stage. Sooner or later we may experience situations where it becomes unavoidably obvious that we are behaving or feeling in ways that are sharply at odds with a self-prescription, and this sets up anxiety and/or other symptoms. A core aspect of therapy in this view is the undoing of involuntarily acquired conditions of worth (e.g., Barrett-Lennard, 1998, pp. 77–78). When certain behaviors and/or inner states of the person are not owned as expressing or belonging to the *self* this can be a (not always reliable) shield against conscious inner conflict and anxiety. The implicit conditions of worth remain unaffected as the person inwardly defends an acceptable view of self. However, the cost of maintaining such a filtered partial view is prone to include a tightness or rigidity of perception, and the potential for intense arousal or over-reactivity.

- How does 'self-defense' break down and forward change ensue? As implied, the psychological costs of screening one's experience can be high. This screening can collapse when an individual runs into situations where their reaction confronts them with such intense or starkly obvious evidence of contradiction between their self-picture and their actual behavior that the defense/denial process fails and acute inner conflict and anxiety or depressed mood occurs. However, the ensuing, painful conflict carries a positive *potential*: the possibility of undoing or dissolving some of the introjected requirements for self-regard. *The communicated unconditional positive regard of an empathically understanding other* is seen to be crucial in facilitating this change. Instances of such response repeated many times, around the same and different conditions of worth and conflict areas, is viewed as the nucleus of a therapeutic change process. The person has become less vulnerable, more open to all sides of their experience, and more steadily regardful of self and others.[2]

- One misunderstanding about UPR is the idea that therapists need to be totally accepting and nonjudgmental toward any and all behaviors of their clients. However, it is not behavior, as such, but feelings and a person's inner experiencing self that is the focus of a nonjudgmental or unconditionally receptive and regardful attitude. A therapist could not be congruently accepting of behaviors that struck him/her as distinctly harmful or dangerous, but may be genuinely accepting toward the personally felt process (perhaps of victimization, deep resentment, anger, or fear) behind these destructive inclinations or actions. As in the case of congruence, unconditional regard and empathic understanding may go hand in hand, each process quality helping to ground and augment the other.

- As in the other exercises, each person records their ratings on the new form immediately following an interview and before any observer feedback and discussion of the session. Each statement should be answered in its own right and according to whatever matches the experience and observation the best – and regardless of what might be the most theoretically positive answer. It is important that the leader keeps to the prearranged times within each mini-group so that time is shared equally in each role. Then all groups will be ready to assemble at about the same time for the concluding discussion.

Most item statements in the R-U form are transparently about positive or negative regard or concerned with conditionality or unconditionality of response, though a couple are intentionally less distinct. Views might differ on what the theoretically most positive answer is in these cases, but ratings are not being summed and scored and what matters in this context are their meanings to participants, the consistency or diversity of particular answers, and the further understanding that can come from the dialogue that the answers (especially divergent ones) help to spark. Participants now have experience in three different mini-groups to reflect and draw on. The earlier substance of facilitator queries may still be relevant and there are of course other possibilities such, for example, as, "If you *felt* a difference in your response in your triad group this time was this change because you had further experience to build on, or a result of being with different people, or because of the further aspects of relationship highlighted this time?" Other issues may spontaneously arise, of course, and inventiveness by the course leader/facilitator and other participants may well lead in added directions.

CONCLUSION

The exercises introduced in this chapter are advanced in quite specific and detailed form, thus to be clear to the interested reader rather than to suggest that they are frozen in stone. Indeed, they evolved somewhat from year to year in my own application and, if my training activity was continuing, fresh experience might well result in further refinements. This said, the rating forms themselves (Appendix 2) have been much considered and tested in practice and I hope that others would not alter them at least until first used

---

[2] If one thinks of the self as naturally diverse and plural the potential conflict is between subselves, one or more of which are mostly submerged and "denied" by a more regnant self (see e.g., Barrett-Lennard, 2005 and/or 2013). The principles of recovery are similar.

as they stand. I have not conducted formal research with data from these exercises though there is potential for this to be done, with suitable planning and consents. In order that participants feel least inhibited in what is already a challenging new call on self-resources, with potential for discovery learning, the triad interviews have not been sound- or video-recorded in my own work. At any subsequent stage of training, especially with actual help-seeking clients, interview recording (to review and go over with a trusted supervisor) is of course highly relevant. One generous way of looking at these exercises is that they arose from creative improvisation. If they are not only useful to others, much as they stand, but add encouragement for further forward-moving improvisations they will have been doubly worthwhile. Chapter 7 introduces a different kind of questionnaire invention and its theoretical grounding. In this further case, the main aim is knowledge advancement, with spin-off value for practice.

Part 2
The Journeying Self in Personal and Group Relations

Chapter 7
The Contextual Selves Inventory: For the Study of Self in its Diversity

Poetry to me has the potential to convey meaning more succinctly than regular prose. It gives the poet "permission" to be expressive and to evoke felt meaning with few words. Its 'voice' complements ordered and reasoned prose communication. In 1985, years before the thought and method advanced in this chapter began to take shape, I wrote a poem that anticipated its thrust. Its focus is on our nature as personal human selves. In particular, are we normally unitary in nature or are we complex, internally diverse beings with varied faces and configurations? As we enter different contexts with others, does our immediate repertoire of behavior and attitude stay the same, or does it shift into another mode? And in times of reverie, if we turn and gaze down our own memory-filled path, do we not feel a kind of empathy for the figure we see back there; so familiar and yet like another self, a self we might wish to have been able to support with wisdom that came to us later? As I began to frame the poem, the sense of it seemed already to be there, 'waiting' for my words. I titled it "A Person" and it begins with the line "One alone and many in one." Differing words catch similar meaning in the phrase "each of us a singular multiplicity", and in the couplet "An abundance answering to one name, Multiple, uncounted but counting as one."

The ending of the same poem (Barrett-Lennard, 2003, p. 179) implies that, even in the healed or well-functioning person, differing self-systems don't disappear. They may change but, more importantly, their relations change. Now "befriended" in the person they can work together in reasonable harmony. I am inclined to think that well-functioning persons are more fluidly diverse than those for whom alternate self-patterns scarcely recognize each other and can repeat in entrenched form. But is all this true? Are we truly diverse, even with subselves, and how can we test this in systematic study of the envisioned diversity? In essence, that is what this chapter is about.

In an inquiry into the nature of self a first question might be "Where does a person's view of self come from?" Considered most generally, one answer seems almost self-evident: children develop their idea or concept of self in large part through relationships with significant others in their lives. But how does this happen and lead to healthy and affirming outcomes for the child, in one case, or plant the seeds of inner dividedness, low self-esteem or serious dysfunction in another instance? What is it that seems to make a crucial difference in generating these and other alternatives? An answering proposition is, in a word, that if parents and caregivers respond with receptive caring that supports the child in their own experiencing the first outcome is very likely. Neither high praise nor sharp criticism play much part in this case. There tends to be an appreciation or prizing of the child person as they express themselves and imagine, construe, and occupy their interactive world. For the alternative contrasting outcomes, the role of strongly conditional attitudes, especially in pivotal childhood relationships, is seen as a major factor. An environment of frequently conditional response evidently has far-reaching effects on the degree *and kind* of self-diversity that develops.

The Relationship Inventory: A Complete Resource and Guide, First Edition. Godfrey T. Barrett-Lennard.
© 2015 John Wiley & Sons, Ltd. Published 2015 by John Wiley & Sons, Ltd.
Companion site: www.wiley.com/go/barrett_lennard/therelationshipinventory

ORIGINS AND MANIFESTATIONS OF SELF-DIVERSITY

The inherent complexity of the human person feeds into diversity of self. It can be said that we have more than one 'nature.' Our biological nature has a great deal in common with the biological nature of other highly evolved species. Our psychological nature includes huge learning ability, the capacity for elaborate language and a lush symbolic life, and linked to these is a highly differentiated, thinking, feeling consciousness. And, we have a social nature, reflected in living interdependently in relationships with our kind. A great deal could be said about each of these three natures and I will single out one aspect. The second and third natures carry the potential for important voices in the child's world, especially ones that convey delighted approval of some personal behaviors and perceived qualities, and aversion to others, to feed into the child's forming self-attitudes.

If there are powerful voices, let's say from parents or major caregivers with distinctly differing attitudes one to another, the child person must learn to negotiate two or more different acceptability patterns and ways of being that are required for responsive regard from adults on whom s/he is dependent. The contrary sets of signals in the child's experience become gradually connected with his or her view of self. Rogers posited that we each develop a need for self-regard, and that the satisfaction of this need may pivot on standards for self that we have internalized, refashioned in some degree, and made our own (Rogers, 1959a, 223–224). He did not suggest that we may internalize more than one kind or set of standards for self but this, to me, is a logical extension of the same direction of thought.

Any very complex dynamic system is likely to display considerable variety of pattern, even passing at times from what seems like one state to another (Barrett-Lennard, 2013, pp. 61-62, and sources therein). Such a system invariably contains distinct subsystems, subsystems that have different functions in the complex whole. Easiest to distinguish in the human organism are the main biological features: our complex brain and nervous system, our skeletal structure and muscle systems, the whole intricate circulation system, our digestive and endocrine systems, our lungs and respiratory system, the liver factory, and numerous others. Any one of these component systems is very complex by itself, and quite distinct from but interdependently related to the working of other component systems. Consciousness, emergent from this incredible biological whole, clearly is no mere onlooker of internal and external events but a semi-autonomous further level of process different in kind from its physiological bedfellows, and with numerous and elaborate properties of its own.

Perception of self, within human consciousness, no doubt hinges on feedback of widely varied kind coming through many channels. Other persons, in all their variety, comprise a primary source. Given a multiplicity of kinds and qualities of feedback, is it plausible to expect that the idea of self that a person acquires would be highly cohesive, unitary, and self-consistent? Or, is it more reasonable to expect qualities of complexity, diversity, even multiplicity?[1] The answer, it would seem, must be of the second kind. Most interpersonal response is more or less conditional depending on the context and influenced by the attitudinal lens of the responding person, which varies from one to another. The strength and impact on the self of evaluative messages from others also would depend partly on the degree of fluidity of the receiving person's sense of identity and thus tend to have a bigger effect in childhood.

In a parent–child context, especially if the parent is holding some of his or her own self-experience at bay and implicitly experiences the child as an extension of self, then violation by the child of the parent's sense of acceptable self can lead to an anxiously or harshly conditional reaction. As a repeated pattern, and in a relationship of dependency (especially one that has nurturing elements as well), the child person begins to deny inwardly the offending aspects of self. I would expect this denial to be relative, applying most strongly in the orbit of that relationship and others felt to be like it. The child's world typically includes further crucial relationships, ones where response is conditional on different aspects of self-experience and behavior. This world may include sibling and other family relationships, and relations with teachers and important carers, and

---

[1] A system can be complex and internally diverse or multiple, and yet have strong internal connection and flow, integration and viability as a whole. The healthy human organism is of this kind (see Seeman, 1989).

models outside the family. As the child gets older, peer relationships are likely to contribute to self-diversity, as will love–partner relationships, friendships, and relations with opponents or "enemies" in the course of life. Engagement in particular groups, organizations, or communities also will both reflect and influence a person's sense of self.

Thus, the self, healthy or unhealthy, cannot be expected to have a single constant pattern. Self-diversity would arise both from the inherent complexity of our nature and the effects (modest to very large) of differing patterns of conditional-relational response from varied significant others. Development of diverse repertoires of self probably would be the norm and generally without troubling effect. If significant inner conflict and anxiety born of marked discrepancy between a person's actual response and emotion in some contexts and an inner prescription for self does occur then personal therapy may be a vital aid. People who are generally at home with their basic nature plausibly would be more accepting of their diversity than individuals pushed from within to hold on to one or more internalized prescriptions for self.

Evidence of diversity or multiplicity of self spans a range of kinds explored in my most recent book (Barrett-Lennard, 2013, pp. 22–31). It is seen in everyday experience and conversation, in serious literary writing, in what many therapy clients say and imply, in the observations and ideas of other theorists, and it has begun to be directly looked for and found in empirical research. To touch on examples of the first kind, people quite often speak of having 'changed their mind(s)' or that they are 'in two minds,' in a way that implies more than one inner view. We may speak of 'pulling ourselves together,' or of having 'come to our senses,' or refer to some behavior that is 'out of character.' Witnessing sporting heroes in action in company with a crowd of aroused others can suggest that a whole other configuration of self is called into play. Shifting from a warrior self in combat action to engagement with a loved partner, or to a tender and playful pattern with one's young child, reflect dramatically different configurations of self.

Literary writing tends to be satisfying to the extent that the main characters are fleshed out as believable fellow humans. The reader's recognition of their humanness hinges on how the inner life as well as outward expressive actions of the characters is subtly portrayed and evoked. The characters are three-dimensional, in a word, complex, intricate, and multifaceted and usually present somewhat different selves in the varied contexts and relationships of their envisioned lives. I have offered a range of illustrations (Barrett-Lennard, 1998, pp. 29–32; 2013, pp. 23–25) of the rich diversity of self invested in leading characters brought strikingly into view by prominent literary artists, both classic and contemporary.

Examples of distinct diversity of self also abound in therapy transcripts and case studies, as also illustrated in my own writing (Barrett-Lennard, 2005, pp. 8–10; 2013, pp. 25–27, p. 81) and evident in accounts within almost any volume of therapy case studies (for example, Farber et al., 1996; Wedding & Corsini, 2001). David Mearns (1999) observed that it is not unusual for a client to identify and even give names to differing inner personalities or subselves. The varied "configurations of self" (his term) can differ from each other in attitude, intention, coping style, and be constrained by somewhat differing moralities. These self-systems live together, he suggests, like members of a family, varying in quality of relation and mutual effect. I think of the "I" who speaks to a therapist as often being a mediating, problem-solving, self mode, threading its way among the self's factions and working at inner dialogue to bring about change in their relations and a more open total self-system. Larger societal systems can play a significant part in self-organization. In one of his demonstration interviews Rogers' client was a psychologist in the civil service in apartheid South Africa, who said of his dilemma, "I want to be honest. And I want to be true to myself. But I have to be a facade, or role." The role was a 'public self' that he knowingly assumed, distinct from a 'true' inner self withheld from view (Farber et al., 1996, 337–338). Many people may live a public 'survivor self' deeply at variance with another private or informal, inner self.

The idea of multiplicity of self is not new. In the late 1800s, William James suggested that a person "has as many different social selves as there are distinct groups of persons about whose opinion he cares." He saw that this diversity need not imply inner discord but may well involve (in his marvelous language) "a harmonious division of labour, as where one tender to his children is stern to the soldiers or prisoners under his command" (James, 1890/1950, p. 294). Among prominent contemporary theorists Gergen (2009) attributes most human language and thought to relationships. Indeed, in his view mental life originates in relationship. He is cautious about the idea of self, but as relationships vary so do our inner and expressive patterns. In Hermans' prolific writing the "dialogical self" is a between-person phenomenon in which "inner" and "outer" are interwoven, diverse social entities "speak through the mouth of the individual" and the "society of mind" is an internalization of the person's relational-social world with its plurality of voices (e.g., Hermans & Hermans-Konopka, 2010).

CONSTRUCTIVE CHANGE IN RELATIONS WITHIN THE PLURAL SELF

This chapter is about therapy only to the extent that it helps to bring out and enliven a more general account of the envisioned nature of the complex multiconfigured self. Clients naturally vary in the troubling issues and circumstances that bring them to therapy, but inner argument and difficulty in *self*-communication is nearly always a feature. Thus, as I now frame it, a key axis and potential of therapy is to open and free up dialogue within the manifold self. This multiself has varied voices; some more sub-merged and out of view than others. In exploratory sharing with a deeply listening therapist, who facili-tates and mediates the inner communication – in the way s/he might help family members to really hear one another (Barrett-Lennard, 2009; Mearns, 1999) – the voices can become more apparent and, in effect, work more collaboratively in the total self. The client person, as mentioned, can be considered to have a mode of self that looks out for the person and may prompt him or her to seek help or relief and in a sense presides over the argument within. This 'mediating self' may be crucially assisted by the ways that a resourceful therapist listens empathically, assists expression from each voice, and supports clarifying inter-change within.

Persons who live rather distinctly differing selves in different life contexts may be quite aware that this is the way they are. Through such awareness, the differing self modes effectively are in communication. People who seem *unaware* of how much they shift when differing subselves come into play suffer an impoverished inner communication that condemns them to more repetitive patterns. At the extreme, the subselves are living as though in different chambers in the total personality. When movement occurs from this chambered state toward more inwardly open awareness and interchange, this is an integrative shift in the working of the overall self-system. The person has become more 'whole,' a whole in whom self-diversity reflects the person's breadth of being and works as a positive and versatile resource.[2] This direction of thought came into sharper focus still when a way to render the subself structure in operational form for research, came to mind.

STUDYING THE SELF *IN CONTEXT* – NEW FOCUS AND METHOD

Considerable research has been devoted to the study of what I refer to as the generalized (or noncontextual) self-concept of individuals. One principal instrument for such study was first used in ground-breaking therapy outcome research reported by Butler and Haigh (1954). It consisted of 100 self-descriptive items (reproduced in Ends and Page, 1959, Appendix), which the respondent sorted into groups on a forced-normal distribution from a "most like me" extreme to "most unlike me." I later reduced this selection to 80 items, arranged in multiple-choice questionnaire form (unpublished, used e.g., by Grabham, 1970). Both the original Q-sort and self-inventory versions were treated by respondents as meaningful ways to describe their present self, self-ideal, past self, and so forth (Butler & Haigh, 1954; Rogers, 1954). It made sense to me to draw on this work but in a new form, a form that allowed for participants to answer for the way they experienced themselves in

---

[2] When a person becomes more at home through therapy with their own inner 'multitude' then fuller presence and attention to the Other in relationships *may* follow. However, if the therapy does not move to include a direct focus on *relational* exploration the potential helping process and gain is incomplete. Therapy can be a resource through which persons come to see further how much they are interwoven in relationship with the life process of other individuals and groups, and gain much of their identity therefrom in a continuing dynamic.

each of a number of important life relationship contexts. The original item arrays were too long for this purpose and a good many statements were dated or reflective of their origin in the therapy research. Through careful scrutiny and informal trials I initially halved the array and adapted a few other statements to provide a working set of 45, including the following illustrative group:

> I have confidence in myself.
> Inwardly, I am on my guard.
> I take initiative, raise issues, start things.
> I experience a lot of inner strain.
> I forgive easily – don't hold grudges or try to "get even."
> I look for alibis and excuses for myself if things go wrong.
> It's difficult for me to share my real feelings.
> I think clearly and am level-headed.

A separate sheet listing the 45 items, with answer spaces, was provided for rating each self-in-context. The answer scale contained the choices: 5) Very (or always) like me; 4) Mostly like me; 3) Equally like and unlike me; 2) Mostly unlike me; and 1) Not like me at all. Participants were asked to rate every item in the way that best described how they felt and saw themselves in that particular context. They were called on to choose five applicable contexts from a list that included:

- A. Me as I feel and see myself, *with my spouse/de facto partner (or closest friend).*

- B. Me as I feel and see myself, *with my parent(s).*

- C. Me as I feel and see myself, with another family member, e.g., "oldest child" (note relation).

- D. Me as I feel and see myself, in my work team or other significant group (note kind).

- E. Me as I feel and see myself, with my clients (or customers/students/another group I serve).

- F. Me as I feel and see myself, with opponents, enemies, or "someone I'm involved with but don't trust."

- G. Me as I feel and see myself, when involved with my ethnic community and/or subculture.

Following the primary ratings, further data-gathering included a repeat of the first-answered Contextual Selves Inventory (CSI) as a reliability check and, finally, ratings for the way the respondent would most like to be in relationships generally (their self-ideal). Most respondents took at least an hour to do all this. Nearly everyone answered for the first four contexts listed and these yielded the primary data for this exploratory study. The mean test-retest correlation (context A, N = 41) was adequate at .77. Correlations *for individuals* between self as seen within the various contexts and their self-ideal covered a very wide range (> .9 to −.5). *Sample averages* of these correlations were in the low positive range. A subset of 11 CSI items (selected from ratings by several psychologist judges) provided an index of self-esteem. Higher self-esteem was linked to degree of convergence between the perceived actual subselves and ideally desired self, as would be expected given sound measurement (mean r = .75). *Direct* overall testing of variation between subselves was not an achieved main focus. As formally summed up elsewhere: "The results of this trial study were broadly encouraging in regard to the underlying conception of relationally based self-diversity and the CSI methodology. They also implied that the original [instrument] was overtaxing and unwieldy for respondents" (Barrett-Lennard, 2008).

The next version of the CSI was radically shortened to 16 self-descriptive statements rated on a similarly anchored seven-point scale, with provision for self-ratings in up to seven relationship contexts (this time including separate columns for each parent). The answer form fitted on one page and there was a separate sheet of directions. For use as an exercise within a workshop context it needed to be compact enough to be answered in about 15 minutes. The workshop participants clearly found the task engaging and one that lead on to useful discussion (see later). Its design as an interesting and feasible resource (initially for use in three overseas workshops conducted by the author in 2006) was serendipitous in terms of research but turned out to be valuable for that purpose as well. The respondents, all with an interest in counselling, were primarily trainees of quite varied age and background studying in freestanding programs. Most of the respondents were women, but specific sample information was not requested in the anonymous take-up of data.

The 16 CSI items were drawn, some with minor revision, from the 45-item form. Screening for similarity of content and retention of the more distinct items helped to avoid any great narrowing of the scope of self-attributes. Relevant feedback and impressions from study of item data also influenced some selection choices. A concern for simple everyday language, combined with a sense of self-qualities that respondents could easily relate to, also played a part. Some items refer explicitly to self-behavior with other people (e.g., I *forgive easily – don't hold grudges or try to "get even"*), while others point to a more interior sense of "I" (e.g., *I have confidence in myself*, and *I think clearly and am level-headed*). In the final analysis I, with my experience in questionnaire design, was the arbiter of necessary choices.

In the workshop application, there was an immediate follow-up that may interest the reader, when everyone had completed their answers on the instrument. Participants were asked to note the range of their answers *on each item* – simply the difference between their lowest and highest rating for the various self-contexts. If a member conceivably gave the same answer to item X in all contexts the range would be zero. On another item a person's answers might vary by three points and, at the extreme, by six points (7 – 1). Going through the items one-by-one, members signaled by a show of hands whether their range on that item was zero, one point and on up to 6 points. As they did this, the numbers of people indicating each possible range were noted on flip charts. We were all interested to see which items drew the widest and the least spread of answers and where people varied most in the degree of distinctions they made.[3] Participants were invited to provide their anonymously completed CSI forms for subsequent evaluation research, and almost all of them did so. All the ratings were later transferred to Excel "workbook" sheets, each person represented by their 16-item ratings for each of the five or six self-contexts. Rating numbers were treated as approximating an equal interval scale, and the mean spread of answers to the same self-attribute served as a simple indication of diversity of perceived self.

Table 7.1 (adapted from Barrett-Lennard, 2008) shows the 16 items and outlines the sample-wide results. The first column simply indicates the mean for each item of all ratings (people X contexts), as counted 1 to 7. Among these, the **bold** figures identify the notionally positive-self statements, the negative-leaning remaining items having generally lower ratings. The second, standard deviation column shows how widely dispersed these ratings were. The third column is of most interest in terms of difference between subselves. The actual spread, *averaged for the 70 respondents*, reached the high level of 4 and 3.8 for items 12 and 16. The remaining mean ranges were all ≥2.5.

Separate statistical study of the data for the 52 participants who provided six contextual-self descriptions yielded a pattern of highly significant (<.01) difference between self-contexts on 14 of the 16 items – items 3 and 11 excepted (though even on these some of the participants gave quite varied answers). Overall, the pattern was one of substantial variation in ways that self was perceived in the differing contexts. An exploratory factor analysis yielded four separable components. The first, identified as Positive Self-Feeling, drew strong loadings (.52 to .71) from items 1 and 2, 4, 7, 10, 12 and 15. The second factor, concerned with protective withholding versus open sharing of self, had strong loadings on items 6, 12 (negative loading), 13 and 16. A third factor involved critical self-feeling as opposed to an easy and confident stance, with loadings on items 3, 5, and (in the opposite direction) on 9 and 10. The fourth factor loaded very strongly and only on the 'maverick' item 11. These meaningful results were useful in preparing the current CSI, mentioned shortly.

Item inter-correlations further implied that, although most items could be gathered into subclusters, no two item statements were merely duplicating each other. The item associations, pairwise comparisons and the factor structure also all provided cues toward preparing a fuller version more suited to general research use. This both fills out the identified domain of self-attributes and adds a little to it. Running to 24 items, this revised version was arranged, initially, for another student study. The first page of the two-page answer form

---

3   A second item-by-item measure of contextual differences was used in some workshops. Taking the rating for the first context (say) as the anchor point, the differences between that rating and each of the others were summed, to give another simple index of variation.

Table 7.1 Variation in self-perception across the relational contexts

Items	Sample mean ratings	Sample mean SDs	Mean range of ratings
1 I have confidence in myself.	5.26	1.26	3.0
2 I take initiative, raise issues, start things.	5.06	1.35	3.3
3 I look for alibis and excuses for myself if things go wrong	3.27	1.11	2.7
4 I feel interesting, present and positive about myself.	5.02	1.16	2.9
5 I notice faults and am critical in my outlook.	4.14	1.25	2.9
6 I forgive easily – don't hold grudges or try to "get even".	4.85	1.36	3.2
7 I'm comfortable with my body and sexuality.	5.10	1.07	2.6
8 It is pretty hard to **be** myself.	3.18	1.48	3.5
9 I am a calm and easy-going person.	4.60	1.18	2.9
10 I think clearly and am level-headed.	4.88	1.08	2.6
11 I am a follower. I let the other(s) take the lead.	3.22	1.06	2.5
12 I am imaginative and can share my dreams.	4.54	1.62	4.0
13 I put on front when I'm uneasy – not showing how I feel	3.87	1.4	3.4
14 I am often tense or anxious.	3.42	1.35	3.2
15 I am full of life and good spirits.	4.84	1.19	2.8
16 It's difficult for me to share my real feelings.	3.60	1.64	3.8
Average of mean ratings for the 16 items	4.30		
Overall average SD across all items		1.28	
Overall average (16 items) of *mean item ranges*			3.08

Source: Adapted from Barrett-Lennard (2008)

includes columns for self-ratings in up to six clearly designated family relationships. The second page provides for the additional (nonfamily) self-in-relationship contexts and includes a column for rating of the "desired/ ideal self in relationships." Respondents are particularly asked to include the option of "self with distrusted person or 'enemy,'" and sample members had no problem doing this. Seven rating choices are now clearly indicated across the page, with three "No (unlike me) answers" of varied strength, a middle "equally like and unlike me" option and provision for three grades of "Yes (like me) answers" (see Appendix 2).[4]

Participants begin by reading the separate "Directions" sheet (Appendix 2), which spells out the full range of self-contexts to select from – also reflected on the Answer form. Any contexts that don't apply are simply skipped (and their columns left blank), leaving the completed columns of answers for ready transfer to dataset forms for analysis. It is of course possible for another investigator to adjust the exact selection of self-contexts – with appropriate amendment to the directions as well as to the answer columns. As an example, two of the recent students were interested in relationships between Internet friends who had not met face-to-face. A column was added for this option – though nothing very distinctive about self-qualities in that context emerged from the small number of people who chose it, and it does not appear in the finalized current form.

---

4 The CSI in its 24-item research form (Appendix 2) can also lend itself to illustrative use in training situations, for example, with participants only needing to select 4 or 5 contexts.

In this most recent research, respondents (mainly undergraduate students) wrote their reactions to the CSI data collection on a feedback form containing a few broad questions. These supplementary data proved to be highly informative in addition to having a debriefing function. The majority of people made comments along the lines of the CSI experience having been an interesting or enlightening experience, as in the following examples:

> To me the process was helpful in raising self-awareness of who I am and how I am in different situations.

> I realize now that my sense of self does tend to shift dramatically with individuals that I get along well with.

> It allowed me to reflect on myself and to see how I act in all of my relationships. It made me realize that I do act differently when I'm with my partner, compared with people at work.

> It made me aware at how different I am with different people, which was both a surprise to me but also quite enlightening.

> I also feel that there are little parts of my character that I reserve for different people in my life, depending on what role they play in my life.

Some people took their variability very much for granted (e.g., "it's a given that I act differently, around different people"). Some were disconcerted by it, as in the following examples:

> I found it interesting to pay attention to the way I differ in my relationships. A little sad that I'm not truly myself all the time – wonder how I could align the "selves" more together.

> This does make me feel a little uneasy because I would prefer to feel like I'm being myself, regardless of the person or situation.

> [It was] quite confronting to actually separate how I am in different relationships.

One student investigator observed that negative feeling about self-variation (a minority in this sample) reflects a cultural mindset, namely, "that unitary theories of self consistency are deeply embedded in the beliefs of Western society" (Fenton, 2011, p. 23). One sample member among the majority noting variation emphasized that the culture she grew up in makes a clear distinction between public and private selves and allows for distinct variability of self in diverse relational contexts (Fenton, p. 27). Almost all the varied feedback from participants "indicated that they had engaged in a level of self-reflection throughout the process of answering the questionnaire" (Van Kampen, 2011, p. 18). In fact, the stimulation of self-reflection emerged as the central underlying theme from a systematic study of the feedback data (Van Kampen, p. 33). Beyond this overall feature, one of the subthemes from respondents was the idea that variability of self was functional, adaptive (Van Kampen, pp. 26–30) and even protective (see also Linville, 1987). This variability need not deny the existence of a core or 'true' inner self. As one person put it "I feel I have a 'core' self which is exposed more or less to others depending on how comfortable I feel around them and the strength/depth of our relationship."

Zec (2011) focused on the eight CSI items indicative of positive self-feeling. Concentrating on complete data from the female majority (N=47), she found substantial differences between the self-descriptions in mother and father relationships, and between partner/spouse and father relationships. (Analysis by another student found, as one might expect, that *self-ideal* ratings summed for the positive self-feeling items were highest of all.) Weir (2011) was especially interested in evidence of stability, as well as variability, across relationships in sense of self, using items deemed to cohere in each of three main factors. A broad conclusion from her correlation data was that several CSI items appeared to yield relatively constant results across relationships, and another group of items reflected considerable variability. (Contrary to expectation there also tended to be more variability of self-descriptions for family relations than across other social relationships.) Future research could throw light on whether there is indeed a bounded domain of subself variation while other qualities of self-as-perceived tend to remain constant across diverse contexts.

THE CSI POISED FOR FRESH INQUIRY

In fresh expression, subselves are viewed as distinctively different patterns of activation of the self, patterns both formed and 'ready for action' but not (usually) cast in stone. Although research to date is positively supportive of the CSI approach, it is limited in extent and ways that leave this area wide open both for related studies and new lines of investigation. Reader interest and inventiveness naturally would be a major determinant of the particular directions of such enquiry. Both quantitative (as with the CSI) and qualitative enquiry occurs to me, as in the following examples. I offer what follows as further input to the reader's reflection and possible planning.

- *Potential subself change, through personally eventful or formative experiences, is one focus of interest.* One context would be to administer CSI before and after therapy to test for shifts. As well, the post-therapy administration might profitably be followed by qualitative interview inquiry around such issues as fluidity or difficulty in turning from one self-context engagement to another, and the participant's sense of whether these are different worlds of experience and/or whether experience in one context is feeding into how they feel and behave in another significant context. This last feature opens into another potential focus.
- Given that the subselves, as conceived, are differing alternatives within a combined whole, exactly how do they interconnect and influence each other? For example, when the immediately manifest self is one of close engagement with a partner, between whom there is a wealth of experience and meaning, how does this pattern flow into, or receive influence from, the subself system activated with one's own parent or child, say, or with another subself configuration outside the family region?
- CSI theory implies that changes in consciousness, feeling and propensity for action occur during the transitions from one self mode to another when immediate engagements change. Turning from one experiential context to another is an everyday experience. This must often involve a considerable and sometimes rapid 'change of gears' in terms of attention, expectation and purpose, past learning and memory called into play, immediate feeling or emotion, and so on. In everyday situations there may be mixed or partial transitions (or shift to another subself system) where a person is simultaneously occupied with two quite different relationships – in a family, say, with one's partner and child. Relevant enquiry might involve use of the CSI and qualitative interviews.
- Feedback data from research participants who have answered the CSI indicates that it promotes self-reflection and can be a consciousness-raising. It evidently comes as an enlightening and sometimes disturbing surprise to respondents when their own answers imply to them that they differ in themselves in distinctly different relationships. These effects could well have practice relevance. One context for study of possible valued effects would be to call on members of experiential groups to answer the CSI and to closely study the group members' communication before and after the CSI experience. (If similar groups with and without exposure to the CSI were available, this would strengthen appraisal of the potential CSI effect.)
- Comparative study of self-diversity in communities known to differ, for example, in respect to the more individualist and more communal outlook of members, may reveal interesting differences in degree or other qualities of self-diversity. Men and women, or older and younger people, or groups sorted in ways having to do with personality styles and from the same culture, may be found to differ in respect to kinds and extent of perceived self-diversity and in attitudes towards consistency and variation of self.

CONCLUSION

The suggested avenues of further research are the end focus of this chapter. Its content, overall, has centered on and around an instrument in which significant relationships provide the context for the study of the self rather than being the direct focus as in use of the BLRI. Here, the self is presumed to develop through and in large measure from engagement in different, and typically diverse, life relationships. It is thus conceived as naturally diverse in its configuration or modalities. The Contextual Selves Inventory is at once reflective of this conception and a new means to test and study it. Work with this instrument shows distinctive promise through a fresh window and method of inquiry, but is at a relatively early stage and wide open to further research and potential practice applications. Within the same underlying thought, the challenge of therapeutic helping includes being ready and prepared to assist clients not just with agonies conceived as personality dysfunctions but with wounds and constraints of consciousness and capacity of the multiself in its varied engagements. The human self has more than one mode and voice, especially, to helpers who are alive to the natural complexity of human self-being in a world of widely diverse lived relationships.

Chapter 8
Tracking Self and Relational Process in Experiential Groups

I have long been interested in intensive groups, and cut my teeth in conducting such groups in the 1960s. The main setting then was in Armidale (University of New England), Australia, and my involvement continued intermittently in Canada, in workshops elsewhere, and back in Australia through the 1990s. The 1960s Australian residential workshops, for people in mental-health-related work and study, were an innovation at the time. With the help of a colleague (P. Pentony), who co-led two of the workshops with me, we planned and I went on to revise short questionnaires that could be answered by each member after each group meeting. Their main aim was to assist participants in their monitoring of self and interactive processes in the group. We naturally wanted the experience to be fruitful for everyone in their own development and experiential helping-process learning. Within the groups, members needed to keep track of how they really felt about what was going on for themselves, for others and in their relationships and the broader process of the group. Albeit with related experience behind us, we were all learning about the potent emergent process and outcomes of open-ended, discovery-oriented experiential groups.

Being in residence together away from home activity there was a lot of opportunity for processing outside the group sessions through informal conversation, topical discussions, reading and use of audio-tapes, and shared recreational activity. This whole context complemented the regular small group sessions. Free exploration, movement, and grounding processes all occurred in a heady mix that included a degree of unsettling that might be part of any concentrated change experience. In my later work with groups I continued to use and develop two end-of-group process rating forms first used in the workshops, which in their content, rationale, application and further potential are the main substance of this short chapter.[1]

One of the two forms this chapter focuses on, the *End-of-Meeting Group Process Questionnaire*, provides a structured opportunity for each person to reflectively evaluate salient qualities of their own felt process, self-with-other experience, and awareness of other-with-other communication, in the group. A main purpose is to help members to stay grounded, especially after intense experiences, and workshop data from its use has been systematically examined. The other questionnaire, called the *Group Atmosphere Form*, is composed of 20 polar opposite pairs of words pertaining to the group experience and process, with a simple scale between each pair for ratings by each member of the group. It can be answered quickly and was used in a 6-month follow-up context as well as session-by-session. Some of the interesting results are reported in my 1998 book (pp. 296–298).

---

[1] Readers interested in further information about the workshops, my theoretical ideas about experiential learning in groups, the use and study of groups in course-educational contexts, and research I've reported from this work – mostly beyond the orbit of this chapter – could select from the following papers: Barrett-Lennard, Kwasnik, and Wilkinson, 1973/1974; Barrett-Lennard, 1974, 1974/1975, 1975/1976, 1979; 1998, Chapter 9; 2003, Chapter 6.

The Relationship Inventory: A Complete Resource and Guide, First Edition. Godfrey T. Barrett-Lennard.
© 2015 John Wiley & Sons, Ltd. Published 2015 by John Wiley & Sons, Ltd.
Companion site: www.wiley.com/go/barrett_lennard/therelationshipinventory

END-OF-MEETING PARTICIPANT PROCESS APPRAISALS

The end-of-meeting member questionnaire in its original (1965) complete form was composed following two previous workshops in the series that brought out the potency of member experience in the groups. We wanted the questionnaire to reflect awareness of this potency with items that could reflect and check on the possibility that some members may feel over-stressed by it. Included questions read, *Did you feel under strain during this session? Did you feel any member of the group was being induced to go further than s/he wanted to go?* and *Did you feel this was a stressful session for some other member?* Generally, however, ratings on personal stress were low (from "somewhat" to "definitely not") and were somewhat higher (means tended to be mid-range) for stress perceived in particular others or for the group more broadly. Correlations between: (1) *Did you find this session a valuable experience* and (2) *Did you feel under strain?* showed no consistency but summed to a low *positive* correlation on average. Generally, the ratings implied that some stress and felt pressure were experienced and were often (though not always) coupled with valued effects of the experience. In light of these results and further experience in intensive groups most of these items were progressively omitted or redesigned (though one current item reads: *Are you left feeling concerned about the impact of the session on someone else?*) This also provided an opportunity for additions beyond the original range without making the form onerous to answer.

Both questionnaires evolved over long experience with their application, and I have made limited further amendment to the End-of-Meeting form for publication in this book. Besides the added last item most items and the basic scope remain as before. The present form opens with several questions asking in simple direct ways about *the value and impact of the session* on other members and for oneself. (In use, each member has a fresh copy at each group session, which they answer at the end before leaving the session.) Most items are positively framed, but the rating scale is equally balanced between agree and disagree, with a strong NO at one end and YES at the other end. The *first* item group draws the respondent's attention to *other members* individually, and calls for his/her sensed appraisal of the value of the session (or otherwise) to others, its impact, and their self-expression. The second item group focuses on self-experience – inner and relational – ending with the question *Do you feel that your presence and/or what you did share mattered to others in the group?* The context for these observations is one of significant engagement and sharing over a 2-hour session. The ratings are assumed to reflect true or actual impressions and in that sense are valid. "Objectivity" is not an issue.

The next questionnaire focus is on qualities of *the group*'s functioning, with a pair of items concerned respectively with attentive listening and genuineness. After that, two items have a dyadic focus again, in inquiring about the respondent's experience (or not) of being understood by and of closely understanding someone else. After touching on another group quality (safety and trust), two items ask about the further important aspect of personal feedback sharing, given and received. The last two questions draw attention to possible active response to felt exchanges *between other members*, and the respondent's sense (or not) of the *whole group 'we'* (see Appendix 2, pp. 172-173).

The residential groups provided a depth of interactive experience and associated interpersonal and self-learning, especially as related to member ability to engage therapeutically with others as counsellors and facilitators (Barrett-Lennard, 1967, 1974, 1975/1976, 1998 pp. 161–167). (Members came from a variety of mental health and counselling backgrounds.) All elements, in this questionnaire, concern features of experience and process considered relevant in truly developmental experience-based learning. Although the groups were low-structure, egalitarian, and member-centered, inevitably the opportunity they provided has a broad direction. This direction, or elements of it, can be seen as reflected in the rating form. Facilitators from person-centered and related backgrounds may have particular resonance to the content of Item 7. Items 8 to 11 are seen as adding something to enduring commonalities of value and approach. This compatible 'something' encompasses a more visibly active and strongly relational stance. Here, it twins empathic responsiveness with the feedback sharing of images of the other from the (still-empathic) responding person. Learning to do this with constructive sensitivity that brings close or fuller relationship is one of the significant *potentials* of intensive groups.

Member appraisals via end of session forms have in my work been anonymous (using a self-selected consistent code to help with collation) and retained for later study. For participants there also has been, I believe, some quality of reflective debriefing in drawing their attention to the discriminations entailed. As seen on the form itself (Barrett-Lennard, 1967, 1974, 1975/1976; 1998, pp. 161–167) respondents are invited to pin down *who* they have in mind, in items that refer to other members. The original workshop form (used first in 1965) did not include all of these aspects (e.g., the sharing of impressions or pictures of others, or attending to communication between others), but there was overlap in substance with most other items. Item ratings by members of the intensive groups that year were inter-correlated, session-by-session. Study of these results revealed a fairly consistent link between several items seen as being concerned with 'personal gain' (such as new or keener awareness of self) and an associated group of items conceived as reflecting estimations of 'group gain,' for example, in terms of genuineness and mutual sensitivity (Barrett-Lennard, 1972). The groups met for 16 or 17 sessions over 11 days with a Sunday intermission in the middle of this period.

From day to day the mean ratings fluctuated considerably. In one group the highest points came at the fifth, 13th and final (17th) sessions, with low points in sessions 11 and 15. Ratings rose more rapidly in the other group, then dipped and rose again. They dipped most sharply in sessions 11 and 13 and then lifted to nearly the same level as the first group, at the end. The two groups differed in their specific 'signatures' from member ratings *and* had broad features in common. Average ratings over the whole workshop were very similar, there was a tendency to build from a lower start in both weeks, go through considerable setbacks or crises in the second week, then 'recover' and rise to a high point again at the end.

As distinct from the other instruments in this book this rating questionnaire taps features of relational life and communication in just-now-experienced interaction. It would be possible to modify and adapt the present form for use in less intensive but interactive developmental or learning groups. For example items 3 (on listening), 4 (honesty), and 7 (trust) would be relevant in most small groups and teams. The item 2 sub-questions and items 10 and 11 easily could be adapted. Even for the intensive group context other users could, of course, add or take out items, remembering that the content has already been refined from extensive application. Although the form is relatively trans-theoretical, other users of distinctive orientation or differing experience might well make adjustments for their own purposes.

The other form, the *Group Atmosphere Form*, in focus here can be answered very quickly. It is less challenging for the participant, and possibly less valuable for member self-monitoring, though surprisingly informative in my experience. In present arrangement and application it too is designed for use at the end of each group session. However, I first included full-length versions of the form in the context of a 6-month follow-up study of outcomes of two workshops. Participants, all on their home grounds and responding independently, were invited to reflect on the overall qualities of their group. Specifically, they were asked to "Please check the scale between each of the following pairs of opposites to describe your perception now of the atmosphere and process in your workshop group. Use a cross to mark the point on the scale that represents the most typical or frequent situation in your group, and also indicate the range of variation in the group process by means of [enclosing] brackets". The scale was and remains seven step, with "Neither or both equally" as the mid-point (as seen in Appendix 2). The ratings of the most 'typical or frequent' quality in the group were systematically examined over a total sample of five groups.

ILLUSTRATIVE RESULTS FROM USE OF THE IN-GROUP QUESTIONNAIRES

There was, naturally, variation among the former members in the way any given group was remembered. Yet the *Group Atmosphere Form* reflected a striking degree of consistency and, even after 6 months, each group's pattern of remembered qualities was distinctive (Barrett-Lennard, 1972, Table 5). For example, group Y was remembered as being harmonious, gentle, caring, warm, quite (not extremely) revealing, and valuable. Generally it was recalled also as being accepting, understanding, more relaxed than tense, tending to be "slow" rather than "fast." Group X, by contrast, was remembered as "conflicting" rather than harmonious, everyone recalled it as turbulent (as opposed to calm), it was mostly remembered as warm but at the same time tense, searching but often upsetting, very active, mostly genuine, tending to be fast, and extremely or quite valuable. Leader differences no doubt played a part, though both leaders were oriented toward active listening, facilitating but not guiding except to encourage members to share immediate experience and tune in to each other, and held the attitude that the group was a joint creation. In this context each group's qualities are viewed as emergent from the unique mix and interaction of participants, including the lead person.

In a previous workshop, in the same series, data were collected at each session with a rating form that included a smaller selection of items similar to both kinds above. Collated results for (at least) three spaced sessions from three concurrent workshop groups, in which this form was used, were examined. Each group was strikingly variable over the course of the workshop on some of the rated aspects. In group S, for example, session 5 was seen as quite gentle (as against harsh), and somewhat revealing, low in turbulence, a little searching, mostly genuine, and middle-of-the-road in terms of upsetting versus comforting. Session 10 zoomed to a different level, and was the high point for this group. It was experienced as gentle, revealing, caring, searching, genuine, understanding, and flowing though also a little upsetting and turbulent. On the other type of item, most members rated it as very productive and a source of new understanding. Four sessions later, however, members found the group quite conflicting, turbulent, and somewhat upsetting. The aspects of genuineness and of understanding versus insensitivity drew a wide range of ratings. Estimations of productivity covered the whole range. Ratings for one of the other groups also varied widely across sessions and between members. Very divergent perceptions of the same session in some cases suggest both different agendas and a low mutuality of awareness and engagement.

The full length *Group Atmosphere Form* (GAF) also lends itself to use in less intensive developmental groups. One illustration involves a whole day experiential group conducted by the author much more recently, during a first course in counselling and toward the end of a demanding academic year. Ten participants completed the 20-item GAF at the end of each of four sessions over a day-long mini-workshop. Relationships did not start from the beginning since people were already acquainted as classmates. On the active/passive scale the modal rating from all sessions was "quite" active. There were shifts over the day and the final session was judged by most as "extremely" active. Notionally "positive" movement occurred on other scales identified here by the poles of "sensitive, genuine, deep (versus shallow), close (versus distant), caring, open, free-moving, warm, flowing and intense." 'Quite' lively, responsive, and searching remained the modal choices on those continua. The "turbulent/calm" axis drew a concentration of ratings in the middle and 'quite calm' categories. A number of people centered on the middle category for the stuck/free-moving element and some also pointed out that they would give different answers for different parts of the same session (e.g., stuck at the beginning, free-moving at the end). Total ratings covered the whole range on reactive/responsive – and I now think that "reactive" is variably understood and have adjusted the wording. The new wording is shown Appendix 2.

The group just mentioned also answered the *End of Meeting Questionnaire* (EMQ) – on the other side of the same sheet as the GAF. From this and previous usage it is clear that, of the two, the EMG is a more textured and informative instrument. However, the GAF is more quickly and easily answered, focuses more on the ambience of the group as a whole, and can be a useful by itself or as a complement to the EMQ. The copy in the Appendix reflects a few recent amendments – as implied. Item 5 was previously a Fast/Slow scale that most often drew a mid-point answer and did not seem very useful in discriminating groups. Item 17 has been amended in the interests of greater clarity of meaning. The last sentence at the top of the form has also been amended to further encourage respondents to *both* identify the most representative scale point and freely indicate the range of variation on this aspect during the session in focus, where they feel this would give greater meaning to their answers.

CONCLUSION

This chapter has an instrument focus in the region of enabling processes in small groups that, in its varied forms, many readers would have first-hand experience of. Those who look for more theory, or who have particular interest in the application *and* study of intensive groups, might well find earlier mentioned sources of interest (see Note 1). Among these is a chapter article (Barrett-Lennard, 2003, chapter 6) in which I spell out a dozen characteristics I see in fruitfully working groups (Barrett-Lennard, p. 59). These features cover issues of belonging, of coming into significant contact through open personal communication, listening, venturing and coming to be unguarded and unjudging of the other, sharing immediate relational experience, experiencing self and other responsibility, providing and receiving personal feedback, communicating in ways that naturally help to open doors of awareness and expression in others, and truly mutual decision-making and facilitative leader engagement over much the same canvas as other members. These aspects are combined into a single textured perspective. In a change of pace, the chapter goes on to include an original exercise, for use with students, to systematically demonstrate the scope of dynamically evolving connections in dyads and larger relational subsystems within small interactive groups.

The two-group process questionnaire forms are both grounded in practice and in broad accord with this perspective. They normally would be used as descriptors by each participant of a group session that has just ended. Although they yield data of potential value for research, as briefly illustrated, their primary purpose has been as an aid to participants in taking stock of the group experience and process in which they were engaged. The content of the forms as they stand (in Appendix 2), while already tested and refined from existing applications is, as implied, not cast in stone. It would be most interesting to me to hear from anyone else about their experience with either or both questionnaires or adaptations of them. And, if the resulting data are studied in research, and assuming I'm still around, investigators could count on my interest in hearing the outcomes or even responding to plans for such work. The next chapter is a major change from this one, in that it revisits many issues and distinguishes new ones in an integrative envisioning of relationship inquiry and application to come – thus with strongest connection to Part I of this book.

Part 3
Reframing: Envisioning the Path Ahead

Chapter 9
Looking Ahead: Fresh Horizons in Relationship Study

My most recent book (2013), although also centered on relationships, gives only passing attention to the BLRI and CSI. Its different mission was to research the phenomenon of human relationship in its basic nature and explore its central role in human life on multiple levels. Although the present work is distinctly different in its aim and content, the perspective evolved in my previous book is seen to have convergent relevance for the future study of relationship.

The aim of this concluding chapter is to offer an extension of possibilities for such fruitful further study. Its content in the first part carries on from Chapter 5, envisioning new paths of study that use recognizable adaptations of the Relationship Inventory (RI). The chapter then unfolds to consider more broadly and argue the need to open new frontiers of multilevel investigation of human relationships, drawing on and reaching beyond the instrumentation that is the focus of this book. It ends with a delineation of ideas for an approach to greatly needed future study of relationships within and between very large human systems, including whole nations. Nations and transnational people systems often involve deeply distrustful relation and may be in open conflict. Some nations continue to be torn by savage internal conflict. The quality of relationships within and between large systems is visibly crucial for human well-being.

A fresh survey discussion of frontiers of enquiry across the RI spectrum is the main focus of the first part of this chapter. Some of these "frontiers" are noted or anticipated in Chapter 5, and others are introduced here for the first time. Not all of the more speculative avenues will appeal to all readers but I hope that they will pique the interest of adventurous souls whose direction and circumstances allow more novel and perhaps 'risky' research enterprises. The first mentioned focus of this kind assumes that the human self is normally complex, with more than one voice and distinct repertoire – discussed in Chapter 7 and my recent book (2013, Chapter 3). This is approached here in a new way outlined next, as one focus in the broader spectrum of potential future study.

INVITATIONS TO CONNECTED FURTHER STUDY OF RELATIONSHIP

A FOCUS ON RELATIONS WITHIN THE SELF

In addition to work with the Contextual Selves Inventory (CSI) (Chapter 7) a direct focus on self-with-self relationships is now possible with an experimental adaptation of the BLRI identified as Form SS-40. This was briefly mentioned in Chapter 5, and the reader's attention is drawn to the arrangement and content of this novel form (see Appendix 1, pp. 156–157) Although this uses the same scoring key as the regular 40-item forms the meanings of the scale measures differ from the meanings in familiar usage of the RI. In this new case, the regard scale provides an estimate of degree of inclusive self-regard, and the empathy scale is essentially concerned with

The Relationship Inventory: A Complete Resource and Guide, First Edition. Godfrey T. Barrett-Lennard.
© 2015 John Wiley & Sons, Ltd. Published 2015 by John Wiley & Sons, Ltd.
Companion site: www.wiley.com/go/barrett_lennard/therelationshipinventory

self-empathy involving a listening inner dialogue (Barrett-Lennard, 1997). The congruence scale in this case taps personal openness and integration generally, not just within a particular relationship. The unconditionality measure is also partly about personal openness but more particularly about self-acceptance or positive receptivity to all sides of self as against a self-judgmental or selectively rejecting tendency.

I hypothesize that self-with-self relational qualities will have bearing on corresponding qualities manifest in the same person's interpersonal relationships. However, the other party in any particular relationship, and the chemistry of the two (or more) people in interaction, clearly would be influential as well. The correlation between RI measures in the self-with-self context and those manifesting in self–other relationships would no doubt vary in strength across the same person's different self–other relationships. I anticipate (somewhat tentatively) that partners in stressed relationships would tend to give rather different self-with-self readings from each other. If this is confirmed, then such differences in fresh combinations of people might usefully predict their likely relationship quality.

Although the possibilities of this form are intriguing, since there is not yet any track record of its application a venturesome user, as of this writing, would be breaking new ground with a fresh relational approach to the study of the self, the value of which can be found through studied application. Correlations between the four component measures may or may not resemble those found in most standard applications of the BLRI where, for example, empathy and congruence tend to be quite strongly correlated, and level of regard and unconditionality show little covariation. If (for example) people's self-regard and self-empathy were found to be quite strongly correlated *and* predictive of their interpersonal relationship quality this would be an interesting result from both practical and conceptual standpoints. This would also be the case with concern to regard and unconditionality and other outcomes of studies with this form.

THE STUDY OF WHOLE "WE" SYSTEMS

Unlike the case of the new form just mentioned, this adaptation has been around for some time even though, to my knowledge, it is rarely used. It is not radically different to the widely used OS and MO forms and the measures it yields have similar although not identical meaning. It is designed to study relationships *viewed as a whole* by the participants (for example, *We feel at ease together, I feel that we put on a role or act with one another, We like and enjoy one another*, and *We each want the other to be a particular kind of person*). This "We-relationship" version, as arranged for use with dyads (Form DW–64 – see Appendix 1), would be especially suited to investigation of couple relationships, and it needs only slight adaptation for use in the study of whole family or group relationships (see pp. 46–47 in Chapter 4). The quality of an experienced *We*, as described by two (or more) participants in the same relationship might be quite similar *or* rather divergent. This similarity/difference taken in conjunction with the score *levels* would help to reveal the health or openness of the relationship itself, and could be useful in counselling as well as lending itself to a distinctive path of research.

The fact that this form focuses directly on the relationship system, not on one party's response to the other, is now more in keeping with my broader view of human relationships as presented elsewhere (Barrett-Lennard, 2013) and later discussed in this chapter. An emergent relationship is a different phenomenon than one person's attitudes and Form DW–64 provides a way of tapping into this relationship as viewed by the participants – or possibly by third persons if the "we/our" designation is changed to "they" and "them." It calls on and obliges the respondents to do something they probably have not tried before in a focused way; in effect, to stand aside and really think about "us" as a single unit of relationship. When the form is presented to participants with the assumption that looking at the relationship as a whole is a natural and meaningful focus participants appear to have no difficulty with the principle of the task even if they find some of the discriminations a challenge to make.

Participants may also appreciate, or expect, that since the data are about their own experience and perspective their answers are likely to differ from that of the other party in the relationship. When used in a practice context with willing partners who compare answers afterwards, especially on items where they differed by more than one point, has potential as a useful exercise in a developmental-enabling context.

It is not uncommon, I believe, for people in a relationship to feel that the other partner has a more or less favorable view of their relation than their own view. This can be tested by calling on each partner to predict on the DW form how they think their partner will answer from their perception of the relation. How well people understand each other's view of their own relationship may be especially important in family counselling contacts, as considered next.

FAMILY RELATIONSHIP CONFIGURATIONS AND STUDY

The 'We' form of the BLRI seems particularly amenable and pertinent to use with couples, though applicable to almost any family relationship configuration, including member perception of their family as a whole. Children not only experience their parents in one-on-one relationships with them but also experience, often vividly, how their parents interact and relate to each other in the child's presence. Parents on their side may connect strongly with the observed and felt relational interaction of their two or more children (or of their single child with a grandparent or other close relative or playmate). The many relationship configurations, such as triads, quartets of two children with the parent couple, and the whole family relational experience (see Barrett-Lennard, 2005, pp. 65–81), are open to study using the BLRI *We* form and related adaptations. Only small adjustments are needed to tap third-person perceptions of relations between other members and inventive further BLRI variations are possible in the family.

INVESTIGATING PERSON–GROUP RELATIONSHIPS

I earlier mentioned use of the BLRI studies of relationships in group therapy and related group contexts (Chapter 5). RI form GS–40, with its plurally worded items referring to the perceived response of the group as a whole would lend itself to exploration in small-group human service and other organizational settings. Since the focus is not on the response of particular individuals the task can feel less revealing than disclosures about dyadic relationships. If a researcher wishes to compare the group-to-member experience with the supervisor-to-member relation these latter could be accessed as well, using the regular OS–40 form. Since many people belong to more than one close group, comparing answers from the same persons for the way "the group responds to me" across different kinds of group would be relevant in some circumstances.

Using the instrument to study relations in *work groups*, teams, and collegial groups is a new field wide open to investigation. Since varied small groups provide the context in which most of the work of organizations takes place qualities of relationship between members and with their team group are vitally relevant to morale and outcomes. The relational response of the designated leader of the group generally would be of shared importance to other members, and relations between certain individual members can matter more still. The member-perceived response of leader/supervisors could be tapped with the regular OS RI. An "ideal-relationship" version could also be used for enquiry into the desired response of supervisors.

STUDYING GROUP-TO-GROUP AND ORGANIZATIONAL RELATIONSHIPS

Relationships *between groups* are often highly consequential and could be studied with a fresh adaptation of the BLRI, bringing a new domain of attributes into view. No such studies have yet been done on the perceived relational response of one group to another group. Appendix 1 includes experimental Form GG–40 of the BLRI adapted for this purpose. Although the same scoring key would apply, what the measures mean is not quite the same as in twosomes or even in group-to-person relationships. Level of regard in the group-to-group context has to do with the degree to which the other group's attitudes are seen as generally respecting, valuing, and friendly toward the respondent group and its membership. The empathy variable is concerned with how well the other group is seen as being attentive, or wanting to be in effective contact with "our" group, to correctly read our messages or actions, and so forth, as opposed to being disinterested in what 'we' are up to, and misreading our group. Resonation to felt experience is not an explicit focus although hinted at in some items. Modified empathy items retain more direct reference to accurate listening and perception, or the lack of this.

Unconditionality has very similar meaning in the group-with-group case as in personal relationship contexts although it is more difficult to frame the items given that the focus is no longer directly on reactions to self-attributes of the other. It is more about acceptance of the distinctive nature of the other *group*, as against selectively judgmental evaluation that weights the acceptability or otherwise of particular qualities, or implies that they should be 'like us.' Congruence has the same kinds of meaning as in one-to-one relationships; around the aspects of whether the group is viewed as open or transparent, responsive to underlying intentions or motives, and thus generally in touch with its own reality – in this case, as a group.

The last-envisioned and so far untried new form, designated OrgS–40 (Appendix 1, pp. 146–148), is designed to tap the qualities of experienced relationship members have with and within their organizations. Nearly everyone is a participant member of one or more organizations (and experiences further such systems from the 'outside'), which come in many shapes, sizes, and qualities, often with hugely consequential effects in the realm of relationship experience and personal wellbeing (see, e.g., Barrett-Lennard, 2013, pp. 95–105). There is a dearth of direct study of *specific relationship qualities* in this context, such as are tapped by the BLRI. My effort to keep each Inventory item both conceptually pertinent and in wordings that respondents can tune into readily will, I expect, soon be tested through application. Refinements are likely, but any difficulties the formulation of an item might pose should not be confused with the challenge of the task to respondents who have before not thought about person-with-organization (or group to group) relationships on the personal and experience-near dimensions involved.

Any association of a person with a system that has "my" in front of it – my organization, my community, my constituency (of people), my state or country, and so on – contributes to that person's identity or sense of self, and is a form of relationship that is potentially amenable to study. Use of Form OrgS–40 is advanced as one salient approach to doing this. The present form, however, is not the only potential 'person-with-system' modification. The wording could be adjusted fairly readily (albeit carefully) to refer to a community or other kind of system, and also could be adapted to tap the way members desire their system to be, or how they expect it be if they have not yet joined it, for example. The scoring key for OrgS–40 is the same as for the basic 40-item forms, although the interpretation of scores would be somewhat different than in one-on-one personal relationships, for example, in the case of empathic understanding. An organization may not literally be empathic, but its members can feel that they are being listened to, or not, that the organization is responsive, or not, to their circumstances or ideas or what it means to them to be part of the system (see discussion of meanings for the group with group form).

Using the Inventory in the way suggested here is not meant to imply that organizations or even small groups are just like an individual expanded in size and scope. It does imply that they are viewed as human systems composed of people and with attributes that reflect this composition. These qualities can be viewed as emergent from the interactive mix, goals, and outlook-in-context of the leadership and members generally. In relationships that involve larger systems (which are themselves relationship entities) emergent new properties can be discernible and earlier ones take on a differing hue. This is especially true when both (or all) parties to the relationship are very big systems, as next discussed.

TOWARDS THE STUDY OF RELATIONS BETWEEN VERY LARGE SYSTEMS

The relationships between big systems, such as nations, clearly are extremely complex and multilayered. The big system has within it many levels and kinds of relationship and interest within a typically cumbersome whole. These include the 'micro' and small-system levels already considered, relationships within and between a diversity of organizations and communities, and relations between ethnic groups and constituent subcultures – to name a few examples. Elsewhere I have touched on the idea of a national relationship audit or census (Barrett-Lennard, 2013, pp. 162). The internal relationships (some typically in tension) *within* large nations would have great bearing on how those nations relate to each other. I have not conceived of specific instrumentation on this level, and my thought is about an approach or path to such study (Barrett-Lennard, pp. 162).

The path I envision includes the study of intra-national relations on a range of levels and representative contexts. My overall framing conception begins on a micro level, with the view that personal relationships and the human self or personality are twin phenomena, different in kind but each dependent on the other. Relationships on this level precede and *flow into* the formation of self (typically beginning with the mother-newborn relation) as much as they *result from* the interplay of selves. Personal and small system relationships both feed into and receive influence from relationships with and between larger systems. My whole perspective "places relationship and interdependence at the core of human life processes" (Barrett-Lennard, 2013, p. 164). Relationships in this paradigm are living human systems, invested in life via their members, and also acting on their person components much as human consciousness acts on the incredibly intricate bodily being that gives rise to it. Relationship as an emergent phenomenon is not just a linkage between two or more islands of individual being but a true "compound" on a different level than the essential human components that underlie it. Relationships exist both observably and in the inner worlds of component members. Each level of system has some measure of autonomy while existing in dynamic relation with its component members and any larger enclosing system(s) (Barrett-Lennard, p. 164).

People identify themselves partly by their nationality and have a direct relation with their big nation system and some of its institutions as well as indirectly through intermediate systems intrinsic to the larger whole. In this sense, we "are intertwined with the working and qualities of the large people-systems we jointly create... [and which in turn] flow into our sense of who we are and influence face-to-face relationships" (Barrett-Lennard, p. 166). There is of course more to my present envisioning spelled out in the relationship paradigm book, but these glimpses suffice to suggest that the study and understanding of large system relations is daunting but possible. While their external relations are not, in the logic presented, wholly explainable by their internal relational processes (given the principle of emergence of new properties), I propose that a vital step would be to systematically study how these "internal" processes feed into each other and the larger whole and what their qualities are. Distinguishing and mapping these wholes would first be necessary for adequate sampling of representative features.

Besides intra-national processes there is, of course, much direct and indirect interchange across national boundaries between component person and subsystem members of each nation in our highly globalized, internet-connected world. I am referring not to economic ties as such, but to the communication, mutual awareness, and qualities of attitude, feeling, and other human exchange both accompanying and separate from economic transactions. An audit of the existing flow across national boundaries of connection and association between persons, groups, organizations and government systems, communities, and subcultures would be part of the essential data in understanding the relation between the national wholes. How to select, gather and integrate the massive array of data within a nation would be a huge undertaking – impractical at first sight. The mapping of the whole structure of kinds of micro- and macro-systems and how they are positioned and engage with each other certainly would be daunting but not impossible given the will and necessary resources, at least for a good approximation. Discriminating a full spectrum of target relational systems would lead on to identification of the specific data to be gathered.

For smaller systems of relation BLRI data as already discussed would be one pertinent source of information and further desirable sources would be considered. For the bigger subsystems, such as relations between organizations and communities, socio-metric and interview data from samples of key informants would be called for. Channels of communication and processes by which transactional and development decisions are made would be among relevant elements to consider. In all, extensive searching enquiry and thought would be involved in choosing the specific forms of data and its collection, and pilot-study testing of these choices would be needed. In keeping with the whole emphasis of this book and chapter, information about mechanisms, programs and channels would not by itself suffice. The emphasis would need to be on qualities of engagement, communication, attitude, and relational interchange. The carefully focused new data along these lines, complemented by pertinent pre-existing information, would need to be drawn and knitted together within an adequate overall conceptual framework of meaning.

Relationships between big systems of people are of such crucial relevance to human and societal well-being that the demanding level of endeavor suggested here is urgently called for. Continued and expanded inquiry into personal and small system relationships remain of priority value but need to be complemented within a common paradigm of thought that sees human relationships as interconnected over multiple levels of association. Without such wider contextual awareness and connected additional knowledge individuals and institutions are trying to manage their complex world with very incomplete information. Fully fledged enquiry into the world of human relationship would recognize and take account of its working over the whole domain sketched here and fully presented in my 2013 book.

CONCLUSION

Needed future research on human relationships has many significant aspects and possibilities. These relationships exist over a great spectrum, from relations between different modalities of self (modes largely born through diverse outer relationships) through interpersonal, inter-group, and other intermediate levels to relations between very big and complex groupings of people including large nations. The many levels and kinds of relationship system are in general interconnected, with smaller systems nested within larger ones, and in two-way relations of influence both "downward" to constituent persons or subsystems and "upward" to the larger systems of which they are part or in contact with. At the micro level of internal relations, preliminary studies with this author's Contextual Selves Inventory support its theoretical base and potential for valuable further and differing applications.

Existing adaptations of the BLRI include the little used but distinctive and promising 'we' form designed for relationship participants to focus on and describe their relationship whole. The slight rewording of items (e.g., to We understand each other), retains the same content and quartet of variables as in previous study, but in this case as they pertain to the relationship system – the experienced 'we' and 'us.' The dyad-we RI form can be used not only with couples but, with minor adjustments, with whole families, and other significantly connected face-to-face groups, as seen by their members. It also can be slightly adapted for the participants to describe how they would most like their relationship to be, or the way they think their partner sees the relationship, or even for use by close outside observers.

One or both parties to a relationship may be a small group and there is inviting scope for original new applications of BLRI Form GS–40 beyond the province of therapy-type groups, for example, in work and learning groups and sporting teams. Small groups within organizations and in other contexts often have significant linkage, awareness of, and association with each other. A new version of the instrument arranged and worded for systematic description of the response of one such group to another group invites application in a fresh way of studying group relations. Nearly everyone is significantly involved with large organizations and such engagement is a further level of human system-to-person relationship. The experimental new OrgS–40 form of the BLRI, also included in Appendix 1 (pp. 146–148), is a unique potential resource in this context, ready for trial application, possible further refinement, and added adaptations.

Although associations between big systems such as whole nations are, in their human relations aspects, multilayered and systemically very complex, they are in principle decipherable. The input of each system to their association, and the existing channels and qualities of communication and other human engagements between them, could be freshly and closely studied and go a long way toward understanding their overall relationship and its potentialities. This means that each big system needs much more comprehensive and versatile scrutiny of its internal relationship processes than heretofore, and the general direction of an approach to this is proposed. The approach rests on a paradigm of thought in which interdependence in relationship is seen as being at the core of human life. A broad conclusion is that secure and intelligent advance of our species as a major partner in its lifeworld rests, in big part, on an outreaching person- and system-sensitive human science of relationships.

Appendix 1
The Relationship Inventory Forms and Scoring Keys

This appendix includes all the principal forms and adaptations of the Barrett-Lennard Relationship Inventory (BLRI), presented in their entirety and with the relevant scoring keys. They comprise a considerable array, and are arranged approximately in order of their original development, but also in keeping with similarities of purpose or usage and shared scoring keys. All of the included forms are in English, but the last part of the appendix lists the other languages in which versions of the BLRI are known to have been used, and shows where possible the names of colleagues originally involved in the translations. General guidelines for the translation process, as supplied to most of these colleagues, are also included.

APPENDIX 1 ANNOTATED CONTENTS

The Relationship Inventory: A Complete Resource and Guide, First Edition. Godfrey T. Barrett-Lennard.
© 2015 John Wiley & Sons, Ltd. Published 2015 by John Wiley & Sons, Ltd.
Companion site: www.wiley.com/go/barrett_lennard/therelationshipinventory

The basic 64- and 40-item forms do not specify a particular category of relationship. They are designed to be applicable in a wide range of contexts, and are referred to extensively in the main text of this book The working illustration of an alternate format for the 64-item forms (preferred by a particular investigator) is worded for a counselling relationship in particular, though this easily could be adjusted for a different context. The 'past tense' illustration (responsive to the interest of another investigator) is worded for adult respondents remembering their relationship with their father during childhood – again another class of relation is easily substituted. The 'coloration' of memory might well change with substantial shifts in mood and/or development of the respondent's own life experience. Desired or anticipated relationships also could be a focus of interest, with small (investigator) adjustments to the regular OS or MO forms.

Your name or code ....   Today's date ....

Barrett-Lennard Relationship Inventory: Form OS–64

Developed by Godfrey T. Barrett-Lennard, PhD

Below are listed a variety of ways that one person may feel or behave in relation to another person. Please consider each numbered statement with reference to your present relationship with _____ (name), mentally adding his or her name in the space provided. If the other person's name is John, for example, then read statement number 1 as "John respects me as a person."

Mark each statement in the answer column on the right, according to how strongly you feel that it is true, or not true, in this relationship. *Please be sure to mark every one.* Write in a plus number (*+3, +2, or +1*), or a minus number (*–1, –2, or –3*), to stand for the following answers:

+3: **YES,** *I strongly feel that it is true*

+2: Yes, *I feel it is true*

+1: (Yes) *I feel that it is probably true, or more true than untrue*

–1: (No) *I feel that it is probably untrue, or more untrue than true*

–2: No, *I feel it is not true*

–3: **NO,** *I strongly feel that it is not true*

	ANSWER
1. _____ respects me as a person...	_____
2. _____ wants to understand how I see things...................................	_____
3. _____ 's interest in me depends on the things I say or do.	_____
4. _____ is comfortable and at ease in our relationship......................	_____
5. _____ feels a true liking for me..	_____
6. _____ may understand my words but he/she does not see the way I feel.........	_____
7. Whether I am feeling or unhappy with myself makes no real difference to the way _____ feels about me.	_____
8. I feel that _____ puts on a role or front with me..........................	_____
9. _____ is impatient with me.	_____
10. _____ nearly always knows exactly what I mean.	_____
11. Depending on my behavior _____ has a better opinion of me sometimes than he/she has at other times...	_____
12. I feel that _____ is real and genuine with me.	_____
13. I feel appreciated by _____.	_____
14. _____ looks at what I do from his/her own point of view.	_____
15. _____ 's feeling toward me doesn't depend on how *I* judge or feel about myself. [Answer 'no' (–1, –2 *or* –3) if the way *you* feel about yourself alters his/her feeling.]	_____
16. It makes _____ uneasy when I ask or talk about certain things.......	_____
17. _____ is indifferent to me.	_____
18. _____ usually senses or realizes what I am feeling.........................	_____

19. _____ wants me to be a particular kind of person... _____

20. I feel that what _____ says expresses exactly what he/she is feeling and thinking at that moment.. _____

21. _____ finds me rather dull and uninteresting. .... _____

22. _____ 's own attitudes toward things I do or say prevent him/her from understanding me... _____

23. I can/could be openly critical *or* appreciative of _____ without making him/her feel differently about me... _____

24. _____ wants me to think that he/she likes or understands me more than he/she really does. .... _____

25. _____ cares for me. .... _____

26. _____ thinks that *I* feel a certain way, because that's the way *he/she* feels....... _____

27. _____ likes or accepts certain things about me, and there are other things s/he does not like in me... _____

28. _____ doesn't avoid or go round anything that is important for our relationship .... _____

29. I feel that _____ disapproves of me.. _____

30. _____ realizes what I mean even when I have difficulty in saying it. .... _____

31. _____ 's attitude toward me stays the same: he/she is not pleased with me sometimes and critical or disappointed at other times................................ _____

32. Sometimes _____ is not at all comfortable but we go on, outwardly ignoring it... _____

33. _____ just tolerates me. .... _____

34. _____ usually understands the whole of what I mean. .... _____

35. If I show that I am angry with _____ he/she becomes hurt or angry with me, too. .... _____

36. _____ expresses his/her true impressions and feelings with me....................... _____

37. _____ is friendly and warm with me.. _____

38. _____ takes no notice of some things I think or feel...................................... _____

39. How much _____ likes or dislikes me is not altered by anything that I tell him/her about myself... _____

40. At times I sense that _____ not aware of what he/she is really feeling with me... _____

41. I feel that _____ really values me. .... _____

42. _____ appreciates exactly how the things I experience feel to me................... _____

43. _____ approves of me in some ways or sometimes, and plainly disapproves of me in other ways/other times .... _____

44. _____ is willing to express whatever is actually in his/her mind with me, including personal feelings about him/herself or me....................... _____

45. _____ doesn't like me for myself... _____

46. At times _____ thinks that I feel a lot more strongly about a particular thing than I really do... _____

47. Whether I happen to be in good spirits or feeling upset does not make _____ feel any more or less appreciative of me................................... _____

48. _____ is openly himself/herself in our relationship................................... _____

49. I seem to irritate and bother_____ .... _____

50. _____ does not realize how sensitive I am about some things we discuss... _____

51. Whether the ideas and feelings I express are "good" or "bad" seems to make no difference to _____'s feeling toward me. .... _____

52. There are times when I feel that _____'s outward response to me is quite different from the way he/she feels underneath......................... _____

53. _____ feels contempt for me. .... _____

54. _____ understands me. .... _____

55. Sometimes I am more worthwhile in _____'s eyes than I am at other times .... _____

56. _____ doesn't hide from himself (herself) anything that he/she feels with me. .... _____

57. _____ is truly interested in *me*. .... _____

58. _____'s response to me is usually so fixed and automatic that I don't get through to him/her. .... _____

59. I don't think that anything I say or do really changes the way _____ feels toward me. .... _____

60. What _____ says to me often gives a wrong impression of his/her whole thought or feeling at the time. .... _____

61. _____ feels affection for me. .... _____

62. When I am hurt or upset _____ can recognize my feelings exactly, without becoming upset him/herself. .... _____

63. What *other* people think of me does (or would, if he/she knew) affect the way _____ feels toward me.. _____

64. I believe that _____ has feelings he/she does not tell me about that are causing difficulty in our relationship... _____

If there is one more page, please enter the 'additional information' requested on that page.

ADDITIONAL INFORMATION[1]

Please fill in the spaces below, about yourself *and* the other person

Yourself	*The other person*

Age ....years   *Age (approx)* ....years

Sex ....(M or F)   *Sex* ....(M or F)

Occupation ....   *Occupation* ....

....

Your position in
this relationship...   *Other person's position in*
this relationship...
(e.g., client, daughter, partner, friend)   (e.g., counsellor, mother, supervisor, best friend)

Duration of this relationship — how long have you known the other person?

All my life ....

OR .... years

OR .... months

OR ....

Is there anything you would like to add about the circumstances or your feeling in this relationship (or how you might wish it to be)?

....

....

....

---

[1] The section "Additional Information" is not part of BLRI proper and researchers may vary its content.

Name or code .... Today's date ....

Barrett-Lennard Relationship Inventory: Form MO–64

Developed by Godfrey T. Barrett-Lennard, PhD

Below are listed a variety of ways that one person may feel or behave in relation to another person.

Please consider each statement with reference to your present relationship with _____, mentally adding his or her name in the space provided. For example, if the other person's name was John, you would read the first statement as "I respect *John* as a person."

Mark each statement in the left margin, according to how strongly you feel that it is true, or not true, in this relationship. Please be sure to mark every one. *Write in a plus number (+3, +2, or +1) when your answer is affirmative, and a minus number (–1, –2, or –3) when your answer is a "no."* Here is the exact meaning of each answer number:--

+3: **YES**, *I strongly feel that it **is true***

+2: Yes, *I feel it is true*

+1: (Yes) *I feel that it is probably true, or more true than untrue*

–1: (No) *I feel that it is probably untrue, or more untrue than true*

–2: No, *I feel it is not true*

–3: **NO,** *I strongly feel that it is* ***not true***

_____ 1. I respect _____ as a person.

_____ 2. I want to understand how _____ sees things.

_____ 3. The interest I feel in _____ depends on what he/she says and does.

_____ 4. I feel at ease with _____.

_____ 5. I really like _____.

_____ 6. I understand _____'s words but do not know how he/she actually feels inside.

_____ 7. Whether _____ is feeling happy or unhappy with him/herself does not change *my* feeling toward him/her.

_____ 8. I am inclined to put on a role or front with _____.

_____ 9. I do feel impatient with _____.

_____ 10. I nearly always know exactly what _____ means.

_____ 11. Depending on _____'s actions, I have a better opinion of him/her sometimes than I do at other times.

_____ 12. I feel that I am genuinely myself with _____.

_____ 13. I appreciate _____ as a person.

_____ 14. I look at what _____ does from my own point of view.

_____ 15. The way I feel about _____ doesn't depend on how she might judge or feel about herself.

_____ 16. It bothers me when _____ tries to ask or talk about certain things.

_____ 17. I feel indifferent to _____.

_____ 18. I usually sense or realize how _____ is feeling.

_____ 19. I would like _____ to have particular qualities as a person.

_____ 20. When I speak to _____ I can say freely just what I'm thinking or feeling at that moment.

_____ 21. I find _____ rather dull and uninteresting.

_____ 22. My own feelings can stop me from understanding _____.

_____ 23. Whether _____ criticizes me or expresses appreciation of me does not (or, would not) change how I feel inside toward him/her.

_____ 24. I would rather that _____ *thinks* I like or understand him/her even when I don't.

_____ 25. I *care* for _____.

_____ 26. Sometimes I think that _____ feels a certain way, because that's the way I feel myself.

_____ 27. I like _____ in some ways, while there are other things about him/her that I do not like.

_____ 28. I don't feel that I have been ignoring (or putting off) anything that is important for our relationship.

_____ 29. I do feel disapproval of _____.

_____ 30. I can tell what _____ means, even when he/she has difficulty in saying it.

_____ 31. My feeling toward _____ stays about the same; I am not in sympathy with him/her one time and out of patience another time.

_____ 32. Sometimes I am not at all comfortable with _____ but we go on, outwardly ignoring it.

_____ 33. I put up with _____.

_____ 34. I usually catch and understand the whole of _____ 's meaning.

_____ 35. If _____ gets impatient or mad at me I become angry or upset too.

_____ 36. I am able to be sincere and direct in whatever I express with _____.

_____ 37. I feel friendly and warm toward _____.

_____ 38. I ignore some of _____ 's feelings.

_____ 39. My liking or disliking of _____ is not altered by anything that he/she says about himself/herself.

_____ 40. At times I just don't know, or don't realize until later, what my feelings are with _____.

_____ 41. I value _____ in our relationship.

_____ 42. I appreciate just how _____ 's experiences feel to him/her.

_____ 43. I feel quite pleased with _____ sometimes, and then he/she disappoints me at other times.

_____ 44. I feel comfortable to express what is in my mind with _____, including feelings about myself or about him/her.

_____ 45. I really don't like _____ as a person.

_____ 46. At times I *think* that _____ feels strongly about something and then it turns out that he/she doesn't.

_____ 47. Whether _____ is in good spirits, or is bothered and upset, does not make me less or more appreciative of him/her.

_____ 48. I can quite openly be myself in our relationship.

_____ 49. Somehow _____ really irritates me (gets 'under my skin').

_____ 50. At the time, I don't realize how touchy or sensitive _____ is about some of the things we discuss.

_____ 51. Whether _____ is expressing 'good' thoughts and feelings, or 'bad' ones, does not affect the way I feel toward him/her.

_____ 52. There are times when my outward response to _____ is quite different from the way I feel underneath.

_____ 53. In fact, I feel contempt toward _____.

_____ 54. I understand _____.

_____ 55. Sometimes _____ seems to me a more worthwhile person than he/she does at other times.

_____ 56. I don't sense any feelings in relation to _____ that are hard for me to face and admit to myself.

_____ 57. I truly am interested in _____.

_____ 58. I often respond to _____ rather automatically, without taking in what he/she is experiencing.

_____ 59. I don't think that particular things _____ says or does alter the way I feel toward him (her).

_____ 60. What I say to _____ often would give a wrong impression of my complete thought or feeling at the time.

_____ 61. I feel deep affection for _____.

_____ 62. When _____ is hurt or upset I can recognize just how he/she feels, _without_ getting upset myself.

_____ 63. What other people think and feel about _____ does help to make _me_ feel as I do toward him/her.

_____ 64. I feel there are things we don't talk about that are causing difficulty in our relationship.

ADDITIONAL INFORMATION

Please add the following information about yourself and the other person:

	Myself	_Other_
Age	_____ years	_____ years (known or estimated)
Sex	_____ (M or F)	_____ (M or F)
Occupation	_____	_____

Positions in this relationship

Examples:	| Mother	<-----/----->	Son
	| Counsellor	<----/---->	Client
	| Husband/partner	<---/--->	Wife/partner
	| Personal Friend	<---/--->	Personal Friend
Actual:			
(_Please fill in_)	_____	<--/-->	_____

Name or code ....   Date answered ....

Barrett-Lennard Relationship Inventory: Form DW–64 (version 4)

Developed by Godfrey T. Barrett-Lennard, PhD

Listed below are various ways that a whole relationship may be experienced from the inside. The listed statements (numbers 1–64) point to qualities of a particular relationship as perceived by a member of that relationship. It is understood that one partner or member would not give exactly the same picture as the other one and that either person's view could change.

Please describe the way it is now in your relationship with _____. While answering, think of actual situations and of the atmosphere of feelings and attitudes between you. Try to bring pictures to mind from your everyday worlds together. You might also think of unusual times that have stayed in your memory. The 'right' answer in each case is how *you* truly feel and see this *whole relationship 'we' or 'us'* as of now.

Mark each statement in the left margin, according to how strongly you feel that it is true, or not true, of this relationship. *Please mark every one.* Write in plus numbers (+3, +2, +1) or minus numbers (−1, −2, or −3) to stand for the following answers:

+3:   **YES**, *I strongly feel that it is true*

+2:   Yes, *I feel it is true*

+1:   (Yes) *I feel that it is probably true, or more true than untrue*

−1:   (No) *I feel that it is probably untrue, or more untrue than true*

−2:   No, *I feel it is not true*

−3:   **NO**, *I strongly feel that it is not true*

_____ 1. We respect each other as people.

_____ 2. We want to know and understand how the other one sees things.

_____ 3. The interest we feel together depends on each one's actions and words.

_____ 4. We feel at ease together.

_____ 5. We like and enjoy one another.

_____ 6. We may hear each other's words but we don't see how the other feels inside.

_____ 7. Either one of us can be 'up' or 'down' in our mood without this changing the other one's attitude toward us.

_____ 8. I feel that we put on a role or act with one another.

_____ 9. We are impatient with each other.

_____ 10. We generally know exactly what the other one means.

_____ 11. Our opinion of the other one goes up or down, according to their behavior and the light they show themselves in.

_____ 12. I feel that we are our real and genuine selves with one another.

_____ 13. We appreciate each other.

_____ 14. We both look at what the other does, from our individual points of view.

_____ 15. How we feel toward the other one doesn't change with swings in their self-feeling or mood. [If it does change, choose one of the "no" answers.]

_____ 16. We get uneasy when the other asks or talks about certain 'sensitive' things.

_____ 17. We are mostly indifferent to each other.

_____ 18. We usually sense or realize what the other is feeling.

_____ 19. We each want the other to be a particular kind of person.

_____ 20. We speak openly to each other, expressing what we are thinking and feeling as we say it.

_____ 21. We tend to find each other dull and uninteresting.

_____ 22. Our attitudes toward certain things the other one says or does get in the way of understanding them.

_____ 23. Either of us can express something that bothers us _or_ that pleases us in the other, without changing their feeling toward us.

_____ 24. We want the other one to think that we like them or understand them more than we really do.

_____ 25. We care for one another.

_____ 26. At times we think that the other feels a certain way, because that's the way we feel ourselves.

_____ 27. We like some things about one another, and there are other things we do not like.

_____ 28. We don't avoid or go round things that are important for our relationship.

_____ 29. We disapprove of one another.

_____ 30. We realize and know each other's meaning even when something is hard to say or find words for.

_____ 31. Our attitude toward each other stays about the same: we are not pleased with the other one sometimes and critical or disappointed at other times.

_____ 32. Sometimes one or other of us is not at all comfortable but we go on, outwardly ignoring it.

_____ 33. We just tolerate each other.

_____ 34. We listen to each other, and usually understand each other's whole meaning.

_____ 35. If one of us shows anger with the other they become hurt or angry too.

_____ 36. Each of us is able to express his/her honest impressions and actual feelings with or toward the other.

_____ 37. There is a friendly warmth in our relationship.

_____ 38. We just take no notice of some things the other one thinks or feels.

_____ 39. How much we like or dislike each other is not altered by particular things we reveal or show about ourselves.

_____ 40. At times we can sense something in the other's feelings that they deny or don't seem to be aware of.

_____ 41. I feel that each of us really values the other person.

_____ 42. We can each appreciate exactly how the other one's experiences feel to them.

_____ 43. Sometimes or in some ways we approve of the other one and there other times or different aspects where we distinctly disapprove.

_____ 44. We can express to each other whatever is actually in our minds, including any feelings about ourselves or about them.

_____ 45. We don't like the other one for themselves, as they are.

_____ 46. We sometimes get things wrong by assuming or imagining that the other feels much more strongly about a particular thing than it turns out they really do.

_____ 47. One of us can be in good spirits, or feeling upset, without causing the other one to feel differently toward us.

_____ 48. We are openly and freely ourselves in our relationship.

_____ 49. We seem to irritate and bother each other – get on each other's nerves.

_____ 50. We often don't realize (at the time) how sensitive or touchy the other is about things that are said or done.

_____ 51. Either of us is can express "good" thoughts or feelings, or "bad" ones, without changing the other person's feeling toward us. [If it does change their feeling, answer 'no.']

_____ 52. At times our outward response to one another is quite different from the way we actually feel underneath.

_____ 53. We feel a kind of contempt for each other.

_____ 54. We understand one another.

_____ 55. We are inclined to judge each other; with a more positive (or negative) estimation sometimes than at other times.

_____ 56. We _don't_ avoid or tiptoe around real feelings in our relationship. [If you feel this is wrong because 'we _do_ avoid or tiptoe around real feelings,' choose a 'no' answer.]

_____ 57. We are truly interested in each other.

_____ 58. Our response to each other is so fixed and automatic that often we don't get through to them, or take in what the other has said.

_____ 59. I _don't think_ that particular things either of us says or does really alter the way the other one feels toward us. (Answer 'no' if it does alter their feeling.)

_____ 60. What one or other of us says often covers up and gives a wrong impression of his/her actual thought or feeling at the time.

_____ 61. We feel real affection for one another.

_____ 62. When one of us is upset or hurting, the other one is able to tune in and recognize the other's feeling exactly without getting really upset.

_____ 63. What _other people_ think of either of us – when we know about it – does affect or rub off on what we think of each other.

_____ 64. I believe there are feelings that we don't talk about together that are causing difficulty in our relationship.

Have you entered an answer for every single item? Please check and make sure. (Thank you.)

Please also provide the following information about yourself and the other person*

Yourself   _Other person_

Age (years) _____   _____ age (known or estimated)

Sex (M or F) _____   _____ (M or F)

Occupation or vocation _____   _____

Kind or context of relationship (e.g., partners, son and father or other family relation, personal friends, client-therapist, colleagues, student and trainee. Please be specific.)

_____

Duration/length of the relationship _____ years

Has the relationship always or for a long time been the way you have described it?

_____

If the relationship has changed, how did this happen and/or how long ago?

_____

_____

_____

* The information section _following item 64_ is not part of the Relationship Inventory proper, and can be varied by other users.

Barrett-Lennard Relationship Inventory: Scoring Key 64–item forms

Developed by Godfrey T. Barrett-Lennard, PhD

Type of relationship …...................................   Code ....

Respondent (e.g., spouse, client).........................   Referent person(s) ....

Level of Regard		Empathy		Unconditionality		Congruence	
Positive items	Answer *example*	Positive items	Answer	Positive items	Answer	Positive items	Answer
1	3	2		7		4	
5	2	10		15		12	
13	2	18		23		20	
25	1	30		31		28	
37	2	34		39		36	
41	–3	42		47		44	
57	1	54		51		48	
61	2	62		59		56	
Sum: Subtotal 1	10						

Level of Regard		Empathy		Unconditionality		Congruence	
Negative items	Answer *example*	Negative items	Answer	Negative items	Answer	Negative items	Answer
9	–2	6		3		8	
17	–3	14		11		16	
21	–3	22		19		24	
29	–2	26		27		32	
33	1	38		35		40	
45	–2	46		43		52	
49	1	50		55		60	
53	–3	58		63		64	
Sum (neg. items)	–13						
Subtotal 2 (–1 × Sum)	13						
Subtotals 1 + 2: *Scale Score*	23						

Illustrative scoring of a whole 64 item Relationship Inventory protocol

Code .... R.I. form .... Date answered ....

Type or class of relationship ....

Respondent (e.g., spouse, client) .... Other person(s) ....

	Level of Regard		Empathy		Unconditionality		Congruence	
	Positive Items	Answer	Positive Items	Answer	Positive Items	Answer	Positive Items	Answer
	1	3	2	2	7	1	4	3
	5	1	10	2	15	2	12	2
	13	2	18	2	23	1	20	1
	25	1	30	2	31	3	28	3
	37	3	34	2	39	2	36	1
	41	2	42	2	47	−2	44	−1
	57	2	54	2	51	2	48	3
	61	−1	62	3	59	2	56	3
Sum: Subtotal 1		13		17		11		15

	Negative Items	Answer	Negative Items	Answer	Negative Items	Answer	Negative Items	Answer
	9	−3	6	−2	3	−2	8	−2
	17	−2	14	−1	11	2	16	−3
	21	−1	22	−3	19	−1	24	−3
	29	−2	26	−1	27	2	32	−2
	33	−2	38	1	35	−2	40	−2
	45	−1	46	−2	43	−1	52	1
	49	−2	50	−2	55	2	60	−2
	53	−2	58	−3	63	−3	64	−3
Sum (for negative items)		−15		−13		−3		−16
−1 × Sum: Subtotal 2		15		13		3		16
Subtotals 1 + 2: Scale Score		28		30		14		31

Note: Plus(+) signs have been omitted, in transposing item answers from an RI protocol.

Barrett-Lennard Relationship Inventory: Form OS–64Couns

Developed by Godfrey T. Barrett-Lennard, PhD
An example of alternate format and wording specifically for counselling relationships (incomplete form)

Below are listed a variety of ways that counsellors may feel or behave in relation to clients. Please consider each numbered statement with reference to your present relationship with your counsellor.

Mark each statement in the answer columns on the right, according to how strongly you feel that it is true, or not true, in this relationship. *Please be sure to mark every one.* Please indicate your answer by placing a tick in the box that most closely matches your response, using the following key:

–3: **No**(!), I strongly feel that it is not true,	+3: Yes(!), I strongly feel that it is true
–2: No, I feel it is not true	+2: Yes, I feel it is true
–1: (No), I feel that it is probably untrue, or more untrue than true	+1: (**Yes**), I feel that it is probably true or more true than untrue

	No −3	No −2	No −1	Yes +1	Yes +2	Yes +3
1. My counsellor respects me as a person	❏	❏	❏	❏	❏	❏
2. My counsellor wants to understand how I see things	❏	❏	❏	❏	❏	❏
3. My counsellor's interest in me depends on the things I say or do	❏	❏	❏	❏	❏	❏
4. My counsellor is comfortable and at ease in our relationship	❏	❏	❏	❏	❏	❏
5. My counsellor feels a true liking for me	❏	❏	❏	❏	❏	❏
6. My counsellor may understand my words but he/she does not see the way I feel	❏	❏	❏	❏	❏	❏
7. Whether I am feeling happy or unhappy with myself makes no real difference to the way my counsellor feels about me	❏	❏	❏	❏	❏	❏
8. I feel that my counsellor puts on a role or front with me	❏	❏	❏	❏	❏	❏
9. My counsellor is impatient with me	❏	❏	❏	❏	❏	❏
10. My counsellor nearly always knows exactly what I mean	❏	❏	❏	❏	❏	❏
11. Depending on my behavior, my counsellor has a better opinion of me sometimes than he/she has at other times	❏	❏	❏	❏	❏	❏
12. I feel that my counsellor is real and genuine with me	❏	❏	❏	❏	❏	❏
13. I feel appreciated by my counsellor	❏	❏	❏	❏	❏	❏
14. My counsellor looks at what I do from his/her own point of view	❏	❏	❏	❏	❏	❏
15. My counsellor's feeling toward me doesn't depend on how I feel toward him/her	❏	❏	❏	❏	❏	❏
16. It makes my counsellor uneasy when I talk about certain things	❏	❏	❏	❏	❏	❏
17. My counsellor is indifferent to me	❏	❏	❏	❏	❏	❏
18. My counsellor usually senses or realizes what I am feeling	❏	❏	❏	❏	❏	❏

	No −3	No −2	No −1	Yes +1	Yes +2	Yes +3
19. My counsellor wants me to be a particular kind of person	❑	❑	❑	❑	❑	❑
20. I feel that what my counsellor says expresses exactly what he/she is feeling and thinking at that moment	❑	❑	❑	❑	❑	❑
21. My counsellor finds me rather dull and uninteresting	❑	❑	❑	❑	❑	❑
22. My counsellor's own attitudes towards things I do or say prevent him/her from understanding me	❑	❑	❑	❑	❑	❑

It is possible to modify any basic OS form (and most adaptations listed) to refer to a relationship remembered from the past. A particular investigator has conducted a study with adult respondents who answered for the way they remembered the response of their father during their childhood, using past tense wording of items. Following for illustration are the directions and first part of the modified (64-item) form – to which a prospective user could add the further items:

Below are listed a variety of ways that one person may feel or behave in relation to another person. Please consider each statement with reference to your childhood relationship with your father by mentally inserting 'my father,' 'dad,' or any other variation of the name you called him by in the spaces provided. For example, if he was known to you as 'Papa,' the question would read, "Papa respected me as a person."

Mark each statement in the answer column on the right, according to how strongly you feel that it was true, or not true, in this relationship. *Please be sure to mark every one.* Write in a plus number (*+3, +2, or +1*), or a minus number (*−1, −2, or −3*), to stand for the following answers:

+3: **YES,** *I strongly feel that it* was true

+2: Yes, *I feel (or think) it was true*

+1: (Yes), *I feel that it was probably true, or more true than untrue*

−1: (No), *I feel that it was probably untrue or more untrue than true*

−2: No, *I feel/think this was not true*

−3: **NO,** *I strongly feel that it was* **not** true

ANSWER

1. _____ respected me as a person. .... _____

2. _____ wanted to understand how I saw things. .... _____

3. _____ 's interest in me depended on the things I said or did. .... _____

4. _____ was comfortable and at ease in our relationship. .... _____

5. _____ felt a true liking for me. .... _____

6. _____ may have understood my words but he did not see the way I felt. .... _____

7. Whether I was feeling happy or unhappy with myself made no real difference to the way _____ felt about me. .... _____

8. I felt that _____ put on a role or front with me. .... _____

9. _____ was impatient with me. .... _____

10. _____ nearly always knew exactly what I meant. .... _____

11. Depending on my behavior, _____ had a better opinion of me sometimes than he had at other times. .... _____

12. I felt that _____ was real and genuine with me. .... _____

13. I felt appreciated by. .... _____

ANSWER

14. _____ looked at what I did from his own point of view. .... _____

15. _____'s feeling toward me didn't depend at all on how *I* was feeling at the time. [Answer "no" (–1, –2 *or* –3) if the way you felt altered his feeling.]..................... _____

16. It made _____ uneasy when I asked or talked about certain things. .... _____

17. _____ was indifferent to me. .... _____

18. _____ usually sensed or realized what I was feeling. .... _____

19. _____ wanted me to be a particular kind of person. .... _____

20. I feel that whatever _____ said to me expressed exactly what he was feeling _____ and thinking at the time. ....

These 20 items are illustrative and a complete 64-item form would continue in past tense wording, and be scored as above for other 64-item forms.

Name or code ....   Answer date ....

Barrett-Lennard Relationship Inventory: Form OS–40 (version 3)

Developed by Godfrey T. Barrett-Lennard, PhD

Below are listed a variety of ways that one person may feel or behave in relation to another person.

Please consider each statement with reference to your present relationship with _____, mentally inserting his or her name in the space provided. For example, if the other person's name was John, you would read the first statement as "John respects me" and the second as "John usually senses or realizes what I am feeling".

Mark each statement in the left margin, according to how strongly you feel that it is true, or not true, in this relationship. Please be sure to mark every one. *Write in a minus number (–3, –2, or –1) when your answer is on the "no" side, and a plus number (+1, +2, or +3) when your answer is a "yes."* Here is the exact meaning of each answer number:–

+3: **YES,** *I strongly feel that it is true*

+2: Yes, *I feel it is true*

+1: (Yes) *I feel that it is probably true, or more true than untrue*

–1: (No) *I feel that it is probably untrue, or more untrue than true*

–2: No, *I feel it is not true*

–3: **NO,** *I strongly feel that it is not true*

_____ 1. _____ respects me.

_____ 2. _____ usually senses or realizes what I am feeling.

_____ 3. _____'s interest in me depends on my words and actions (or how I perform).

_____ 4. I feel that _____ puts on a role or front with me.

_____ 5. _____ feels a true liking for me.

_____ 6. _____ reacts to my words but does not see the way I feel.

_____ 7. Whether I am feeling happy or unhappy with myself makes no real difference to the way he/she feels about me.

_____ 8. _____ doesn't avoid or go round anything that matters between us.

_____ 9. _____ is indifferent to me.

_____ 10. _____ nearly always sees exactly what I mean.

_____ 11. Depending on my behavior, _____ has a better (or a worse) opinion of *me* sometimes than s/he has at other times.

_____ 12. I feel that _____ is genuine with me.

_____ 13. I know I'm valued and appreciated by _____

_____ 14. _____'s *own attitudes* get in the way of understanding me.

_____ 15. No matter what I tell about myself _____ likes (or dislikes) me just the same.

_____ 16. _____ keeps quiet about his/her real inner impressions and feelings.

_____ 17. _____ finds me rather dull and uninteresting.

_____ 18. _____ realizes what I mean even when I have difficulty in saying it.

_____ 19. _____ wants me to be a certain kind of person.

_____ 20. _____ is willing to say whatever is on his/her mind with me, including feelings about either of us or how we are getting along.

_____ 21. _____ cares for me.

_____ 22. _____ doesn't listen and pick up on what I think and feel.

_____ 23. _____ likes certain things about me, and there are other things he/she does not like in me.

_____ 24. _____ is openly himself (herself) in our relationship.

_____ 25. I feel that _____ disapproves of me.

_____ 26. _____ usually understands the whole of what I mean.

_____ 27. Whether thoughts or feelings I express are 'good' or 'bad' makes no difference to _____'s feeling toward me.

_____ 28. Sometimes _____ is not at all comfortable but we go on, outwardly ignoring it.

_____ 29. _____ is friendly and warm toward me.

_____ 30. _____ does not understand me.

_____ 31. _____ approves of some things about me (or some of my ways), and plainly disapproves of other things (or ways I act and express myself).

_____ 32. I think _____ always knows exactly what s/he feels with me: s/he doesn't cover up inside.

_____ 33. _____ just tolerates or puts up with me.

_____ 34. _____ appreciates exactly how the things I experience feel to me.

_____ 35. Sometimes I am more worthwhile in _____'s eyes than I am at other times.

_____ 36. At moments I feel that _____'s outward response to me is quite different from the way s/he feels underneath.

_____ 37. _____ feels affection for me.

_____ 38. _____'s response to me is so fixed and automatic that I don't get through to him/her.

_____ 39. I don't think that anything I say or do really changes the way _____ feels toward me.

_____ 40. I believe that _____ has feelings s/he does not tell me about that affect our relationship.

Please double check and make sure that you have given an answer to every item. _Thank you for doing so._

Please note the other person's relation to you, e.g., a personal friend, spouse or partner, mother, or other family member, teacher or supervisor, counselor/therapist ....

....

Name or code ....   Answer date ....

Barrett-Lennard Relationship Inventory: Form MO–40 (version 3)

Developed by Godfrey T. Barrett-Lennard, PhD

Below are listed a variety of ways that one person may feel or behave in relation to another person.

    Please consider each statement with reference to your present relationship with _____, mentally inserting his or her name in the space provided. For example, if the other person's name was John, you would read the first statement as "I respect John as a person" and the second as "I usually sense or realize what John is feeling."

    Mark each statement in the left margin, according to how strongly you feel that it is true, or not true, in this relationship. Please be sure to mark every one. *Write in a minus number (–3, –2, or –1) when your answer is on the 'no' side, and a plus number (+1, +2, or +3) when your answer is a 'yes.'* Here is the exact meaning of each answer number:–

+3:   **YES,** *I strongly feel that it is true*   *–1:*   (No) *I feel that it is probably untrue, or more untrue than true*

+2:   Yes, *I feel it is true*   *–2:*   No, *I feel it is not true*

+1:   (Yes) *I feel that it is probably true, or more true than untrue*   *–3:*   **NO,** *I strongly feel that it is not true*

_____   1. I respect _____ as a person.

_____   2. I usually sense or realize how _____ is feeling.

_____   3. The interest I feel in _____ depends on his/her words and *actions*.

_____   4. I tend to put on a role or front with _____.

_____   5. I *like* _____.

_____   6. I hear _____ 's words but don't know how s/he feels inside.

_____   7. Whether _____ is feeling happy or unhappy with himself (herself) doesn't make me feel more or less positive toward him (her).

_____   8. I don't avoid or put off dealing with anything that matters between us.

_____   9. I feel indifferent to _____.

_____   10. I nearly always see exactly what _____ means.

_____   11. Depending on _____'s actions, I have a better opinion of him/her sometimes than I do at other times.

_____   12. I feel that I am genuinely myself with _____.

_____   13. I appreciate and value _____, as a person.

_____   14. My own feelings or attitude tend to get in the way of understanding _____.

_____   15. My liking or disliking of _____ isn't changed by anything s/he reveals or says about her/himself.

_____   16. I don't show my inner impressions and feelings with _____.

_____   17. I find _____ rather dull and uninteresting.

_____ 18. I can tell what _____ means, even when s/he has difficulty saying it.

_____ 19. I would like _____ to be a particular kind of person.

_____ 20. I'm willing to say whatever is in my mind with _____, including feelings that come up in me about either one of us, or how I see us getting along.

_____ 21. I care for _____.

_____ 22. I screen out and don't pick up on some of _____ 's feelings.

_____ 23. I like or respect certain things about him/her, and there are other things that really put me off.

_____ 24. I am able to be openly myself in our relationship.

_____ 25. I do feel disapproval of _____.

_____ 26. I usually can tune in and understand all of _____ 's meaning.

_____ 27. Whether _____ is expressing 'good' thoughts and feelings, or 'bad' ones, does not affect the way I feel toward him/her.

_____ 28. Sometimes I am not at all comfortable with _____ but we go on, outwardly ignoring it.

_____ 29. I feel friendly and warm toward _____.

_____ 30. I really don't understand _____.

_____ 31. I am quite pleased with _____ sometimes, and then s/he disappoints me at other times.

_____ 32. I know fully what I feel in relation to _____. I don't sense anything that's hard for me to admit to myself.

_____ 33. I put up with _____, as s/he is.

_____ 34. I appreciate just how _____ 's experiences _feel to him/her_.

_____ 35. Sometimes _____ seems to me a more worthwhile person than s/he does at other times.

_____ 36. There are times when my outward response to _____ is quite different from the way I feel underneath.

_____ 37. I feel affection for _____.

_____ 38. I respond to _____ rather automatically, not really taking in what _s/he is experiencing_.

_____ 39. The different things _____ says or does don't alter my feeling toward him/her.

_____ 40. I feel there are things that we don't bring up and talk about that are causing difficulty in our relationship.

Please double-check and make sure that you have given an answer to every item. _Thank you._

Please also note the other person's relation to you, e.g., personal friend, spouse/partner, mother, father or other family member, teacher or supervisor, client, counsellor. ....

....

Observer's name/code .... Person observed .... Answer date ....

Barrett-Lennard Relationship Inventory: Form Obs–40 (Version 3)
Developed by Godfrey T. Barrett-Lennard, PhD

Listed below are different ways that one person may feel and behave in relation to another. Please consider each numbered statement with reference to your present sense and perception of person A's (_____) attitude, feeling and way of relating to person B (_____). First, note in the spaces here who "A" and "B" are.

Try to suspend any reaction of approval or disapproval you may have in giving your own best sense and estimate of how A is responding to B, as you focus on each item-aspect. The 'right' answer is whatever is truest to your personal sense and view from what you have observed and have to go on.

Mark each statement in the left margin, according to how strongly you feel that it is true, or not true, in *this relationship. Please be sure to mark every one. Write in a minus number (–3, –2, or –1) when your answer is on the "no" side, and a plus number (+1, +2, or +3) when your answer is a "yes."* Here is the exact meaning of each answer number:–

+3: **YES,** *I strongly feel that it is true*

+2: Yes, *I feel it is true*

+1: (Yes) *I feel that it is probably true, or more true than untrue*

–1: (No) *I feel that it is probably untrue, or more untrue than true*

–2: No, *I feel it is not true*

–3: **NO,** *I strongly feel that it is not true*

_____ 1. A is personally respecting of _____ [write in name/identity of B, as above]

_____ 2. She/he senses or realizes how B is *feeling.*

_____ 3. Her/his interest in B depends on B's communication and style of behavior.

_____ 4. S/he assumes a role or front with B.

_____ 5. S/he evidently feels a responsive personal warmth and liking for B.

_____ 6. S/he reacts to B's words but does *not* see the way B feels inside

_____ 7. Whether B is feeling happy or unhappy *with him/herself* doesn't (or wouldn't) affect A's own feeling toward him/her.

_____ 8. S/he doesn't avoid or shy away from anything that's important in the relationship with B.

_____ 9. S/he is indifferent to B as a person.

_____ 10. S/he nearly always sees exactly what B means.

_____ 11. Depending on B's behavior, s/he has a better (or worse) opinion of B sometimes or at some moments than s/he has at other times/moments.

_____ 12. My sense is that s/he is genuine and honest with B.

_____ 13. The way that A responds conveys a personal appreciation and valuing of B.

_____ 14. A's personal reaction to something about B gets in the way of her/his understanding.

_____ 15. A's attitude and responsiveness (or lack of response) stays essentially the same no matter what feelings and self-qualities B expresses.

_____ 16. S/he keeps quiet about his/her own inner impressions and feelings with B.

_____ 17. S/he evidently finds B pretty dull and uninteresting.

_____ 18. S/he somehow grasps what B means even when B has difficulty in saying it.

_____ 19. S/he judges B's reactions and style, with definite preference for certain characteristics.

_____ 20. A is willing to say what is on her/his mind with B, including personal feelings and sense of how they are getting along.

_____ 21. S/he isn't going through motions; s/he *cares* about B.

_____ 22. S/he doesn't listen and pick up on what B actually thinks and feels.

_____ 23. S/he seems to like and respect B in some ways, but not to like other things about her/him.

_____ 24. S/he is personally straightforward and open in their relationship.

_____ 25. S/he disapproves of B – as s/he sees her/him.

_____ 26. S/he usually understands the whole of B's expression and meaning.

_____ 27. No matter whether B's feelings/reactions are 'good' or 'bad', healthy or unhealthy, her/his attention and response to B remains the same.

_____ 28. At some moments s/he is not comfortable, but they go on, outwardly ignoring it.

_____ 29. S/he is friendly and warm toward B.

_____ 30. S/he really doesn't understand B's experienced world and feelings.

_____ 31. Her/his reaction to B seems to range from acceptance to disapproval.

_____ 32. I sense that s/he is quite in touch with her/his own feelings and reactions with B; s/he is not covering up inside.

_____ 33. S/he just tolerates B, because that's part of her/his job or role.

_____ 34. S/he appreciates just how the things B is going through feel *to her/him.*

_____ 35. At some moments she warms to B and then at other times she seems cool or indifferent to what B expresses or feels.

_____ 36. Her/his outward response is different from my sense of the way she/he is feeling underneath.

_____ 37. S/he responds very warmly to B, even with a kind of affection.

_____ 38. Her/his response with B is so fixed and automatic that B does not get through to him/her.

_____ 39. Nothing B expresses alters A's basic attitude and felt response to her/him.

_____ 40. There are things going on but unspoken in their communication that make the relationship somewhat unreal.

Have you answered all the items, even ones that were not straightforward or where you had to go out on a limb a bit? Please double check and make sure there are no gaps. Add qualifying comments if you wish. (Godfrey T. Barrett-Lennard. Adapted 2007 from RI forms OS–40 & MO–40 (and a prior 64-item observer form)).

Barrett-Lennard Relationship Inventory: Scoring Sheet – 40-item OS, MO, and Obs–40 (adult) forms

Developed by Godfrey T. Barrett-Lennard, PhD

Name/code .... Date answered ....

Class of relationship .... Form: OS MO Obs40 (circle one) ....

Position of respondent .... Note if other RI data on same relationship ....

Enter the answer for each item in its space, below, after reversing the sign (from +to –, or – to +) for the item numbers shown in **bold**. *(The* **bold** *items are worded "negatively.")*

Level of Regard (R)		Empathy (E)		Unconditionality (U)		Congruence (C)	
Item No.	*Answer*	Item No.	*Answer*	Item No.	*Answer*	Item No.	*Answer*
1		2		**3**	Reverse sign	**4**	Reverse sign
5		**6**	Reverse sign	7		8	
9	Reverse sign	10		**11**	Reverse sign	12	
13		**14**	Reverse sign	15		**16**	Reverse sign
17	Reverse sign	18		**19**	Reverse sign	20	
21		**22**	Reverse sign	**23**	Reverse sign	24	
25	Reverse sign	26		27		**28**	Reverse sign
29		**30**	Reverse sign	**31**	Reverse sign	32	
33	Reverse sign	34		**35**	Reverse sign	**36**	Reverse sign
37		**38**	Reverse sign	39		**40**	Reverse sign
R Scale Score->		E Scale Score->		U Scale Score->		C Scale Score->	

Add the 10 values in each answer column to obtain the score for that scale, which might be a positive or negative number. The *possible* range of scale scores is –30 (or –3 × 10) to +30 (+3 × 10). If avoidance of negative values is necessary, add a constant of +30 to each obtained scale score, to yield 'converted scores' with a *possible* range of 0 to 60.

FORMS FOR TEACHER-STUDENT AND YOUNG CHILD RELATIONSHIPS

The BLRI form that follows next is designed for research with school students above a grade 5 reading level. It is believed to be suitable for use in the study of teacher to student relationships at least through junior high and to about grade 10. Compared to the basic 40- and 64-item forms for adults this young-student version is somewhat simpler in its language, and the items consistently refer to the teacher by her or his gender. The form as shown here is worded for female teachers. The twin form that is needed where reference teachers are male simply requires separately preparing for use after adjusting the pronouns to 'he' and 'him.' The small numbers in the right hand margin refer to the numbering of corresponding items in the 64-item form. The items most changed in formulation, though of the same or of very similar thrust, have an "r" after the number on the right hand side. Those reversed in wording valence have a minus sign in front of the small number. *The whole righthand column of small numbers is best deleted before reproducing the Inventory for use.*

In the parallel form for teachers, respondents rate their attitude and response to a whole class or other grouping of students. It is thus a distinctive MO type person-to-group form. The items are worded distinctively for teacher respondents though they follow in their thrust, item for item, those in the student form. Users of the teacher form may wish to contribute to its validation by also gathering other pertinent scaled data or qualitative information.

The separate form for *young child* respondents is open in respect to class of relationship. It accords with the student form in the idea content of each item though with further simplification of language and discrimination. The yes and no answers, scored +1 and −1, give a theoretical maximum range of −10 to +10 on each scale. Since the item composition and sequence corresponds to the student and teacher versions, the same scoring key works with all three forms in this group. A student worked with me to develop a more general "low literacy" form. I was not quite satisfied with the result, though it helped a bit in revising the original "Child" form – which remains the simplest version of the BLRI (and may be used with older respondents whose lack fluency in the level of English required for the adult forms). My estimate is that this requires at least an average third-grade reading and verbal comprehension level and the presence of an encouraging administrator who can be consulted about any difficulties. Even younger children may be able to give reliable answers verbally if the items are read out to them. The form may be preferred for primary school children generally, except where the present teacher-student forms are appropriate.

Name or code .... Answer date ....

Barrett-Lennard Relationship Inventory: Form OS–40: T-S (Student form) (version 3)

Developed by Godfrey T. Barrett-Lennard, PhD

- Before doing anything else, please write in your <u>first</u> name _____
- Below are listed different ways you might feel about your teacher: M _____

(Write in the teacher's name if it is not there already).

Each numbered statement might be true OR not true of the way *you see and feel* about your teacher. Write in on the left a plus number (+3, +2, or +1) to stand for "yes" answers, and a minus number (–1, –2, or –3) to stand for "no" answers. This is about *your experience* in relation to someone, and is not a test. Select the answer numbers that match *your own idea or sense* of what is true. *Be sure you write in a number beside every statement.* Here are the answers to choose from:

+3:	**YES,** I strongly feel that it *is true*		*–1:*	(No) I think it's *probably untrue.*
+2:	Yes, I feel it's mostly true.		*–2:*	No, I feel it mostly isn't true.
+1:	(Yes) I think it *might be true*		*–3:*	**NO,** I definitely feel it's *not true.*

		OS–64
_____ 1.	She respects me.	1
_____ 2.	She wants to know what I think and mostly can see what I mean.	10r
_____ 3.	Her interest in me depends on how well I learn and perform.	3
_____ 4.	I feel that she is genuine – talks to me (to us) straight.	12
_____ 5.	I'm a bother to her and she gets impatient and annoyed with me.	9
_____ 6.	She reacts to what I do, but doesn't understand how I feel and see things.	6r
_____ 7.	Whatever *my* mood is, her attitude with me stays the same.	7
_____ 8.	She keeps quiet about what she really thinks and feels inside.	36
_____ 9.	I'm just another student and don't matter to her.	17
_____ 10.	She sees what I mean (or am trying to say) *and* how I'm feeling as I say it.	10/18r
_____ 11.	Depending on how I behave, she has a better (or worse) opinion of *me*.	11
_____ 12.	She doesn't "beat about the bush" or avoid saying things.	28
_____ 13.	I feel she is pleased to see me.	13/41r
_____ 14.	She looks at things from her angle, never through my eyes.	22r
_____ 15.	No matter what I express, her feeling toward me stays the same.	39r
_____ 16.	It's like she's acting a part with me/with us.	8
_____ 17.	I feel she sees me as dull and uninteresting.	21
_____ 18.	She realizes what I mean even when I have trouble saying it.	30
_____ 19.	She wants me to be a *certain kind* of person.	19

_____ 20. She is open about her mood and what's on her mind. 44

_____ 21. She is concerned and cares about me. 25

_____ 22. She doesn't listen to me, or notice what I think and feel. 38

_____ 23. She doesn't/wouldn't change her mind about *me* when I succeed or fail. 11~

_____ 24. She just seems to be her real or natural self in our relationship. 48

_____ 25. I feel that she disapproves and looks down on me. 29

_____ 26. When I tell or ask her something, she truly sees what I mean. 34

_____ 27. If I say something I'm ashamed of, she still treats me the same. 39

_____ 28. Sometimes she's tense or uncomfortable, but goes on without mentioning it. 32

_____ 29. She's friendly and warm toward me. 37

_____ 30. She does *not* understand me. –54

_____ 31. I feel she is always judging us as 'good' or 'bad' (or, dumb or smart). –51

_____ 32. What she is thinking or feeling shows out in the open. –60

_____ 33. She tolerates or 'puts up' with me (feels she has to). 33

_____ 34. She listens to hear *me* properly and see my problem – or excitement. 42

_____ 35. *She sees* different things in me, some okay, some she doesn't approve of. 43

_____ 36. At times what she says out loud is different from the way I think she's feeling inside herself. 52

_____ 37. She responds very warmly; feels a sort of affection for me. 61

_____ 38. She reacts to me automatically, without listening or thinking about it. 58

_____ 39. I don't have to be cautious with her: I can come straight out without affecting her attitude toward me. 59r

_____ 40. She has concerns she doesn't show us, and I have to guess what she *really* wants or thinks. 64

Please go back and make sure that you have answered every single question. If there is another page, please fill that in too.

Thanks for helping us to understand more about how it is for students, with their teachers!

Name or code ....Student group ....Answer date ....

Barrett-Lennard Relationship Inventory: Form MO(G)–40: TS (for teachers)

Developed by Godfrey T. Barrett-Lennard, PhD

Below are listed various ways that one person may feel or behave in relation to others. Please consider each statement with reference to your present relationship with your students – in a particular class or group (note above, or your students generally if arranged).

Mark each statement in the left margin, according to how strongly you feel that it is true, or not true, in this relationship. Please be sure to mark every one. *Write in a minus number (–3, –2, or –1) when your answer is on the "no" side, and a plus number (+1, +2, or +3) when your answer is a "yes."* Here is the exact meaning of each answer number:–

+3: **YES,** *I strongly feel that it is true*

+2: Yes, *I feel it is true*

+1: (Yes) *I feel that it is probably true, or more true than untrue*

–1: (No) *I feel that it is probably untrue, or more untrue than true*

–2: No, *I feel it is not true*

–3: **NO,** *I strongly feel that it is not true*

		ref. MO–64
_____	1. I respect them individually.	1
_____	2. I like to know *their* ideas and nearly always see what they mean.	10
_____	3. The interest I feel in them depends on their behavior and how well they learn.	3r
_____	4. I feel that I am genuinely myself with them.	12
_____	5. I do at times get impatient and annoyed with them.	9
_____	6. I teach and manage the class group, but don't know how they feel inside.	6r
_____	7. Whatever mood they are in (such as pleased *or* unhappy with themselves), my own attitude toward them remains the same.	7
_____	8. I don't show my inner impressions and feelings, with them.	–36
_____	9. I have a job to do, but feel pretty much indifferent to them, personally.	17
_____	10. I usually do sense and realize how they feel about things.	10/18r
_____	11. Depending on their actions and effort, I have a better personal opinion of them sometimes than I do at other times.	11
_____	12. I'm "up front" with them. I am *not* avoiding anything – or expressing it indirectly, hoping they will get the message.	28r
_____	13. I feel personally interested and pleased to see them.	13/41r
_____	14. The classroom situation and my own reactions don't allow me to be sensitive to each one or see things from their angle.	22r

_____ 15. My liking or disliking of them isn't changed by anything they say or show about different sides of themselves. 39

_____ 16. I tend to put my real self on one side and play a role in front of them. 8

_____ 17. On the whole, I find the youngsters rather dull and uninteresting. 21

_____ 18. I see what *they mean*, even when they have difficulty saying it. 30

_____ 19. I have a definite idea or image of the kind of people I wish they would become. 19

_____ 20. I'm happy to acknowledge *my* mood, and say what is on my mind with them – whether it's about our classroom work or how we are getting along. 44

_____ 21. I feel concern and *caring* for them. 25

_____ 22. I screen out and ignore some of their feelings and ways they think. 38

_____ 23. How I feel toward a student doesn't change when he/she succeeds or fails. 31r

_____ 24. I am able to be openly myself in our relationship. 48

_____ 25. They are rather a sorry lot—on a lower or different level than I look for. 29r

_____ 26. I screen out and ignore some of their feelings and ways they think. 38

_____ 27. If any of them tell me things they are ashamed of, I might not like the behavior but it does not affect my attitude or basic feeling toward them. 39

_____ 28. Sometimes I'm tense or uncomfortable with them but I go on, outwardly ignoring it. 32

_____ 29. I feel friendly and warmly toward them. 37

_____ 30. They baffle me: I really don't understand them. –54

_____ 31. I feel some students are generally 'good,' others mostly 'bad,' and that some are smart, others are 'dumb.' –51

_____ 32. I'm pretty "transparent" with them. What I think and feel generally shows through. –60

_____ 33. I put up with them, since I have to. 33

_____ 34. I listen to hear their problems and ideas, including how they feel in class. 42

_____ 35. A student may do well, seem worthwhile and please me at one stage, then at another time he/she disappoints me. 43

_____ 36. My outward response to them can be quite different from the way I feel underneath. 52

_____ 37. It's more than a professional relation with my students; I feel a bond and affection for them. 61r

_____ 38. I know what to expect and often do react rather automatically, not listening each time or taking in what they think and feel. 58

_____ 39. Students don't have to be cautious with me: They can come straight out with things without affecting my attitude toward them. 59

_____ 40. I don't always show my own feelings and wishes, and unspoken things can cause difficulty in our relationship. 64

Code .... Date ....

Barrett-Lennard Relationship Inventory: Form OS–40CH (adapted from teacher-student and adult forms) (version 3)

Developed by Godfrey T. Barrett-Lennard, PhD

☺❄   ☺❄   ☺❄   ☺❄   ☺❄   ☺❄

Please start by writing your own first name here _____

- Down below is a list of ways one person might react and feel toward someone else. If you think about a person you know, you will be able to say which things are true and which ones are not true, in the way *you feel* they are with you.

- You need to be thinking of the same person as you answer all the questions. Please write on the next line the name you call that person by:_____.

- You can see each sentence below has a number, and a short line in front of the number. While you keep thinking about the other person, mark the short line to show whether you feel the sentence is true, or is not true. Put in a tick (✓) to stand for "yes" answers; and a cross (X) for "no" answers. Your answers are not checked right or wrong. They simply show how *you feel* that person is with you. Be sure to write in an answer in front of every number.

_____ 1. He respects me.

_____ 2. He wants to know what I think – how I look at things.

_____ 3. He thinks I'm okay sometimes, and other times he doesn't like the way I am.

_____ 4. He speaks true to me.

_____ 5. He gets annoyed or mad at me.

_____ 6. He reacts to what I do but doesn't see the way I feel.

_____ 7. If I'm happy or upset it doesn't change how he feels about me.

_____ 8. He keeps quiet about what he really feels.

_____ 9. He doesn't seem to care about me.

_____ 10. He can tell exactly what I mean.

_____ 11. He likes me better or worse, depending on the way I behave.

_____ 12. He shows or tells me what he really feels.

_____ 13. He is pleased to see me.

_____ 14. He just goes by *his* idea, and doesn't see what I think.

_____ 15. No matter what I tell him, he feels the same way about me.

_____ 16. He pretends, like an actor, and doesn't show what he truly feels.

_____ 17. He is not interested in me.

_____ 18. He sees or knows what I'm feeling.

_____ 19. He wants me to be a certain way.

_____ 20. He lets me see his mood and thoughts.

_____ 21. He really likes me.

_____ 22. He doesn't listen or notice what I feel.

_____ 23. He doesn't change his mind about me when I succeed or fail at something.

_____ 24. He shows how he really is with me.

_____ 25. He looks down on me – like I'm low and don't count.

_____ 26. He sees what I mean even when I can't quite say it.

_____ 27. If I tell what I'm guilty about, he still treats me the same.

_____ 28. He can be tense or uncomfortable but never mentions it.

_____ 29. He is warm and friendly with me.

_____ 30. He doesn't understand me – how I feel.

_____ 31. I feel he is always judging that I'm "good" or "bad."

_____ 32. What he is thinking or feeling shows out in the open.

_____ 33. He doesn't like me being around.

_____ 34. He listens to know what I mean.

_____ 35. Sometimes I please him, other times he doesn't approve of me.

_____ 36. What he says out loud is different from his inside feeling.

_____ 37. He cares for me in a loving way.

_____ 38. He reacts without really noticing or thinking about it.

_____ 39. I can say things straight out and he keeps the same feeling toward me.

_____ 40. I have to guess what he really wants or feels inside.

Please check and MAKE SURE that you have answered every sentence.

Thank you for sharing the way you feel!

Barrett-Lennard Relationship Inventory: Scoring sheet T-S and CH forms

Developed by Godfrey T. Barrett-Lennard, PhD

Date answered .... Type/class of relationship ....

Form: OS or MO (circle one) .... Position of respondent ....

Note if there are other RI data on same relationship ....

Enter the answer for each item in its space, below, changing the sign (from + to –, or – to +) if the item number is shown in **bold**, *as you go along. (The* **bold** *items are worded "negatively".)*

Level of Regard (R)		Empathy (E)		Unconditionality (U)		Congruence (C)	
Item No.	**Answer**	Item No.	**Answer**	Item No.	**Answer**	Item No.	**Answer**
1		2		**3**	Reverse sign	4	
5	Reverse sign	**6**	Reverse sign	7		**8**	Reverse sign
9	Reverse sign	10		**11**	Reverse sign	12	
13		**14**	Reverse sign	15		**16**	Reverse sign
17	Reverse sign	18		**19**	Reverse sign	20	
21		**22**	Reverse sign	23		24	
25	Reverse sign	26		27		**28**	Reverse sign
29		**30**	Reverse sign	**31**	Reverse sign	32	
33	Reverse sign	34		**35**	Reverse sign	36	Reverse sign
37		**38**	Reverse sign	39		**40**	Reverse sign
R Scale Score->		E Scale Score->		U Scale Score->		C Scale Score->	

The value of answer signs must be reversed for items shown in **bold.**

For T-S forms: Sum the (ten) resulting answer values in each column to obtain scale scores. The possible range is –30 (i.e., –3 × 10) to +30 (+3 × 10). (Negative values *could be* avoided by adding a constant of +30 to each total, to yield "converted scales scores" with a possible range of 0 to 60.

For CH forms: Child respondents tick the items for which their answer is "Yes" (counted as +1) OR put in a cross to indicate "No" (counted as –1). After appropriate reversal of answer signs the *possible* range is –10 to +10, to which a constant (+10) *could be* added to avoid any negative scale score values.

THE LIFE RELATIONSHIPS FORM

I referred to this substantial adaptation as the Relational Life Space form in Chapters 4 and 5 (see pp. 46, 59 & 62) in keeping with its earlier history, but I prefer the more indicative and simpler designation given here. It does not span all *levels* of human relationship I am now interested in (discussed in the later part of Chapter 9) but samples the vital interpersonal (face-to-face) relationships that people experience. Where an investigator is interested in these lived worlds of relationships this form can be a pertinent resource, and one that may also be helpful in selected practice contexts. It's a bigger more demanding task than other individual forms of the BLRI, as well as unique in the range of information it yields.

Three distinct documents are entailed and follow this page. The first is a detailed but hopefully clear "Directions" section. The multipage answer form follows, in which the items are virtually the same as those in the basic 40-item OS form. Last is the distinctive single page form on which to record and score the answers. It would be a big practical advantage if a suitably experienced investigator were to set the instrument up for computer administration and automatic scoring. A client who has a healing or otherwise fruitful therapy experience must, in the theory on which the BLRI is based, be receiving a deeper level of empathy and/or other measured qualities in the therapy relationship than in any of his/her current life relationships. This proposition would be testable using this form and the corresponding Other-to-Self (OS–40) form on the therapy relationship. Among other research applications the form would be relevant in studying loneliness or searching into the relative impoverishment or richness of life relationships in diverse social groups and cultures.

In order to accommodate the width of this form the relevant pages are presented landscape for ease of reproduction.

Barrett-Lennard Relationship Inventory: Form OS-LR-40

Developed by Godfrey T. Barrett-Lennard, PhD

DIRECTIONS

This questionnaire provides a means to describe the kind of world you live in in the area of relationships with other people. It is concerned with *your* experience of the attitudes, feelings, and behavior of others toward you, in your everyday life. The first step in responding to the questionnaire is to *pick out and note which relationships you will be describing*. Guidelines for this are given below. The second step is to consider each of the statements in the Answer Section and record how true or untrue you feel it is, in each relationship. A more detailed explanation follows.

RELATIONSHIP STATEMENTS AND ANSWER SCHEME

If you turn to the Answer Section you will see that each statement with a number in front contains a blank space, where a word has been left out. The spaces stand for the other person(s) in a relationship with you. The name to put in these blank spaces would differ for each relationship, and can be added mentally as you go along.

You will notice that there are 11 columns to the right of the statements. All your answers within the same column (column 2, say) refer to the same relationship – to be written in under the number at the top of that column. Your answers go in the boxes opposite each statement. Every time, select the answer that's closest to the way you feel and write in its number. There are three positive numbers (+3, +2, and +1) that stand for "Yes" answers of different strength, and three negative numbers (–1, –2, and –3) that stand for "No" answers. Here are the six answers to choose from:

YES answers	NO answers
+3: **YES**, *I strongly feel it is true*	–1: (No) *I feel it is probably untrue, or more untrue than true*
+2: *Yes, I feel it is true*	–2: *No, I feel it is not true*
+1: (Yes) *I feel that it is probably true, or more true than untrue*	–3: **NO**, *I strongly feel that it is not true*

GUIDELINES FOR CHOOSING AND IDENTIFYING THE RELATIONSHIPS TO DESCRIBE

Our relationships with other people can be arranged in three broad groups: (1) relationships with family members; (2) friend and acquaintance relationships; and (3) relations with people we know at work or as a result of special interests or public responsibilities.

1. *FAMILY MEMBERS* can include parents, brothers and sisters, spouse or partner, one's own children, grandparents, and/or other close relatives. Please select and show on the Answer Section the relationships you *will be* describing, as follows:

   Parents. Use column **1** for your relationship with whomever you call Mum/mom/mother or Dad/father: If there is no parent figure now in your life, go by your memory of them if this does not upset you. If *both* of your parents are living choose either one and enter the name you call them by. If you would rather describe your parents' response *together*, write "my parents" at the top of the column, and mentally substitute 'they' and 'them' for 'he/she' and 'him/her,' as you answer. If you have a quite different relationship with each parent, column 5 is available for any other family relationship you choose, and could be used for your second parent. Do not use **column 2** for a parent.

Brother/sister. Use column **2** to describe the relationship with the brother or sister – if you have any living – who is nearest to you in age. Write in 'brother' or 'sister' *and* the name you call them by, at the top of the column. (If you have no brother or sister, leave this column blank.)

Spouse/partner. If you are married, or have an intimate partner that you live with, use column **3** for your relationship with them. Otherwise leave the column blank). Write in "husband," "wife," "partner," etc., *and* the name you call them by, at the top of the column. (*Friend* relationships fit in later.)

Son/daughter. Use column **4**, if you have any children (otherwise leave the column blank), for the relationship with your *oldest child*. Write in 'son' or 'daughter,' and their first name or initial, at the top of the column.

Other relative/family member. Column **5** may be used for your relationship with another relative who is important in your life, *or* a further member of your immediate family, Write in the kind of relationship ('grandmother,' for example) under the number "5."

2. *FRIENDS AND PERSONAL ACQUAINTANCES* may include individuals of either sex and people you link up with in a group, by personal choice.

Use column **6** for a particular *same sex friend*. Write in your friend's first name or initial as an aid to keep her/him clearly in mind. If you have no one particular friend, answer for the way friends or acquaintances of the same sex most often respond to you. Write in a name for them and mentally substitute 'they' and 'them' for 'he/she' and 'him/her', as you answer.

Using column **7**, proceed in the same way as just above, either for a particular friend, *or* for your friends and acquaintances generally, of the *opposite sex*. Again, write in the relationship (and name) at the top.

Reserve column **8** to describe the way that members of a *group you belong to* relate to you. Choose a group that is important to you – say, a sports club or team, a church group, neighborhood group, a support or growth group. Note at the top the name or kind of group it is. Again, imagine 'they' and 'them' in place of 'she/he' and 'her/him', etc. (If you do not belong to any self-chosen group leave this column blank.)

3. *PEOPLE IN YOUR WORK OR PUBLIC LIFE* fall in three groupings, defined broadly so that they apply to most people, employed or not:

Use column **9** for your relationship with people in your *work* group or team, or your immediate colleagues, fellow-students, or co-workers in a volunteer organization. In answering think about the way this set of people generally respond or treat you.

Use column **10** specifically for relationship with *your boss* or *supervisor*, the person you report to, or your main teacher or professor, for example. If you are employed focus on your employment supervisor or boss, unless you have only slight contact with them. Show the position of the person.

Use the final column (**11**), if it applies, for your relationship with *persons working under you* or assisting you, your students if you are a teacher, *or* your clients, patients or constituents whom you know on a face-to-face basis. Again, you may need to mentally substitute 'they' and 'them' for s/he and him/her, in answering the items. Be sure to note the kind of group at the top.

ADVICE ON COMPLETING THE QUESTIONNAIRE

- After you have finished planning and recording – at the top of the columns – the full set of relationships you are going to describe, refer back to the three possible 'yes' and three 'no' answer choices listed on the first page of the Directions.

- The next step is to go down the whole list of 40 items, putting in column 1 all your answers just for that relationship. By the time you have done this, you will be familiar with the answering system and the items.

- We suggest that you then go back to the start and answer one item at a time across the page for your remaining family relationships. Then start at the top again for the groupings of friend and work relations.

This Inventory is about your life with other people, your world of relationships as they are to you. This means there are no generally 'correct' answers. What matters, at each step, is how *you experience and see* the other person's attitude and response to you. You will need to concentrate to get all your answers in the right rows and columns. Because there are so many answers to give, you might need a break along the way!

If you have problems or questions, speak to the person who has given you this questionnaire. When you are quite clear about what to do, and have shown what each selected relationship is at the top of the columns you are ready to begin answering. Remember, please start by going right through the form, answering for one relationship only. After that, come back to the beginning, and answer across the page, one item at a time, for your remaining family relationships. Then, go back and answer for your friend relationships and for your work relationships.

Barrett-Lennard Relationship Inventory: Form OS-LR–40 Answer Section

Developed by Godfrey T. Barrett-Lennard, PhD

Statements regarding the other person's response or attitude	1 Mother and/or Father	2 Brother or Sister	3 Spouse/ Partner	4 Son/ Daughter	5 Other relative	6 Same sex friend	7 Opposite sex friend	8 Personal group	9 'Work' group	10 Boss/ Supervisor	11 Clients or ? ....
			Family relationships				*Friendships*			*'Work' relations*	
1. ____ respects me											
2. ____ usually sees or senses what I am feeling.											
3. ____'s interest in me depends on my words and actions (or how I perform)											
4. I feel ____ puts on a role or front with me											
5. ____ feels a true liking for me											
6. ____ reacts to my words but does not see the way I feel											
7. Whether I am feeling happy or unhappy with myself makes no real difference to the way ____ feels about me											
8. ____ does *not* avoid anything that's important for our relationship. (Answer "no" if you feel s/he does avoid an important issue.)											
9. ____ is indifferent to me											
10. ____ nearly always can see exactly what I mean											
11. Depending on my behavior, ____ has a better (or worse) opinion of me sometimes than at other times											
12. I feel that ____ is genuine with me											
13. I feel valued and appreciated by ____											

Relationships (write in)

(Continued)

Statements regarding the other person's response or attitude	Relationships (write in)										
	1 Mother and/or Father ……	2 Brother or Sister ……	3 Spouse/ Partner ……	4 Son/ Daughter ……	5 Other relative ……	6 Same sex friend ……	7 Opposite sex friend ……	8 Personal group …… ……	9 'Work' group …… ……	10 Boss/ Supervisor …… ……	11 Clients or ? ……
	Family relationships					*Friendships*			*'Work' relations*		
14. _____'s own attitude toward things I do or say gets in the way of understanding me											
15. No matter what I reveal about myself, _____ likes (or dislikes) me just the same											
16. _____ keeps quiet about his (her) real impressions and feelings											
17. _____ finds me rather dull and uninteresting											
18. _____ realizes what I mean even when I have difficulty in saying it											
19. _____ wants me to be a particular kind of person											
20. _____ is willing to express whatever is on his/her mind with me, including feelings about either of us or how we get along											
21. _____ cares for me											
22. _____ doesn't pick up on what I think and feel											
23. _____ likes certain things about me and there are other things he/she does not like											
24. _____ is openly himself (herself) in our relationship											
25. I feel that _____ disapproves of me											
26. _____ usually understands the whole of what I mean											
27. Whether thoughts I express are 'good' or 'bad' makes no difference to _____'s feelings toward me											

28. Sometimes _____ is not at all comfortable but we go on, outwardly ignoring it										
29. _____ is friendly and warm toward me										
30. _____ does *not* understand me										
31. _____ approves of some things about me (some of my ways) and disapproves of other ways I am or express myself										
32. I think _____ always knows exactly what s/he is feeling with me (S/he doesn't cover up inside, not seeing his/her own feelings)										
33. _____ just tolerates or puts up with me										
34. _____ appreciates exactly how the things I experience feel to me										
35. Sometimes I am more worthwhile in _____'s eyes than I am at other times										
36. At moments I feel that _____'s outward response to me is quite different from the way he/she feels underneath										
37. _____ feels real affection for me										
38. _____'s response to me is so fixed and automatic that I don't get through to him/her										
39. I don't think that anything I say or do really changes the way _____ feels toward me										
40. I believe that _____ has feelings he/she does not tell me about, that affect our relationship										

Reminder: Please check to make sure that you have completely filled in all of the relationship columns you have used. It's important to include an answer for every item, *leaving no gaps.*

Through this work we are attempting to add to knowledge to the field of human relationships, and appreciate your contribution to this work through the time and care it takes to respond to this questionnaire. *Thank you for doing this!*

LIFE RELATIONSHIPS FORM (OS-LR–40)

Barrett-Lennard Relationship Inventory: Scoring Sheet Form OS-LR-40

Developed by Godfrey T. Barrett-Lennard, PhD

Name/code ....

Test date ....

Level of Regard (R) scale

Item data for each relationship (r)
Negatively worded items in **bold** and shaded spaces – require reversal of answer signs

Item # & sign ⇒	r1	r2	r3	r4	r5	r6	r7	r8	r9	r10	r11
1+											
5+											
9–											
13+											
17–											
21+											
25–											
29+											
33–											
37+											
Sum =>											

Empathy (E) scale

Item data for each relationship (r)
Negatively worded items in **bold** and shaded spaces – reversal of answer signs

Item # & sign ⇒	r1	r2	r3	r4	r5	r6	r7	r8	r9	r10	r11
2+											
6–											
10+											
14–											
18+											
22–											
26+											
30–											
34+											
38–											
Sum =>											

Unconditionality (U) scale

Item data for each relationship (r)
Negatively worded items in **bold** and shaded – reversal of answer signs

Item no. & sign ⇓	r1	r2	r3	r4	r5	r6	r7	r8	r9	r10	r11
3–											
7+											
11–											
15+											
19–											
23–											
27+											
31–											
35–											
29+											
Sum =>											

Congruence (C) scale

Item data for each relationship (r)
Negatively worded items in **bold** and shaded – require reversal of answer signs

Item no. & sign ⇓	r1	r2	r3	r4	r5	r6	r7	r8	r9	r10	r11
4–											
8+											
12+											
16–											
20+											
24+											
28–											
32+											
36–											
40–											
Sum =>											

FORMS FOR RELATIONSHIPS WITH AND BETWEEN GROUPS AND WITH ORGANIZATIONS

Barrett-Lennard Relationship Inventory (BLRI) forms of 64 items adapted for the case where one party to the relationship is a group have been used in reported research (see Chapter 3, p. 32; Ch. 5, pp. 57–58). I now consider these to be out of date and the versions that follow are each of 40 items that correspond in content with the primary OS–40 forms. Those that tap "my perception of the group's response to me" have precedent in previous versions and are deemed available for use without further validation. The version for *group-with-group relationships* has interesting potential, but is untried in research and thus provisional in some of the details and in need of further validation. Another investigator could make careful minor changes, for example, to item wordings or instructions, without adjustment to my authorship. More substantial amendments, for example, to the total number, selection and/or category of items, would lead to a designation such as "after Barrett-Lennard". In this case, I also suggest giving footnote indication on the actual form of the name of the user-editor and date of his/her modification.

A draft form for organization-with-member relationships (Form OrgS–40) is also included. This also is untried in research and I recommend that an informed user (e.g., an organizational psychologist or related consultant) test the form in a small-scale pilot study with a view to minor amendments before extended application. The wording of items has already been considerably adapted and before making further adjustments a user needs to be well versed in the underlying theory and distinction between scales.

A scoring key does not follow these forms since it is the same as the score form already given for the basic 40-item forms (see p. 122). However, the scale measures need to be understood in context. They have meanings adapted to those contexts as discussed in Chapter 9 (pp. 93–96).

Today's date ....   Your name or code ....

Barrett-Lennard Relationship Inventory: Form GS–40 (version 2, adapted from forms OS-G–64 and OS–40)

Developed by Godfrey T. Barrett-Lennard, PhD

Below are listed various ways that one could experience the other members of a group as feeling and behaving toward oneself. There are many kinds of face-to-face or small groups and we ask you at the end of this form to spell out the kind of group your answers below are about.

Please consider each numbered statement with reference to the way the other people in this group typically are with you. Answer each item separately, to show how you really see their response to you. Don't worry about whether your reply fits your answer to any other item or applies to every single member. This questionnaire is about *your sense* of the other people's response, attitude, or reaction to you, in the group. Thus there are no generally 'correct' answers.

Mark each statement in the answer column on the right, to show how much you feel it is true, or is not true. *Please be sure to mark every one.* Write in a positive number (+3, +2, or +1), or a negative number (–1, –2, or –3), to stand for one of the following answers:

+3: YES, *I strongly feel that it **is true**.*

+2: Yes, *I feel it is true.*

+1: (Yes) *I feel that it is probably true, or more true than untrue.*

–1: (No) *I feel that it is probably untrue, or more untrue than true*

–2: No, *I feel it is not true.*

–3: NO, I *strongly feel that it is **not true**.*

ANSWER

1. I feel they respect me as a person. .... _____
2. They want to understand how I see things. .... _____
3. Their interest in me depends on my words and actions (or how I perform). .... _____
4. I feel that they put on a role or front with me. .... _____
5. They feel a true liking for me. .... _____
6. They react to my words but they don't see the way I *feel*. .... _____
7. How *I'm feeling* at the time in or about myself – maybe okay or out of sorts – makes no real difference to *their* feeling about me in response. .... _____
8. They don't avoid or go round anything that matters between us .... _____
9. They are indifferent to me. .... _____
10. They nearly always see exactly what I mean. .... _____
11. Depending on what I do and express, their opinion *of me* goes up or down. .... _____
12. I feel that they are open and genuine with me. .... _____
13. I know that I'm valued and appreciated by them. .... _____
14. Their own attitudes toward things I say or do get in the way of understanding me. ..... _____
15. No matter what I say about myself, they like (or dislike) me just the same. .... _____
16. They mostly keep quiet about their real inner impressions and feelings. .... _____
17. They see me as rather dull and uninteresting. .... _____

18. They realize what I mean even when I have difficulty saying it. .... _____

19. They want me to be a particular kind of person. .... _____

20. They generally are willing to say whatever they think with me, including feelings about how we are getting along. .... _____

21. They care for/about me as a person .... _____

22. They don't listen and pick up on what I think and feel. .... _____

23. They like or accept certain things about me, and there are other things they don't like in me .... _____

24. They are openly themselves in our relationship .... _____

25. I feel that they disapprove of me .... _____

26. They usually understand my whole meaning .... _____

27. Whether personal feelings or ideas I express are 'good' or 'bad' makes no difference to their feeling toward me. .... _____

28. Sometimes they are not at all comfortable but we go on, outwardly ignoring it. .... _____

29. They are friendly and warm toward me. .... _____

30. They don't understand me. .... _____

31. They approve or go along with some things about me and plainly disapprove of other things about me (or ways I act and express myself). .... _____

32. I think they always know exactly what they feel with me; they don't cover up within themselves. .... _____

33. They just tolerate or put up with me. .... _____

34. They are able to appreciate exactly how things I experience feel to me. .... _____

35. Sometimes I am more worthwhile in their eyes than I am at other times. .... _____

36. At moments I feel that their outward response to me is quite different from the way they feel underneath. .... _____

37. I feel they enjoy me, even with a kind of affection. .... _____

38. Their response to me is so fixed and automatic that I don't get through to them. .... _____

39. Things I say and do don't shift the way they feel toward me. .... _____

40. I believe they have feelings that aren't expressed that affect our relationship. .... _____

Please tell us what kind of group this is, and your own position or role in it: Is it, for example, a personal development or therapy group, is it a work team or staff/colleague group, are the members classmates or in a study group, is it a working committee with particular responsibility, is it a group with some special or even dangerous mission, is it a group on a spiritual path (church or other), or is it a whole family? *Please write in the kind of group and its size (approx. number of people)*:

....

In accord with the kind if group it is, please briefly say what your own position, role, or category is:

_____

How long have you been in this group? .... Your age .... and gender ....

Thank you for completing this form, and helping in our research!

Your name/code ....   Today's date ....

Your group ....   Their group ....

Barrett-Lennard Relationship Inventory: Form GG–40

(adapted by Godfrey T. Barrett-Lennard from forms OS–40 and GS–40)

Below are listed various ways that one group could experience the response of another group (or family, etc.) in their general attitude, feeling, and behavior toward the first group.

Please consider each numbered statement with reference to the way the other group of people typically are with your group. (Be sure to fill in the top of this page, and further information about the groups at the end.) Answer each item separately, to show how you really see their response. Don't worry about whether your reply fits your answer to any other item. This questionnaire is about *your experience and perceptions*, and there are no 'right' or 'wrong' answers.

Mark each statement in the answer column on the right, to show how much you feel it is true, or is not true. *Please be sure to mark every one.* Write in a positive number (+3, +2, or +1), or a negative number (–1, –2, or –3), to stand for one of the following answers:

+3: YES, I strongly feel that it **is true**.

+2: Yes, I feel it is true.

+1: (Yes) I feel that it is probably true, or more true than untrue.

–1: (No) I feel that it is probably untrue, or more untrue than true

–2: No, I feel it is not true.0

–3: NO, I strongly feel that it is **not true**.

ANSWER

1. The membership of their group respects us as a group. .... _____

2. Generally, they want to understand and be in touch with how *we* view things. .... _____

3. Their response to us depends on how our group presents itself and performs. .... _____

4. I feel that their group puts on a role or front with us. .... _____

5. I think they generally like our group. .... _____

6. They react to our words or practices without seeing what these mean or how we feel in our group. .... _____

7. The ups and downs of how happy or satisfied *we feel* in and with our group doesn't affect *their* view and feeling towards us. .... _____

8. They are willing to face and explore anything that matters between our groups. .... _____

9. As a group they are indifferent to us. .... _____

10. They nearly always see and understand messages and actions of our group. .... _____

11. Depending on how our group is doing, they have a better (or worse) opinion of us. .... _____

12. I feel that their group is open and genuine in relations with our group. .... _____

13. I know that as a group we are valued and appreciated by them. .... _____

14. Their group's attitudes toward our group get in the way of understanding us. .... _____

15. No matter what we disclose or show from our group, their same response holds. .... _____

16. They keep quiet about their group's real intentions and feelings. .... _____

17. I believe they see us as a rather dull and uninteresting lot. .... _____

18. They seem to realize what we mean even if we have difficulty conveying it. .... _____

19. They want us to have particular qualities in our group's outlook and activity. .... _____

20. They are generally willing to express whatever they think about us, including any problems they see. .... _____

21. They have a caring interest in our group. .... _____

22. They don't listen and pick up on what our group thinks. .... _____

23. They accept certain things about our group, and there are other things they reject or don't like. .... _____

24. Their group's membership is open in its expression and dialogue with us. .... _____

25. I feel that they disapprove of us or what we stand for as a group. .... _____

26. They usually understand the whole of what we convey and mean in communications between our groups .... _____

27. Whether our group is deemed 'good' or 'bad' in its own working makes no difference to their feelings and response to us. .... _____

28. I think that they are not at all comfortable with our group but prefer to go on, outwardly ignoring it. .... _____

29. They are most responsive and friendly in relations with our group. .... _____

30. Their members don't understand our group.................................. _____

31. They approve or go along with some things about our group and disapprove of some other things. [Only say 'yes' if you feel these are both true.] .... _____

32. I think they are open to their experience with our group and see clearly how they actually feel about us. .... _____

33. As a group they just tolerate or put up with the presence of our group. .... _____

34. They seem able to appreciate exactly what our group's view is. .... _____

35. Sometimes our group is more worthwhile or acceptable in their eyes than the way they regard us at other times. .... _____

36. I sense at moments that their outward behavior toward our group is quite different from their private response. .... _____

37. The membership of their group tends to radiate a warm regard toward our group. ..... _____

38. Their response to us as a group appears so fixed and automatic that we can't get our ideas or perspective through to them. .... _____

39. We needn't worry about varied views and reactions coming to them from our group. Their group's attitude and response to us doesn't change. .... _____

40. I believe their group has views and feelings toward our group that aren't expressed, but which affect our relation with them. .... _____

Please add the following information about your own and the other group in this relationship:

Your group

What is your group's position in this context? Are you, for example, another parallel group in the same organization; or does your group have a different kind of responsibility or status? What is the position and role of your group, as best you can say in sentence or two?

_____
_____
_____
_____
_____
_____

The other group

Who are the other group? What is their role or position? Are they similar or unlike yours in their nature and function? Does the history of your own and the other group have particular bearing on their relationship? Please answer briefly.

_____
_____
_____
_____
_____
_____

Today's date .... *[WORKING VERSION]*   Your name or code ....

Barrett-Lennard Relationship Inventory: Form OrgS–40
(version 1 adapted by Godfrey T. Barrett-Lennard from related BLRI forms)

Below are listed various ways that individuals in an organization could experience the organization's response as a people system (of many members with diverse roles).

Please consider each numbered statement with reference to the way this organization of people typically is with you. (First, what is the system? Please write in _____). Answer each item separately, to show how you really see this organization's response to you as a member person. Don't worry about whether your reply fits your answer to any other item. This questionnaire is about *your own experience and perceptions*, which are the only 'right' answers.

Mark each statement in the answer column on the right, to show how much you feel it is true, or is not true. *Please be sure to mark every one.* Write in a plus number (+3, +2, *or* +1), or a minus number (–1, –2, *or* –3), to stand for one of the following answers:

+3: YES, *I strongly feel that it is **true**.*

+2: Yes, *I feel it is true.*

+1: (Yes) *I feel that it is probably true, or more true than untrue.*

–1: (No) *I feel that it is probably untrue, or more untrue than true*

–2: No, *I feel it is not true.*

–3: NO, I *strongly feel that it is **not true**.*

	ANSWER
1. I feel respected within my organization.	_____
2. The organization wants to understand how its members, including myself, see things and what's important to us.	_____
3. Their interest in me depends on what I do, especially on how I perform..................	_____
4. I feel that the organization puts on a front and image of how it wants to be seen even by its members.	_____
5. The organization has a kind of personality and I feel liked and supported by it...........	_____
6. The organization may respond to some messages but has no ability to see or take account of the way its members *feel*.	_____
7. How I feel in and about myself or my strengths makes no difference to the way the organization views me.	_____
8. This system is straightforward and without pretense in relation to its members	_____
9. The organization is indifferent to me as a member-person.	_____
10. They (the organization or its leadership) nearly always see what I mean in my communications.	_____
11. Depending on what I do and express, they make a more positive or negative appraisal of me.	_____

12. I feel that the organization is open and transparent in my association with it. .... _____

13. I know that I'm valued and appreciated by this organization. .... _____

14. Their policies and attitudes give very little room for understanding me as a person. .... _____

15. No matter what I express about myself, the system responds in the same way. .... _____

16. The organization tends to conceal its inner values and ambitions. .... _____

17. The organization treats me like an unthinking, uninteresting cog in a machine. .... _____

18. I feel that messages from me generally get through in the system even
    when my meaning is difficult to express. .... _____

19. The organization wants me to fit in as a particular kind of person. .... _____

20. I feel a climate of openness on all matters, including my relation and role here. .... _____

21. The organization has no caring interest in me or my well-being. .... _____

22. I don't feel listened to and understood around my ideas and what I feel. .... _____

23. I feel accepted in what I bring, in some aspects, and that there are other
    things about me that aren't liked or valued in this system. .... _____

24. The organization is openly itself, without pretense, in my association with it. .... _____

25. I feel disapproved of in and by this system. .... _____

26. I usually feel understood in what I convey within the organization. .... _____

27. Whether ideas of feelings I express are 'good' or 'bad' makes no difference
    here in whether I'm regarded favorably or not. .... _____

28. Sometimes I feel marked tensions and stress in the organization, but it goes
    on as though nothing was wrong. .... _____

29. I experience an atmosphere here of friendly warmth. .... _____

30. I don't feel understand generally in this organizational environment. .... _____

31. I feel a certain valuing here of some things I do and represent, and a disinterest
    or disapproval toward other things about my activity or style. .... _____

32. I think people here know clearly what they feel in relations with me;
    they don't cover up or fool themselves. .... _____

33. Generally I feel that others in the organization just tolerate or put up with me............ _____

34. People here seem able to see or catch on to how things *look and feel to me*. .... _____

35. Whether I'm seen as a worthwhile or valued member shifts and changes...................... _____

36. At moments I feel that outward responses to me here are quite different
    from the way the same people feel underneath. .... _____

37. I almost feel enjoyed or regarded with affection in the organization. .... _____

38. The often fixed and automatic response of people here means that I don't really
    feel in touch and able to get through to them. .... _____

39. The different things I say and do evidently don't change the way 'bosses'
    or other members regard me. .... _____

40. I believe there are perceptions and feelings that are not expressed that
    affect my relations in the organization. .... _____

Please put your answers in context by adding information, as follows:

What is your position in the system and
your main role or task?

What kind or class of organization is this?

....

....

Please also note the position of the person or
group you report to:

Approx. size (numbers) in this system, (1) overall
and (2) in the division or branch of your work?

....

(1)............................... (2).....................

How long have you been a member and
has your position or job changed?

Where is the organization based (if you know)?

....

....

[These questions after Item 40 are tentative and open to variation]

THE OS AND MO ADAPTATIONS FOCUSED ON *EMPATHIC UNDERSTANDING*

As indicated in the outline of studies in Chapter 5, and noted in Chapter 9, many investigators have focused specifically on the empathy scale and measure from the Relationship Inventory. It is possible that if the empathy items are presented consecutively by themselves that some respondents will be influenced by what I call a 'consistency response bias'. It can be more difficult to answer each item in its own right, without consideration of any other answers. Thus the arrangement of the new form that follows, containing a strong complement of 12 empathy items separated by a mix of items from the other scales. Rather than a random selection there are four selected items (in both positive and negative wording) from each of the further three scales. These can be treated merely as filler statements or used to give an approximation of the other measures, single or combined. Although this exact form is quite new, it seems a reasonable assumption that at least the empathy component 'borrows' reliability and validity from the same scale in the basic 4-scale BLRI forms.

The empathy form as presented here does not identify any particular class of personal (dyadic) relationship but the instructions at the top could be amended slightly to, for example, specify that the other person in the relationship is the respondent's counsellor or therapist (or other particular category). If/when this is done, some investigators also have put a term such as "my therapist" in the blank spaces within the actual items.

In all, I commend this new form to investigators who wish to focus specifically or mainly on the measure of empathic understanding and would be pleased to hear of their experience and response to its availability.

Your first name/initials/code .... The other person .... Answer date ....

Barrett-Lennard Relationship Inventory: Form OS-Emp+

Developed by Godfrey T. Barrett-Lennard, PhD

Below are listed a variety of ways that one person may feel or behave in relation to another person.

Please consider each statement with reference to your present relationship with _____. Think of him or her ('seeing' their name in the blank spaces) as you answer each numbered statement.

Mark each statement with a number, out in the left margin, according to how strongly you feel that it is true, or not true, in this relationship. Answer each item as though it was by itself, not to agree with another answer. Please be sure to mark every one. *Write in a minus number (–3, –2, or –1)* when your answer is on the 'no' side', and a plus number *(+1, +2, or +3)* when your answer is a grade of 'yes'. Here is the meaning of each answer number:

–3: NO, I *strongly feel* that it is *not true*.
–2: No, I feel it is not true.
–1: (No) I feel that it is *probably untrue*, or more untrue than true.
+1: (Yes) I feel that it is *probably true*, or more true than untrue.
+2: Yes, I feel it is true.
+3: YES, I *strongly feel* that it *is true*.

_____

_____ 1. _____ respects me.

_____ 2. _____ usually senses or realizes what I am feeling.

_____ 3. _____'s interest in me depends on how I present myself or perform.

_____ 4. _____ reacts to my words but does not see the way I feel.

_____ 5. I feel that _____ puts on a role or front with me.

_____ 6. _____ nearly always sees exactly what I mean.

_____ 7. _____ is friendly and warm toward me.

_____ 8. _____ appreciates just how the things I experience *feel* to me.

_____ 9. _____ finds me rather dull and uninteresting.

_____ 10. _____ does not understand me.

_____ 11. I feel that _____ is genuine with me.

_____ 12. _____'s *own attitude* toward things I do or say gets in the way of understanding me.

_____ 13. No matter what I say about myself, _____ likes (or dislikes) me just the same.

_____ 14. _____ realizes what I mean even when I have difficulty in saying it.

_____ 15. _____ expresses his/her true inner impressions and feelings with me.

_____ 16. _____ doesn't listen and pick up on what I think and feel.

_____ 17. _____ wants me to be a particular kind of person.

_____ 18. _____ usually understands the whole of what I mean.

_____ 19. Whether I express 'good' thoughts or 'bad' feelings/desires makes (or would make) no difference to his/her attitude toward me. (Answer 'no' if this does make a difference to his/her attitude.)

_____ 20. _____ doesn't realize how sensitive I am about some of the things we discuss. (Answer with one of the 'no' ratings if you feel s/he *is aware* of your sensitivity.)

_____ 21. I feel that _____ does not like me.

_____ 22. _____'s response to me is so fixed and automatic that I don't get through to him/her.

_____ 23. I believe that _____ has feelings s/he does not tell me about that affect our relationship.

_____ 24. When I am hurting or upset _____ recognizes my painful feelings without becoming upset him/herself.

Please check that you answered every item. *Thank you.*

(Form adapted by Godfrey T. Barrett-Lennard, 2012)

Your first name or code .... The other person .... Answer date ....

Barrett-Lennard Relationship Inventory: Form MO-Emp+

Developed by Godfrey T. Barrett–Lennard, PhD

Below are listed a variety of ways that one person may feel or behave in relation to another person.

Please consider each statement with reference to your present relationship with _____ [add first name]. Think of him or her ("seeing" their name in the blank spaces) as you answer each numbered statement.

Mark each statement in the left margin, according to how strongly you feel that it is true, or not true, in this relationship. Answer each item as though it was by itself, not to agree with another answer. Be sure to mark every one. Write in a negative number (–3, –2, or –1) when your answer is on the "no" side, and a positive number (+1, +2, or +3) when your answer is a grade of "yes.". Here is the meaning of each answer number:

–3: NO, I *strongly feel* that it is *not true*.
–2: No, I feel it is not true.
–1: (No) I feel that it is *probably untrue*, or more untrue than true.
+1: (Yes) I feel that it is *probably true*, or more true than untrue.
+2: Yes, I feel it is true.
+3: YES, I *strongly feel* that it *is true*.

_____ 1. I respect _____ as a person.

_____ 2. I usually sense and realize how _____ is feeling.

_____ 3. My interest in _____ depends on his/her actions and performance.

_____ 4. I can hear or react to _____'s words without sensing the way s/he feels inside.

_____ 5. I tend to put on a role or front with _____.

_____ 6. I nearly always can see exactly what _____ means.

_____ 7. I feel friendly and warm toward _____.

_____ 8. I appreciate just how _____'s experiences feel to her/him.

_____ 9. I find _____ rather dull and uninteresting.

_____ 10. I really *don't* understand _____.

_____ 11. I feel genuinely myself with _____.

_____ 12. My own feelings or attitude get in the way of understanding _____.

_____ 13. My liking or disliking of _____ isn't changed by anything s/he says about her/himself. (Answer on the 'no' side if your feeling does change.)

_____ 14. I can tell what _____ means even when he/she has difficulty saying it.

_____ 15. I can express my true inner impressions and feeling with _____.

_____ 16. I don't (or can't) listen well to _____ and pick up on what s/he feels and thinks.

_____ 17. I would prefer _____ to be a different or particular kind of person.

_____ 18. I usually catch and understand the whole of what _____ means.

_____ 19. Whether _____ is expressing "good" thoughts or "bad" feelings or desires makes no difference to my attitude toward him/her.

_____ 20. I don't realize how sensitive or touchy _____ is about some of the things we discuss.

_____21. I really don't *like* _____.

_____22. I often respond to _____ rather automatically, not taking in what s/he is thinking or feeling.

_____23. I feel there are things I/we don't talk about that are affecting our relationship.

_____24. When _____is hurting or upset I can recognize his/her pain *without* it becoming my pain so that I feel hurt and upset. [Answer "no" if his/her pain triggers your own upsetting pain.]

Please check that you answered **every** item. *Thank you.*

(Form adapted by Godfrey T. Barrett-Lennard, November 2012.)

Barrett-Lennard Relationship Inventory: Scoring key for 24-item empathy OS/MO FORMS

Developed by Godfrey T. Barrett-Lennard, PhD

Name/code ....   Date answered ....

Class/category of relationship ....

Position of respondent in the relationship ....,

Enter the answer for each item in its space, below, *after reversing the sign* (from + to –, or – to +) **IF** the item number is shown in **bold**. (The **bold** items are worded "negatively," so that answers to these items have the opposite meaning to answers to positively worded items.)

Empathy (E)		Level of Regard (R)		Unconditionality (U)		Congruence (C)	
Item No.	*Answer*	Item No.	*Answer*	Item No.	*Answer*	Item No.	*Answer*
2		1		**3**	Reverse sign	5	Reverse sign
4	Reverse sign	7		13		11	
6		**9**	Reverse sign	**17**	Reverse sign	15	
8		**21**	Reverse sign	19		**23**	Reverse sign
10	Reverse sign	R Total>		U Total>		C Total>	
12	Reverse sign					+U Total>	
14						+R Total>	
16	Reverse sign						
18							
20	Reverse sign						
22	Reverse sign						
24							
E Scale Score->						R+U+C Total –>	

Add the 12 item values in the E answer column, after reversing answer signs where indicated, to obtain the score for empathic understanding. The *possible* score range is –36 (or –3 × 12) to +36 (+3 × 12). A composite total for the R, U, and C items will also have the same potential score range as for the E scale. For statistical manipulation a constant may be added to scale scores, to avoid any negative score totals. (Adding +36 would yield a maximum possible range for empathy of 0 to 72.)

EXPLORATORY ADAPTATION FOR SELF-WITH-SELF RELATIONS

This is a tentative "experimental" version of the BLRI, reflected on, worked over, discussed with colleagues, but so far untried in research. I include it here because I view the self as normally complex with more than one voice or mode, which co-exist in interaction comprising an 'inner' form of relationship. (The CSI in Appendix 2, though developed outside the frame of the BLRI, is built on a similar basic idea.) The items, though following one-by-one in broad idea from the items in basic 40-item forms, have had to be significantly reformulated for the self-with-self context.

This form can be scored with same key as for the basic OS–40 and MO–40 inventories. However (as also noted in Chapter 9, pp. 93–94) the scale measures have rather different meanings than in the other RI forms. In this case, the regard scale provides an estimate of regard level within the diverse self and the empathy scale is essentially concerned with self-empathy involving a listening inner dialogue (Barrett-Lennard, 1997). The congruence scale in this case taps personal openness and integration generally, rather than within particular relationships. The unconditionality measure is also partly about personal openness but more particularly about self-acceptance or positive receptivity to all sides of self as against a self-judgmental or selectively self-rejecting tendency.

Barrett-Lennard Relationship Inventory: Form SS–40 (version 3, adapted from forms OS–40 and MO–40)

Developed by Godfrey T. Barrett-Lennard, PhD
(Tony Weston contributed to the arrangement of this experimental form)

Other forms of the Relationship Inventory are about between person relationships, but the focus of this form is on *how a person regards and relates to him- or herself*. Please consider each numbered statement with reference to your self-attitudes and inner communication. The 'right' answers here are those that fit the way *you* work and see all of yourself when you reflect on it.

Mark each statement in one of the answer columns on the right, according to how strongly you feel that it is true or right, or not true/not right. *Be sure to mark every one.* Show your answer by placing a tick in the box that is the best fit to what you really think and feel. The full meaning of each answer is outlined below.

–3:	NO, I strongly feel that it is *not true*,	+3:	YES, I strongly feel that it *is true*
–2:	No, I feel it's not true	+2:	Yes, I feel it is true
–1:	(No), I feel that it is probably untrue, or more untrue than true	+1:	(Yes), I feel that it is probably true or more true than untrue

	DISAGREE			AGREE		
	NO –3	No –2	(No) –1	(Yes) +1	Yes +2	YES +3
1. I respect myself – all of me in my world	❑	❑	❑	❑	❑	❑
2. I usually sense or realize what my inner feelings are	❑	❑	❑	❑	❑	❑
3. My own evaluation of me as a person depends on how well I say and do things (or how I see myself performing)	❑	❑	❑	❑	❑	❑
4. I put on different outer self to try to keep the inner me happy	❑	❑	❑	❑	❑	❑
5. I quite like the person that's me as I am overall	❑	❑	❑	❑	❑	❑
6. I often don't notice (or only realize later) what my inner feelings are (or have been)	❑	❑	❑	❑	❑	❑
7. Whether *I'm* happy or unhappy with my outer behavior, another or deeper part of me rides on undisturbed	❑	❑	❑	❑	❑	❑
8. I *don't avoid* facing my inner me. I see inward as well as outward, and am in touch with whatever goes on in me	❑	❑	❑	❑	❑	❑
9. I feel indifferent, not positive, looking at myself as I am	❑	❑	❑	❑	❑	❑
10. I nearly always know exactly what my inner self-feeling is.	❑	❑	❑	❑	❑	❑
11. Depending on my outward behavior, I have a better (or worse) opinion of myself	❑	❑	❑	❑	❑	❑
12. I think I am open and genuine in the way I relate to myself	❑	❑	❑	❑	❑	❑
13. I'm appreciative of and glad to be the self I've become	❑	❑	❑	❑	❑	❑
14. I have attitudes or beliefs that get in the way of facing some feelings that weigh on me or that I see only in glimpses	❑	❑	❑	❑	❑	❑

	DISAGREE			AGREE		
	NO −3	No −2	(No) −1	(Yes) +1	Yes +2	YES +3
15. Whatever my inner conversation or argument, alongside it all there's a core in me that hears and doesn't judge	❏	❏	❏	❏	❏	❏
16. I mostly don't ask myself about my "real" or deep down impressions and feelings – and prefer things that way	❏	❏	❏	❏	❏	❏
17. I see myself as a rather dull and uninteresting person	❏	❏	❏	❏	❏	❏
18. I sense or realize the way I feel inside even when it would be hard for me to express it	❏	❏	❏	❏	❏	❏
19. I want, and tell myself, to be a particular kind of person	❏	❏	❏	❏	❏	❏
20. I can freely 'say' or think to myself how I'm feeling and getting along with all the parts or sides of me	❏	❏	❏	❏	❏	❏
21. I care for and feel good about me	❏	❏	❏	❏	❏	❏
22. I don't give that much attention to the inner me or dwell on what I 'really' feel	❏	❏	❏	❏	❏	❏
23. I like certain things about me, and there are other things I do not like in my total me	❏	❏	❏	❏	❏	❏
24. I'm open and straightforward with myself, and can live what I deeply feel and think	❏	❏	❏	❏	❏	❏
25. I disapprove of myself as a person	❏	❏	❏	❏	❏	❏
26. I usually understand and could say to myself the whole of what I'm feeling	❏	❏	❏	❏	❏	❏
27. Whether the ideas or desires that arise in me are 'good' or 'bad' don't affect how I feel toward myself as a person	❏	❏	❏	❏	❏	❏
28. Sometimes I am really not comfortable inside but I go on, ignoring my discomfort or telling myself everything is OK.	❏	❏	❏	❏	❏	❏
29. I am friendly and warm toward the inner person that's me	❏	❏	❏	❏	❏	❏
30. I can't understand or make sense of my whole complicated self	❏	❏	❏	❏	❏	❏
31. I approve of some things about me (some of my ways), and disapprove of other things about me (or my other ways)	❏	❏	❏	❏	❏	❏
32. I seem to always know exactly what I feel: I don't cover up inside or hide things from myself	❏	❏	❏	❏	❏	❏
33. Inside I just tolerate or put up with my outer self as I am	❏	❏	❏	❏	❏	❏
34. I keep track of how I feel about things happening around me	❏	❏	❏	❏	❏	❏
35. Sometimes I am more (or less) worthwhile in my own eyes than I am at other times	❏	❏	❏	❏	❏	❏
36. At times what I say to myself or assume about me is quite different from the way I actually feel deep down	❏	❏	❏	❏	❏	❏
37. When I stand back and think of myself in life, I feel a kind of empathy and warmth of regard for that 'me' person	❏	❏	❏	❏	❏	❏
38. My outer patterns or ways of responding are pretty much automatic so I don't notice the way I feel deep inside	❏	❏	❏	❏	❏	❏
39. I don't think that anything I find myself saying or doing changes the way I inwardly feel towards me as a person	❏	❏	❏	❏	❏	❏
40. I sense feelings in me that I tend to skirt around and ignore	❏	❏	❏	❏	❏	❏

GUIDELINE SUGGESTIONS TO TRANSLATORS OF THE BL RELATIONSHIP INVENTORY

These guidelines assume that the translator begins with a regular current English-language form of the BLRI[2] and that it is being translated into another language that I will refer to here as N-E (Non-English). The principle behind these suggestions is that trial translations in both directions (English to Non-English, and then Non-English to English) yield a better result than one-way translation achieves by itself. In accord with this principle, the following steps are recommended:

Step 1. Draft translation of the RI from English to other language.

Step 2. Reverse translation from this draft, back into English, by one or more bilingual persons working independently of the original translator.

Step 3. Original translator to closely review the "back-translation" for discrepancy with the original English version. There will never be a perfect match, but particular differences may be substantive or stylistic. In the stylistic case, meanings are very little changed even though some words are different. In the substantive case, meaning and implication have been affected, and refinement of the draft Non-English text is called for.

Step 4. Having amended the initial draft translation, the original translator desirably would now consult the back-translator(s) for their opinion on whether equivalence of meaning has *now* been achieved. This consultation may lead to some further refinements. Since different languages do not encompass an exactly equivalent spectrum of distinctions in meaning, translators will at times have to fall back on a formulation of 'best available fit.' *It is helpful if the primary translator has a good grasp of the defined underlying interpersonal qualities* measured by the RI (empathic understanding, congruence, level of regard, and unconditionality). A few of the negatively worded items imply a kind of "double-negative" – when a person does not agree with a statement and needs to answer with a grade of 'no' (−1, −2, or −3). This feature might produce confusion unless the intent of the item is well understood, and special care is taken to maximize clarity of wording.

Step 5. Where possible, a small pilot study or trial run application of the translated RI, with actual respondents in real relationships, is desirable before its full-scale research application. If respondents report difficulty, say, with some particular item(s), it would be *a matter of judgment* whether this was due to any deficiency that might be remedied in the translation *or* a result of inherent subtlety of meaning in the item itself.

When administering the RI in *final* form, it can happen that someone finds difficulty answering a particular item, and asks for clarification. Their difficulty might actually arise from uncertainties within the referent relationship, or a lack of confidence in their own perception, in which case the answer choice of 'probably true' or 'probably untrue' may be the best fit. In any case, making sure that the person is considering all the answer choices, and gently encouraging them to go by their own best sense, is usually appropriate and sufficient. (If they literally don't know what a particular word means, explain it simply.)

---

[2]   Even if a translator starts with a previous translation of the RI, it may be based on an *earlier* English language form that was later revised or amended in some details. Thus my recommendation is to work from a current English form and the earlier translation, together, to achieve a result equivalent to Step 1, above. The other steps can then follow, essentially as described.

TRANSLATIONS AND THE TRANSLATORS

The following list of languages and translator-users taken from my records is indicative but not comprehensive, given that communications happened over a long period and the information was not entered into a cumulative list while fresh. All translations are from the original English form(s).

American Sign Language: Barbara A. Brauer (PhD, 1979, NYU) translated OS–64 form into AMSELAN, presented on video tape for rating by deaf students (studied after an initial interview).

Arabic: (1995 contact) Prof. A. M. Soliman (United Arab Emirates University, Al Ain, UAE) had translated and successfully used the original 'client' RI form in Arabic.

Chinese: Mandarin &/or Taiwanese, OS E scale by Cheng-I Chu, Department of Public Health, Tzu Chi University (see References). Contact (2013): lyndon@mail.tcu.edu.tw. Other translations possible.

Czech Republic: Translated (2011) by Jana Mitaczova, Charles Univ., Prague jmitasczova@gmail.com

Dutch: (1) Prof. G Lietaer germain.lietaer@ppw.kuleuven.be (Catholic University of Leuven). Translation and revision of OS RI forms, 1974 and 1976 (see References); (2) Dr. Alexandra Verwaaijen: her translation is in her dissertation (1990) at the Catholic University of Nijmegen (see References).

French: Early translations in Quebec by Prof. D. Marceau (Univer. Sherbrooke) and by F. Belpaire & Y. Archambault at Centre D'Orientation, Montreal. No info. on a probable translation in France.

German: First full translation presented in K. Sander's doctoral dissertation in 1971 at the University of Hamburg. R. Jorgen gives shortened versions in his 1975 dissertation at University of Hamburg, and there could be later versions in German. (Prof. R. Tausch was involved in supervising the early work.)

Greek: Transl (1998) by V. Kosmatos (University of Patras) of teacher-student forms. Dr G. Mouladoudis, School of Education, University of Ioannina, also corresponded about a Greek translation.

Hebrew: (1996). (Mrs) G. Arad, ralfia@study.haifa.il. Haifa University, Israel.

Iran (Persian?): Dr Abdollah Ahmadi saag_zi@yahoo.com (2007), Azarbaijan, Iran. Planned to translate and use the BLRI. Probably did so, but no confirming follow-up.

Italian: (1) Translation of teacher-student forms by G. Sulprizio and colleagues at IACP, Rome (1996–1997). (2) R. Montirosso rmontirosso@bp.Inf.it (1999) translation of Form MO–40.

Japanese: At least one translation was made, but its source not retrieved.

Korean: Park Nam-Sook, Yonsei University. Contact (1999): pnsmom@hotmail.com

Malaysian: For example, N. Yusoff, Medical Faculty, University of Malaya, Kuala Lumpur (2009).

Polish: (1990) Krzysztof Cieslak, PhD, from Institute of Psychology, Jagiellonian University, Crakow, Poland. (Draft translation in GBL file)

Portuguese: (1) Prof. Joao Marques-Teixeira et al. translated and used OS–40 ca. 1993. Contact (2013) jemto1@gmail.com. (2) Claudia C. Martins carmo.claudia@clix.pt (2002). (3) Amarlis Rocha (2004–2008 amarilisrocha@hotmail.com) translated and used 40-item student *&* teacher forms.(4) Prof. Sueli de Carvalho Vilela wrote 11/ 2009 from Universidade Federal de Alfenas, Brazil re potential use of BLRI in translation for her doctoral study in nursing at University of São Paulo. (5) Much earlier, Dr. Rachel Rosenberg had used an adapted RI form with groups, in São Paulo.

Slovak: Dr. Vladimír Hlavenka (1995) Psychology Dept, Univerzity Komenského, Bratislava.

Spanish: (1) Celis, A. (1999) University of Chile. Translated Form OS–64 (trans. in pub. report – ref. listed); (2) Rodríguez Irizarry (1993) University of Puerto Rico. E scale translation in listed dissertation; (3) Xavier Cleries i Costa (1995) Servei de Formacio, Institut d'Estudis de la Salut, Barcelona.

Swedish: Translation by Anders Bergehamn andersbergehamn@hotmail.com (1999). Translated both the 40-item *and* 64-item OS forms. Worked with 40-item version after 3 or 4 item changes.

Turkish: Translation of OS Empathy scale (1996) by Bulant Turin, Ortakoy, Istanbul.

Appendix 2
Contextual Selves Inventory and Triad and Group Rating Forms

This appendix includes the questionnaire instruments and rating forms, discussed fully in their rationales and application in Chapters 6, 7, and 8. They are included here without added comment beyond the information on this page.

ANNOTATED CONTENTS

The Relationship Inventory: A Complete Resource and Guide, First Edition. Godfrey T. Barrett-Lennard.
© 2015 John Wiley & Sons, Ltd. Published 2015 by John Wiley & Sons, Ltd.
Companion site: www.wiley.com/go/barrett_lennard/therelationshipinventory

CONTEXTUAL SELVES INVENTORY – DIRECTIONS SECTION
(Developed by Godfrey T. Barrett-Lennard, PhD)

This inventory taps into your own view of yourself as you feel **YOU are** in different relationships. It is about what each context calls forth in you. There are two parts to the answer section:

1. Part A is entirely concerned with your sense of self with partner and family members. Answer if possible for at *least four* of these contexts.
2. Part B is concerned with relationships beyond your family. Please answer for every mentioned context you can. Be sure to include contexts 8 and 12. (Answer for your self-ideal last of all).

The right answer is always the one that best fits your own personal sense of yourself, as *you are* in the particular relationship involved. Skip contexts that don't apply, leaving the columns blank.

Please *read through* this list of contexts (they are similarly numbered on the answer pages. Write in what the particular relation is, where requested. Do this as soon as you decide.

1. *Me as I see and feel about me when engaged with my spouse or partner:* If you have no spouse or partner, answer if possible for "Me with an intimate or special friend".
2&3. *The way I feel and see* myself *with my Mother and, separately, with my Father:* Step or adoptive parents count here. If a parent is no longer in your life, picture how you remember you were with them (though if this confuses or troubles you then leave out any answers for that context).
4. *The way I am in myself when involved with the brother or sister nearest to me in age:* If you have no brother or sister (or step-brother/sister), but have a long active relationship with a cousin then please substitute that context and write in "cousin." Otherwise, just leave this column blank.
5. *Me as I am with my own child (or step or adoptive child) – assuming you have one:* If you have more than one child, please choose the oldest (thus the longest relationship).
6. *Me as I am/have been with another close relative of particular importance in my life:* This might be a grandparent, aunt, uncle or cousin, for example. (Leave the column blank only if no one fits.)
7. *Me as I am (or was) with fellow-students in my school experience or later studies.*
8. *The way I am with someone I'm involved with but don't trust, or who I've experienced as antagonistic, judgmental and down on me, or a bully or an "enemy":* No doubt, in your life, there is or was someone (or possibly a group) who fits this description – whether an extreme instance or not. Hold that person or group in mind as you answer. *Note if it's a group.* (Don't skip this context.)
9. *Me as I am with fellow-workers or colleagues – or a non-work team, volunteer, or special hobby or interest group:* Choose your work/employment situation if applicable. Note on the form whether it's you in your job situation or another context.
10. *Me as I am with my boss, group leader, direct supervisor, senior officer, or present teacher:* These are seen as varied forms of authority relation (directive or not).
11. *Me as I am with people I serve:* You could think of this as "me as I am in a particular role," say, as a teacher, supervisor, salesperson, health worker, minister/priest, police officer. Remember to note *in a word or two what the context or role is, above your answers.*
12. Finally! *Me as I would <u>most</u> like to be, in most situations of relationship with other people.* As you rate each item on the 1 to 7 scale you can mentally adjust it, for example, to "I *would* have confidence in myself". It is usually straightforward to describe one's ideal self and we ask you please to include it.

Note: Answering this Inventory can be interesting or even enlightening. But, IF you find it distressing to think about yourself in any particular relationship don't force yourself to go on with it. You could cross out that heading or omit the column and proceed to the next context.

Contextual Selves Inventory (CSI) – Part A of Answer Section

Developed by Godfrey T. Barrett-Lennard

Name or code ....   Date ....

Age .... yrs   Sex: M or F (please circle)

This questionnaire lists ways that a person might feel about him/herself in different life relationships. The directions that follow are more fully explained on an accompanying sheet (read first). *This* answer page is concerned with relationship contexts in your personal/family life. *Select all of the contexts that apply in your case. Skip a column*, leaving it empty, *if it simply doesn't apply.* It is okay to describe yourself in a past relationship (perhaps with a parent) that still lives in your memory.

   Please answer each of the statements below to describe how *you are*, as you feel and see yourself, within each chosen context. It's best to start by *answering all of the items for a single context, putting your mind carefully to each statement.* Then go on to further contexts, ignoring previous answers. Try to picture yourself with the other person, or bring images to mind of particular situations. Then ask yourself "How do I really feel about myself, the way *I* am, when I'm' engaged in that relationship." Use numbers from 1 to 7 to show your answers for the way you see yourself in each relation. Numbers 1, 2, and 3 stand for different degrees of 'No, not like me/not the way I am.' A '4' answer sits in the middle, implying both like and unlike about equally. The higher numbers 5, 6, and 7 stand for different degrees of 'Yes, like me/like the way I am' *in that relationship*. The more exact meaning of the answer numbers is as follows:

1	2	3	4	5	6	7
Never/not at all like me	Mostly not like me	More unlike me than like me	Equally like and unlike me	More like than unlike me	Mostly like me	Very or always like me

	Self statements	(1) With partner/ spouse (note if friend)	(2) With my Mother	(3) With my Father	(4) With brother/ sister/cousin (circle)	(5) With own child: M or F? Age ___yrs	(6) With other relation (who? _____)
1.	I have confidence in myself.						
2.	I notice faults and am critical in my outlook.						
3.	I take initiative, raise issues, start things.						
4.	I look for alibis and excuses for myself if things go wrong.						
5.	I feel interesting, capable, and positive about myself.						
6.	I tend to follow, letting the other people take the lead.						
7.	I forgive easily – don't hold grudges or try to "get even".						

8.	I'm comfortable with my body and sexuality.						
9.	It is pretty hard to be myself.						
10.	I think clearly and am level-headed.						
11.	I put on a front when I'm uneasy—not showing how I feel.						
12.	I am imaginative and can share my dreams.						
13.	I am often tense or anxious.						
14.	It's difficult for me to share my real feelings.						
15.	I am a calm and easy-going person.						
16.	I am aloof and reserved, I keep my distance.						
17.	I am optimistic and seldom "down" in my mood.						
18.	I often feel resentful or angry.						
19.	I am full of life and good spirits.						
20.	I am self-oriented, concerned about me.						
21.	I am inwardly on my guard.						
22.	I am a considerate and mostly gentle person.						
23.	I'm fairly easily confused and can freeze or get in a panic.						
24.	I am agreeable and tend to fit in with what others want.						

Contextual Selves Inventory (CSI) – Part B of Answer Section

Developed by Godfrey T. Barrett-Lennard

Name or code ....   Date ....

Age .... yrs   Sex: M or F (please circle)

This questionnaire lists ways that a person might feel about him/herself in important life contexts. This page is for contexts outside your family. Use *all* the columns you can. In particular, please make sure to include and enter answers for columns 8 and 12.

Please answer each of the statements below to describe how *you are*, as you feel and see yourself, within each chosen context. Try to picture yourself with the other person, or bring images to mind of particular situations. Then ask yourself "How do I really feel about myself, the way *I am*, when I'm engaged in that relationship." Use numbers from 1 to 7 to show your answers for the way you see yourself in each relationship. Numbers 1, 2, and 3 stand for different degrees of 'No, not like me/not the way I am.' A '4' answer sits in the middle, implying both like and unlike about equally. The higher numbers 5, 6, and 7 stand for different degrees of 'Yes, like me/like the way I am' *in that relationship*. The more exact meaning of the answer numbers is as follows:

'No' (unlike me) answers				'Yes' (like me) answers		
1	2	3	4	5	6	7
Never/Not at all like me	Mostly not like me	More unlike me than like me	Equally like and unlike me	More like than unlike me	Mostly like me	Very or always like me

	Self statements	(7) Self at school/ university or other learning group	(8) With distrusted person or "*enemy*"	(9) Self with others at Work, or _____?	(10) Self with boss/authority _____?	(11) Self with people I serve?_____	(12) Desired/ **ideal self** in relationships
1.	I have confidence in myself.						
2.	I notice faults and am critical in my outlook.						
3.	I take initiative, raise issues, start things.						
4.	I look for alibis and excuses for myself if things go wrong.						
5.	I feel interesting, capable, and positive about myself.						
6.	I tend to follow, letting the other person/people take the lead						

7.	I forgive easily – don't hold grudges or try to "get even".						
8.	I'm comfortable with my body and sexuality.						
9.	It is pretty hard to be myself.						
10	I think clearly and am level-headed.						
11	I put on a front when I'm uneasy—not showing how I feel.						
12	I am imaginative and can share my dreams.						
13	I am often tense or anxious.						
14	It's difficult for me to share my real feelings.						
15	I am a calm and easy-going person.						
16	I am aloof and reserved, I keep my distance.						
17	I am optimistic and seldom "down" in my mood.						
18	I often feel resentful or angry.						
19	I am full of life and good spirits.						
20	I am self-oriented, concerned about me.						
21	I am inwardly on my guard.						
22	I am a considerate and mostly gentle person.						
23	I'm fairly easily confused and can freeze or get in a panic.						
24	I am agreeable and tend to fit in with what others want.						

Please check for any gaps, to be sure you've answered all 24 items in each column used. Thank you.

Triad Participant Record Form E

Developed by Godfrey T. Barrett-Lennard, PhD

Please fill in the next line first

Today's date .... Your first name ....

Partners' names .... and ....

Below are listed ways that one person (a listener) might feel and respond to another (e.g., a sharing speaker). *Answer Part A immediately after your turn as listener, Part B right after being the 'client'/speaker, and Part C after your experience as the observer.* In the Part you are answering first write in the relevant name(s) in the space (s) in Item 1. (Afterwards just think the name[s].)

   Do the ratings before discussion or feedback so that your observations are independent of each other. (Listeners keep a record of their partners' ratings in the columns to the right of your ratings.)

   Mark each statement in the main answer column on the right, according to how strongly you feel that it is true, or not true, in this interaction. Please be sure to mark every one. Write in a positive number *(+3, +2, or +1)* for each "yes" answer, and negative numbers *(−1, −2, or −3)* to stand for "no" answers. Here is the meaning of each answer number:

+3: **Yes (!)**, *I strongly feel that it is true.*

+2: Yes, *I feel it is true.*

+1: (Yes) *I feel that it is probably true, or more true than untrue*

−1: (No) *I feel that it is probably untrue, or more untrue than true.*

−2: No, *I feel it is not true.*

−3: **No(!)**, *I strongly feel that it is not true, or not that way.*

ANSWERS

	LISTENER	Speaker	Observer

A. *How I found myself responding when I was the listener:*

1. I *wanted* to understand _____'s [name] own feeling and perspective.

2. I needed more of the picture to understand _____, and struggled to tune in.

3. I heard _____'s words but couldn't sense the quality of his/her inner feelings.

4. I concentrated on closely following _____'s own view and feeling.

5. I tried too hard to form my responses, so that I was not consistently absorbed in listening and making inner connection with him/her.

6. My response seemed to help _____ to see or feel something more clearly.

7. I probably put my own meanings onto her/his experience.

8. I was able to follow and see exactly what _____ was expressing.

B. *How I experienced the listener when I was the client/speaker:*   SPEAKER

1. I felt that _____[name] wanted to understand how I see things.   _____

2. I had to build up a picture before ____began to lock on to *my* issues and feelings.   _____

3. _____ picked up on my words but did not show awareness of my *feelings*.   _____

4. I felt that _____ was closely following my meaning and feeling.   _____

5. _____ may have been trying too hard; caught up in the task more than truly   _____
   absorbed in listening to me and connecting with my felt meaning.

6. _____'s response actually helped me to see something more distinctly   _____

7. I felt _____ tended to put his/her own meanings onto my experience.   _____

8. _____ caught the exact gist or essence of what I felt and meant.   _____

C. *My perception of the listener's response when I was the observer:*   OBSERVER

1. I felt _____ *wanted* to understand _____'s own perspective and feeling.   _____

2. _____ needed a good bit of information on the way to an effortful notion of the   _____
   speaker' issue and feeling.

3. _____ picked up on words/ideas but didn't convey a sense of _____'s *feeling*.   _____

4. _____ seemed to be closely following _____'s actual meaning and feeling.   _____

5. _____ appeared to try too hard to make 'good' responses, rather than being   _____
   totally absorbed in listening and connecting with _____.

6. _____'s response helped _____to feel and see something more clearly.   _____

7. I thought that _____ put his/her own meanings onto _____'s experience.   _____

8. _____seemed right on target, catching the essence of what_____ expressed.   _____

(Godfrey T. Barrett-Lennard, 2004)

Triad Participant Record Form C

Developed by Godfrey T. Barrett-Lennard, PhD

Please fill in the next line first

Today's date .... Your first name ....

Partners' names .... and ....

Below are listed ways that one person (a listener) might feel and respond to another (e.g., a sharing speaker). Answer Part A immediately after your turn as listener, Part B right after being the "client"/speaker, and Part C after your experience as observer. In item 1 write in the relevant name(s) in the underline space.

Mark each statement in the main answer column on the right, according to how strongly you feel that it is true, or not true, in this interaction. Please be sure to mark every one. Write in a positive number *(+3, +2, or +1)* for each 'yes' answer, and negative numbers *(–1, –2, or –3)* to stand for 'no' answers. Here is the meaning of each answer number:

+3: **Yes (!)**, *I strongly feel this is true.*
+2: Yes, *I feel that this is true.*
+1: (Yes) *I feel that this is probably true, or more true than untrue*

–1: (No) *I feel that this is probably untrue, or more untrue than true.*
–2: No, *I feel that this is not true.*
–3: **No(!)**, *I strongly feel that this is not true.*

	LISTENER self-rating	Speaker rating	Observer rating
A. *How I found myself responding when I was the listener:*			
1. At moments with _____ [name] I was distracted or not able to concentrate, although I didn't mention it.	_____	|___|	|___|
2. I felt comfortable in showing uncertainty or non-understanding when this was uppermost in me.	_____	|___|	|___|
3. I felt self-conscious and that I was putting on something of a role with _____.	_____	|___|	|___|
4. I let _____ see the way I was truly responding to her/him in the situation.	_____	|___|	|___|
5. I wanted to form good responses, while trying not to seem artificial.	_____	|___|	|___|
6. I felt at ease with _____ in the situation, and unguarded in my response.	_____	|___|	|___|
7. Various impressions and reactions went on in me that I didn't express at all.	_____	|___|	|___|
8. I felt very absorbed and "all there" with my immediate self, as we went along.	_____	|___|	|___|

B. *How I experienced the listener when I was the sharing speaker:* SPEAKER

1. _____ [name] seemed a bit uneasy or distracted, but we didn't speak of it. _____

2. _____ could tell me when s/he was uncertain or had trouble connecting with me in anything I expressed. _____

3. I had the feeling _____ was watching her/himself, in the listener role that s/he wanted to manage correctly. _____

4. _____ let me see the way s/he was truly responding to me in the situation. _____

5. _____ seemed caught up in trying to express her/himself properly as a listener-helper, while also wanting to be natural. _____

6. I felt _____ was genuinely at ease and open in his/her response to me. _____

7. I sensed _____ reacting to me or to my issues more than s/he expressed. _____

8. _____ seemed very engaged and "present," sharing his/her response as it came. _____

C. *My perception of the listener's (L's) response when I was the observer:* OBSERVER

1. At moments _____ seemed distracted or tense, although s/he did not say so. _____

2. _____ seemed at ease in showing uncertainty or non-understanding when this was her/his honest reaction. _____

3. I felt that the listener (__L__) was watching her/himself, trying to conform to the role s/he had in mind. _____

4. L let the speaker see the way s/he was truly responding, in the situation. _____

5. I could sense L's effort to make 'good' responses without seeming artificial. _____

6. L seemed to me truly at ease and open in his/her response to the speaker. _____

7. I sensed L feeling/reacting in ways that were left unsaid, in their exchange. _____

8. L struck me as responding transparently from his/her immediate engaged self and presence. _____

(Godfrey T. Barrett-Lennard, 2004)

Triad Participant Record Form R-U

Developed by Godfrey T. Barrett-Lennard, PhD

Please fill in the next line first

Today's date .... Your first name ....

Partners' names .... and ....

Below are ways that one person might feel and respond to another. Please consider each numbered statement, *noting names in the first item of each section.* Answer Part A *immediately* after your turn as listener, Part B right after being the speaker, and Part C after being the observer.

   Mark each statement in the main answer column on the right, according to how strongly you feel that it is true, or not true, in this interaction. Please be sure to mark every one. Write in a positive number *(+3, +2, or +1)* for each 'yes' answer, and negative numbers *(–1, –2, or –3)* to stand for 'no' answers. Here is the meaning of each answer number:

+3:   **Yes (!)**, *I strongly feel this is true.*

+2:   Yes, *I feel that this is true.*

+1:   (Yes) *I feel that this is probably more true than untrue.*

–1:   (No) *I feel that this is probably untrue, or more untrue than true.*

–2:   No, *I feel that this is not true.*

–3:   **No(!)**, *I strongly feel that this is* not *true*

PERSPECTIVES

A. *How I found myself responding when I was the listener:*   LISTENER   Speaker   Observer

1. I felt a personal *respect for* _____ [name] as s/he spoke on in the session.   _____ |___| |___|

2. I found myself *evaluating* or sizing up _____'s problem, and how s/he came across.   _____ |___| |___|

3. Whether _____ was self-critical *or* shared positive feelings about her/himself didn't and wouldn't affect my own feeling toward her/him   _____ |___| |___|

4. I felt an inner warmth and reaching out as _____ shared and expressed her/himself.   _____ |___| |___|

5. I couldn't help feeling some discomfort or disapproval in relation to _____.   _____ |___| |___|

6. Some things s/he expressed triggered feelings I have and was feeling in myself.   _____ |___| |___|

7. I did feel some impatience with _____ , and maybe a sense of 'so what'.   _____ |___| |___|

8. My own reaction to_____ held steady: I didn't feel "turned off" toward her/his process at some moments, and more responsive to her (him) during other sharing.   _____ |___| |___|

9. I wanted to help _____ get a better perspective or handle on her/his problem and *develop a solution*.   _____ |___| |___|

B. *How I experienced the listener when I was the client/speaker:*   SPEAKER

1. I felt respected by _____ [name] as a feeling person with my own view.   _____

2. I sensed that_____ was evaluating me or my world, and how I came across.   _____

3. Whether I was expressing painful or troubling things about myself/my life, or more positive ones, did not seem to effect _____'s attitude and response to me.   _____

4. I felt a warmth and caring interest from _____ as I spoke about myself.   _____

5. I couldn't help feeling at moments that _____ was disapproving of me.   _____

6. I felt that _____'s own attitudes and feeling toward the issues I spoke about were affecting his/her response to me.   _____

7. I sensed _____ was impatient with me, maybe uninterested or critical.   _____

8. I sensed that I *could* say anything, or show different sides of myself, without it changing _____'s attitude or feeling toward me.   _____

9. _____ tried to help me to get a better perspective or handle on my problem and figure out a solution.   _____

C. *My view of the listener's (L's) response, from the position of observer:*   OBSERVER

1. L was visibly respecting of _____ [name] as a person with *his/her* own view.   _____

2. I sensed that L was appraising and trying to see through _____'s style and messages.   _____

3. L's attitude and responsiveness seemed to me to be the same, whether _____ was expressing conflicted negative feelings *or* positive things about self.   _____

4. I sensed a warmth and caring from L as _____ spoke on about him/herself.   _____

5. I felt that in some way L disapproved of _____.   _____

6. I thought that L's response tended to come from his/her own attitudes rather than from what _____ was trying to say.   _____

7. I sensed that L was impatient with _____, maybe uninterested or critical.   _____

8. It seemed _____ could express and show anything s/he experienced without disturbing or changing L's attitude in response to him/her.   _____

9. I felt that L wanted _____ to get a fresh grip and perspective on his/her problem and then come to a solution.   _____

End-of-Meeting *Group Process Questionnaire*

Developed by Godfrey T. Barrett-Lennard, PhD

Your code/first name ....   Date ....

Group ....   Time ....

Check each rating scale at the point that best describes your feeling regarding the whole group session or meeting that has just ended. Also, please enter names where you can for the questions requesting this information. If you cannot give any meaningful rating to an item, write in 'uncertain' over the rating line. (Please use this last option sparingly.)

		YES!	Yes	Somewhat/ sometimes	No	NO!

1. Please think about other members of the group.

   A. Was this time valuable for anyone, do you feel? If so, who, especially (name)?

   B. Are you left feeling concerned about the impact of the session on someone else? Who?

   C. Did anyone express him/herself more freely than before, or on new levels? Who?

2. A. Was this time beneficial or productive *for you*?

   B. Did *you,* on the other hand, feel uninvolved or 'out of it' at times?

   C. Were you able to open up and say/share whatever *you wanted to* in the group, in this session?

   D. Do you feel that your presence and/or what you did share *mattered to others* in the group?

3. Do you feel that members of the group really *listened* to each other, this time?

4. Did there seem to you to be a quality of genuineness and honesty in the group?

5. Did you at any time(s) feel personally understood in a helpful or easing way, by someone in the group? Which person(s)?

6. Did you *feel* closely in touch with someone else in their feelings and situation, during this session? Which person(s)?

7. Was an atmosphere of safety and trust present or growing in the group, as you sense it?

8. Did anyone directly share *their* impression or picture of you or your style in a way that you were glad of? Which person(s)?

9. Did you directly share with anyone else in the group |____ . ____ | ____ . ____|
    the way you picture them or see or react to their style?
    Who, and was it okay?

10. Did you find yourself actively responding to what |____ . ____ | ____ . ____|
    you saw going on *between others* in the group?
    Which persons especially?

11. What about the whole group? Is it a whole 'we' |____ . ____ | ____ . ____|
    with a feel and character you presently sense?

    If so, can you, in 4 or 5 words, picture or list some aspects or qualities you see?

Any other comments about the process this time, or your own feelings _____

....

Group Atmosphere Form

Developed by Godfrey T. Barrett-Lennard, PhD

Name/code .... Group .... Date & time ....

Please circle the scale point between each of the following pairs of opposite words that best describes your perception of the atmosphere and process in the *group,* during the session in which you have just taken part. Add brackets to show the range *if* and where you saw big variation over the session.

		Extremely	Quite	A little	Neither or both equally	A little	Quite	Extremely	
1.	Active	+++	++	+	•	+	++	+++	Passive
2.	Harsh	+++	++	+	•	+	++	+++	Gentle
3.	Turbulent	+++	++	+	•	+	++	+++	Calm
4.	Guarded	+++	++	+	•	+	++	+++	Trusting
5.	Connected	+++	++	+	•	+	++	+++	Separate
6.	Safe	+++	++	+	•	+	++	+++	Risky
7.	Tense	+++	++	+	•	+	++	+++	Relaxed
8.	Perceptive	+++	++	+	•	+	++	+++	Insensitive
9.	False	+++	++	+	•	+	++	+++	Genuine
10.	Deep	+++	++	+	•	+	++	+++	Shallow
11.	Distant	+++	++	+	•	+	++	+++	Close
12.	Caring	+++	++	+	•	+	++	+++	Hostile
13.	Closed	+++	++	+	•	+	++	+++	Open
14.	Stuck	+++	++	+	•	+	++	+++	Free-moving
15.	Warm	+++	++	+	•	+	++	+++	Cold
16.	Lively	+++	++	+	•	+	++	+++	Lethargic
17.	Erratic	+++	++	+	•	+	++	+++	Steady
18.	Flowing	+++	++	+	•	+	++	+++	Static
19.	Superficial	+++	++	+	•	+	++	+++	Searching
20.	Intense	+++	++	+	•	+	++	+++	Subdued

Explain any rating, or add some further dimension, if you wish to
Please go back and *fill in the top line* (name/code, date, etc.), if you have not already done so.

References

Abramowitz, S. I., & Abramowitz, C. V. (1974). Psychological mindedness and benefit from insight-oriented group therapy. *Archives of General Psychiatry, 30*, 610–615.

Abramowitz, S. I., & Jackson, C. (1974). Comparative effectiveness of there-and-then versus here-and-now therapist interventions in group psychotherapy. *Journal of Counseling Psychology, 21*, 288–293.

Adorno, T. W., Frenkel-Brunswik, F., Levinson, D. J., & Sanford, R. N. (1950). *The authoritarian personality*. New York: Harper.

Alvarado, V. I. (1976/1977). Perception of counselors: A function of culture. *Dissertation Abstracts International, 37-A,* 3407.

Bandura, A. (1969). *Principles of behaviour modification*. New York: Holt, Reinhart and Winston.

Bandura, A. (1977). *Social learning theory*. Englewood Cliffs, NJ: Prentice-Hall.

Barkham, M., & Shapiro, D. A. (1986). Counselor verbal response modes and experienced empathy. *Journal of Counseling Psychology, 33*, 3–10.

Barrett-Lennard, G. T. (1959a). *Dimensions of perceived therapist response related to therapeutic change* (Unpublished doctoral dissertation). University of Chicago.

Barrett-Lennard, G. T. (1959b). Therapeutic personality change as a function of perceived therapist response. *American Psychologist, 14*, 376.

Barrett-Lennard, G. T. (1962). Dimensions of therapist response as causal factors in therapeutic change. *Psychological Monographs, 76*, 43 (Whole No. 562).

Barrett-Lennard, G. T. (1964). *The Relationship Inventory. Forms OS-M–64, OS-F–64, MO-M–64 and MO-F–64.* University of New England, Australia.

Barrett-Lennard, G. T. (1967). Experiential learning in small groups: The basic encounter process. *Proceedings of the Canadian Association of University Student Personnel Services*, 2–12.

Barrett-Lennard, G. T. (1972). *Group process analysis from post-session and follow-up data. Group Process Study Papers, Whole No. 4.* University of Waterloo, Ontario.

Barrett-Lennard, G. T. (1974). Experiential learning groups. *Psychotherapy: Theory, Research and Practice, 11*, 71–75.

Barrett-Lennard, G. T. (1975/1976). Process, effects and structure in intensive groups: A theoretical-descriptive analysis. In C. L. Cooper (Ed.), *Theories of Group Processes* (pp. 59–86). London: Wiley. (Published 1975; corrected edition, 1976.)

Barrett-Lennard, G. T. (1976). Empathy in human relationships: Significance, nature and measurement. *Australian Psychologist, 11*, 173–184.

Barrett-Lennard, G. T. (1978). The Relationship Inventory: Later development and applications. *JSAS: Catalog of Selected Documents in Psychology, 8*, 68 (MS. 1732).

Barrett-Lennard, G. T. (1979). A new model of communicational-relational systems in intensive groups. *Human Relations, 32*, 841–849.

Barrett-Lennard, G. T. (1981). The empathy cycle: Refinement of a nuclear concept. *Journal of Counseling Psychology, 28*, 91–100.

Barrett-Lennard, G. T. (1984). The world of family relationships: A person-centered systems view. In R. F. Levant & J. M. Shlien (Eds.), *Client-centered therapy and the person-centered approach: New directions in theory, research and practice* (pp. 222–242). New York: Praeger.

Barrett-Lennard, G. T. (1986). The Relationship Inventory now: Issues and advances in theory, method and use. In L. S. Greenberg and W. M. Pinsof (Eds.), *The psychotherapeutic process: A research handbook* (pp. 439–476). New York: Guilford Press.

Barrett-Lennard, G. T. (1993). The phases and focus of empathy. *British Journal of Medical Psychology, 66,* 3–14.

Barrett-Lennard, G. T. (1997). The recovery of empathy – toward others and self. In A. C. Bohart & L. S. Greenberg (Eds.), *Empathy reconsidered: New directions in psychotherapy* (pp. 103–121). Washington, DC: APA Books.

Barrett-Lennard, G. T. (1998). *Carl Rogers' helping system: Journey and substance.* London: Sage.

Barrett-Lennard, G. T. (2003). *Steps on a mindful journey: Person-centred expressions.* Ross-on-Wye: PCCS Books.

Barrett-Lennard, G. T. (2005). *Relationship at the centre: Healing in a troubled world.* London: Whurr Edition/ Wiley.

Barrett-Lennard, G. T. (2007). Origins and unfolding of the person-centred innovation. In M. Cooper, P. F. Schmid, M. O'Hara, & G. Wyatt (Eds.), *The handbook of person-centred psychotherapy and counselling* (pp. 19–29). Houndmills/New York: Palgrave Macmillan.

Barrett-Lennard, G. T. (2008). The plural human self under study: Development and early results from the Contextual Selves Inventory. *Proceedings of the 43rd Annual Conference of the Australian Psychological Society,* 11–15.

Barrett-Lennard, G. T. (2009). From personality to relationship: Path of thought and practice. *Person-Centred and Experiential Psychotherapies, 8(2),* 79–93.

Barrett-Lennard, G. T. (2013). *The relationship paradigm: Human being beyond individualism.* Houndmills: Palgrave Macmillan.

Barrett-Lennard, G. T., Kwasnik, T. M., & Wilkinson, G. R. (1973/1974). Some effects of participation in encounter group workshops: An analysis of written follow-up reports. *Interpersonal Development, 4,* 35–41.

Barron, F., & Leary, T. F. (1955). Changes in psychoneurotic patients with and without psychotherapy. *Journal of Consulting Psychology, 19,* 239–245.

Bebout, J. (1971/1972). Personal communications, including detailed results from factorial analyses of the RI. Berkeley, Talent in Interpersonal Exploration Project, 1971/ 72.

Bebout, J., & Gordon, B. (1972). The value of encounter. In L. N. Solomon and B. Berzon (Eds.), *New perspectives on encounter groups* (pp. 83–118). San Francisco: Jossey-Bass.

Beck, A. T. (1976). *Cognitive therapy and the emotional disorders.* New York: International Universities Press.

Berlin, J. (1960). *Some autonomic correlates of therapeutic conditions in interpersonal relationships.* (Unpublished doctoral dissertation), University of Chicago.

Berzon, B. (1962). *"Relationship Inventory" pilot study: Helping relationship project.* Unpublished report, Western Behavioral Sciences Institute, LaJolla, CA.

Berzon, B. (1964). The self-directed therapeutic group: An evaluative study. LaJolla, California: *Western Behavioral Sciences Institute Reports, 1.*

Bills, R. E. (1975). *A system for assessing affectivity.* Tuscaloosa: University of Alabama Press.

Blatt, S. J., Quinlan, D. M., Zuroff, D. C., and Pilkonis, P. A. (1996). Interpersonal factors in brief treatment of depression: further analyses of the NIMH Treatment of Depression Collaborative Research Program. *Journal of Consulting and Clinical Psychology, 64,* 162–171.

Bleecker, E. R. (1964). *An exploratory field investigation of student counselors' judgements of selected counselee characteristics.* (Doctoral dissertation) University of Wisconsin, MI. *University Microfilms,* No. 64-13,861.

Boettcher, R. E. (1977). Interspousal empathy, marital satisfaction, and marriage counseling. *Journal of Social Service Research, 1,* 105–113.

Bohart, A. C., & Greenberg, L. S. (1997). *Empathy reconsidered: New directions in psychotherapy.* Washington, DC: American Psychological Association.

Bohart, A. C., & House, R. (2008). Empirically supported/validated treatments as modernist ideology. 1: Dodo, manualization, and the paradigm question. In R. House & D. Loewenthal (Eds.), *Against and for CBT: Towards a constructive dialogue* (pp. 188–201). Ross-on-Wye: PCCS Books.

Bown, O. H. (1954). *An investigation of the therapeutic relationship in client-centered psychotherapy.* (Unpublished doctoral dissertation). University of Chicago.

Bozarth, J. (1998). *Person-centered therapy: A revolutionary paradigm.* Ross-on-Wye: PCCS Books.

Bozarth, J. D., & Wilkins, P. (Eds.). (2001). Unconditional positive regard. Vol. 3 of *Rogers' therapeutic conditions. Evolution, theory and practice* (Series Ed. G. Wyatt). Ross-on-Wye, UK: PCCS Books.

Braaten, L. J. (1961). The movement from non-self to self in client-centered psychotherapy. *Journal of Counseling Psychology, 8,* 20–24.

Brauer, B. A. (1979/1980). The dimensions of perceived interview relationship as influenced by deaf persons' self-concepts and interviewer attributes as deaf or non-deaf. *Dissertation Abstracts International, 40,* 1352-B.

Brown, J. T. S. (1981). Communication of empathy in individual psychotherapy: An analogue study of client perceived empathy. *Dissertation Abstracts International, 41,* 2748-B.

Brown, O. B., & Calia, V. F. (1968). Two methods of initiating student interviews: Self-initiated versus required. *Journal of Counseling Psychology, 15*, 402–406.

Burgess, E. W., & Cottrell, L. S. (1939*). Predicting success or failure in marriage*. New York: Prentice-Hall.

Butler, J. M., & Haigh, C. V. (1954). Changes in the relation between self-concepts and ideal concepts consequent upon client-centered counseling. In C. R. Rogers & R. F. Dymond (Eds.), *Psychotherapy and personality change* (pp. 55–75). Chicago: University of Chicago Press.

Byrne, B. (1983). Trainee uses of reciprocal peer supervision and of faculty supervision in psychotherapy training. *Dissertation Abstracts International, 44*, 111A.

Cahoon, R. A. (1962). Some counselor attitudes and characteristics related to the counseling relationship (Doctoral Dissertation). Ohio State University. *University Microfilms* No. 63-2480.

Carter, J. A. (1981/1982). Couple's perceptions of relationship variables, marital adjustment and change before and after treatment. *Dissertation Abstracts International, 41*, 3172-B.

Cartwright, D. S. (1957). Annotated bibliography of research and theory construction in client-centered therapy. *Journal of Counseling Psychology, 4*, 82–100.

Cartwright, D. S., Kirtner, W. L., & Fiske, D. W. (1963). Method factors in changes associated with psychotherapy. *Journal of Abnormal and Social Psychology, 66*, 164–175.

Cartwright, D. S., Robertson, R. J., Fiske, D. W., & Kirtner, W. L. (1961). Length of therapy in relation to outcome and change in personal integration. *Journal of Consulting Psychology, 25*, 84–88.

Celis, A. (1999). Proceso de adaptacion del inventario de la relación de ayauda *de* G. T. Barrett-Lennard. *Revista de Psicología* (University of Chile), *8* (1).

Chu, C.-I., & Tseng, C.-C. (2013). A survey of how patient-perceived empathy affects the relationship between health literacy and the understanding of information by orthopaedic patients. *BMP Public Health, 13*, 155. Retrieved from http:/www.biomed.com/1471-2458/13/155

Churukian, G. A. (1970/1971). An investigation of relationships between the compatibility of supervisor-supervisee interpersonal needs and the quality of their interpersonal relations and productivity of supervision. *Dissertation Abstracts International, 31-A*, 5656–5657. University Microfilms No. 71–2045.

Clark, J. V., and Culbert, S. A. (1965). Mutually therapeutic perception and self-awareness in a T group. *Journal of Applied Behavioral Science, 1*, 180–194.

Cline, E. W. (1970). Confirming behavior of school executives. (Doctoral dissertation). University of Florida. *University Microfilms*, No. 70-14,867.

Cooper, C. L. (1969). The influence of the trainer on participant change in T-groups. *Human Relations, 22*, 515–530.

Cooper, C. L. (1973). A follow-up study on the influence of the T-group trainer on participant change. *Journal of European Training, 2*, 181–188.

Cooper, C. R. (1974/1975). The impact of marathon encounters on teacher-student relationships. *Interpersonal Development, 5*, 71–77.

Cramer, D. (1985). Psychological adjustment and the facilitative nature of close personal relationships. *British Journal of Medical Psychology, 58*, 165–168.

Cramer, D. (1986a). An item factor analysis of the original Relationship Inventory. *British Journal of Medical Psychology, 59*, 121–127.

Cramer, D. (1986b). An item factor analysis of the revised Barrett-Lennard Relationship Inventory. *British Journal of Guidance and Counselling, 14*, 314–325.

Cramer, D. (1987). Self-esteem, advice-giving, and the facilitative nature of close personal relationships. *Person-Centered Review, 2*, 99–110.

Cramer, D. (1989). Self-esteem and the facilitativeness of parents and close friends. *Person-Centered Review, 4*, 61–76.

Cramer, D. (1994). Self-esteem and Rogers' core conditions in close friends: A latent variable path analysis of panel data. *Counselling Psychology Quarterly, 7*, 327–337.

Cramer, D., & Jowett, S. (2010). Perceived empathy, accurate empathy and relationship satisfaction in heterosexual couples. *Journal of Social and Personal Relationships, 27*, 327–349.

Darwin, C. (1872). *On the origin of species* (6th ed.). London: John Murray.

Desrosiers, F. -X. (1968). A study of the personal growth of counseling trainees as a function of the level of therapeutic conditions offered by their supervisory groups and by their supervisors. *Dissertation Abstracts, 29-A*, 119–120.

Dettlaff, A. J. (2005). The influence of personality type on the supervisory relationship in field education. *Journal of Baccalaureate Social Work, 11*(1), 71–86.

Dymond, R. F. (1954). Adjustment changes over therapy from self-sorts. In C. R. Rogers & R. F. Dymond (Eds.), *Psychotherapy and personality change* (pp. 76–84). Chicago: University of Chicago Press.

Elkin, I., Shea, M. T., Watkins, J. T., Imber, S. D., Sotsky, S. M., Collins, J. F., ... Parloff, M. B. (1989). National Institute of Mental Health treatment of depression collaborative research program: General effectiveness of treatments. *Archives of General Psychiatry, 46*, 971–982.

Emmerling, F. C. (1961/1962). A study of the relationships between personality characteristics of classroom teachers and pupil perceptions of these teachers. *Dissertation Abstracts, 22*, 1054–1055. (Ann Arbor, MI: University Microfilms No 61–3002.)

Ends, E. J., & Page, C. W. (1959). Group psychotherapy and concomitant psychological change. *Psychological Monographs, 73* (10): Whole number 480.

Epstein, N., & Jackson, E. (1978). An outcome study of short term communication training with married couples. *Journal of Consulting and Clinical Psychology, 46*, 207–212.

Farber, B. A., Brink, D. C., & Raskin, P. M. (Eds.). (1996). *The psychotherapy of Carl Rogers. Cases and commentary.* New York/London: Guilford Press.

Feldstein, J. C. (1982). Counselor and client sex pairing: The effects of counseling problem and counselor sex role orientation. *Journal of Counseling Psychology, 29*, 418–420.

Fenton, K. (2011). *Self variability: A qualitative investigation of participant responses motivated by the Contextual Selves Inventory* (Unpublished BPsych thesis). Murdoch University, Perth.

Fiedler, F. E. (1950). A comparative investigation of early therapeutic relationships created by experts and non-experts of the psychoanalytic, non-directive and Adlerian schools. *Journal of Consulting Psychology, 14*, 436–445.

Fike, C. & van der Veen, F. (1966). *Adolescent perceptions of the family: A pilot study.* Unpublished manuscript (University of Wisconsin).

Follette, W. C., Darrow, S. M., & Bonow, J. T. (2009). Cognitive behaviour therapy: A current appraisal. In W. O'Donohue & J. E. Fisher (Eds.), *General principles and empirically supported techniques of cognitive behavior therapy* (pp. 42–62). Hoboken, NJ: Wiley.

Freire, E. (2001). Unconditional positive regard: The distinctive feature of client-centred therapy. In J. D. Bozarth and P. Wilkins (Eds.), *Rogers' therapeutic conditions: Evolution, theory and practice. Vol 3: Unconditional positive regard* (pp. 145–155). Ross-on-Wye: PCCS Books.

Fretz, B. R., Corn, R., Tuemmler, J. M., & Bellet, W. (1979). Counselor nonverbal behaviors and client evaluation. *Journal of Counseling Psychology, 26*, 304–311.

Fuertes, J. N., Mislowack, A., Brwon, S., Shval, G-A., Wilikinson, S., & Gelso, C. J. (2007). Correlates of the real relationship in psychotherapy: A study of dyads. *Psychotherapy Research, 17*, 423–430.

Gallagher, J. J. (1953a). Manifest anxiety changes concomitant with client-centered therapy. *Journal of Consulting Psychology, 17*, 443–446.

Gallagher, J. J. (1953b). MMPI changes concomitant with client-centered therapy. *Journal of Consulting Psychology, 17*, 334–338.

Ganley, R. M. (1989). The Barrett-Lennard Relationship Inventory (BLRI): Current and potential uses with family systems. *Family Process, 28*, 107–115.

Gergen, K. J. (2009). *Relational being: Beyond self and community.* New York/Oxford: Oxford University Press.

Gilmour-Barrett, K. C. (1973). *Managerial systems and interpersonal treatment processes in residential centers for disturbed youth* (Unpublished doctoral dissertation). University of Waterloo, Ontario.

Goldfarb, N. (1978). Effectiveness of supervisory style on counselor effectiveness and facilitative responding. *Journal of Counseling Psychology, 25*, 454–460.

Gomes, W. B. (1981). *The communicational-relational system in two forms of family group composition* (Unpublished master's thesis). Southern Illinois University, Carbondale.

Gore, E. J. (1985). *An objective measure of belief systems.* Doctoral dissertation, University of Colorado, Boulder. UMI dissertations publishing 8608604.

Grabham, A. R. (1970). *Phenomenal self-esteem as a criterion of mental health: A comparison of delinquent and 'normal' adolescent boys* (Unpublished master's thesis). University of Waterloo, Ontario.

Greenberg, L. S., & Geller, S. M. (2001). Congruence and therapeutic presence. In Wyatt, G. (Ed.), *Rogers' therapeutic conditions: Evolution, theory and practice. Vol 1: Congruence* (pp. 131–149). Ross-on-Wye: PCCS Books.

Griffin, E. J. (1977/1978). A study of effects of a curriculum-centered college reading course and an affectively oriented curriculum focused course on reading achievement and attitude toward reading. *Dissertation Abstracts International, 38-A*, 6496. University Microfilms No. 71–24372.

Griffin, R. W. (1967/1968). Change in perception of marital relationship as related to marital counseling. *Dissertation Abstracts International, 27-A*, 3956. University Microfilms No. 67–6466.

Gross, W. F., Curtin, M. E., & Moore, K.B. (1970). Appraisal of a milieu therapy environment by treatment team and patients. *Journal of Clinical Psychology, 26,* 541–545.

Gross, W. F., and DeRidder, L. M. (1966). Significant movement in comparatively short term counseling. *Journal of Counseling Psychology, 13,* 98–99.

Gurman, A. S. (1977). The patient's perception of the therapeutic relationship. In A. S. Gurman and A. M. Razin (Eds.), *Effective psychotherapy: A handbook of research* (pp. 503–543). Oxford/New York: Pergamon.

Halkides, G. (1958). *An investigation of therapeutic success as a function of four variables* (Unpublished doctoral dissertation). University of Chicago.

Hall, K. E. (1972/1973). The effects of a teacher-led guidance program on selected personal and inter-personal variables among fourth grade pupils. *Dissertation Abstracts International, 33-A,* 1436. University Microfilms No. 72-27,194.

Handley, P. (1982). Relationship between supervisors' and trainees' cognitive style and the supervision process. *Journal of Counseling Psychology, 29,* 508–515.

Hart, K. L. (2005/2006). An initial study of attachment style and its relationship to perception of therapist empathy. *Dissertation Abstracts International, 66 (4-B),* 2307.

Hermans, H. J. M., & Hermans-Konopka, A. (2010). *Dialogical self-theory: Positioning and counter-positioning in a globalizing society.* New York: Cambridge University Press.

Hines, M. H., & Hummel, T. J. (1988). The effects of three training methods on the empathic ability, perceived spousal empathy, and marital satisfaction of married couples. *Person-Centered Review, 3,* 316–336.

Holland, D. A. (1976). *The Relationship Inventory: Experimental Form OS-S–42: A validity study* (Unpublished honors bachelor's thesis). University of Waterloo, Ontario.

Hollenbeck, G. P. (1961). The use of the Relationship Inventory in the prediction of adjustment and achievement. (Doctoral dissertation, University of Wisconsin). *Dissertation Abstracts, 22 (6),* 2063–2064. University Microfilms No. 61-5940.

Hollenbeck, G.P. (1965). Conditions and outcomes in the student-parent relationship. *Journal of Consulting Psychology, 29,* 237–241.

Hornblow, A. R., Kidson, M. A., & Jones, K. V. (1977). Measuring medical student's empathy: A validation study. *Medical Education, 11,* 7–12.

Hough, S. (2001). The difficulties in the conceptualisation of congruence: A way forward with complexity theory? In Wyatt, G. (Ed.), *Rogers' therapeutic conditions: Evolution, theory and practice. Vol 1: Congruence* (pp. 116–130). Ross-on-Wye: PCCS Books.

Hummel, M. H., & Hummel, T. J. (1988). The effects of three training methods on the empathic ability, perceived spousal empathy, and marital satisfaction of married couples. *Person-Centered Review, 3,* 316–336.

Iberg, J. R. (2001). Unconditional positive regard: Constituent activities. In J. D. Bozarth & P. Wilkins (Eds.), *Rogers' therapeutic conditions: Evolution, theory and practice. Vol 3: Unconditional positive regard* (pp. 109–125). Ross-on-Wye: PCCS Books.

Jaeger, T. K. (1989). Principal/teacher interpersonal relations and school climate. *Dissertation Abstracts International, 49,* 3571A.

James, W. (1890/1950). *The principles of psychology* (Vol. 1). New York: Henry Holt & Co.

Junek, W., Burra, P., & Leichner, P. (1979). Teaching interviewing skills by encountering patients. *Journal of Medical Education, 54,* 402–407.

Kagan, M. (1968). *A study of selected dimensions of the field instructor-student relationship* (Doctoral dissertation). University of Minnesota. *University Microfilms* No. 68-12,265.

Koffka, K. (1935). *Principles of Gestalt psychology.* London: Kegan Paul.

Kouzes, J. M., & Posner, B. Z. (1993). Psychometric properties of the Leadership Practices Inventory – updated. *Educational and Psychological Measurement, 53,* 191–199.

Kramer, R. (1997). *Leading by listening: An empirical test of Carl Rogers' theory of human relationship using interpersonal assessments of leaders by followers.* (Doctoral dissertation, School of Business & Public Management) George Washington University.

Kurtz, R. R., & Grummon, D. L. (1972). Different approaches to the measurement of therapist empathy and their relationship to therapy outcomes. *Journal of Consulting and Clinical Psychology, 37,* 106–115.

La Crosse, M. B. (1977). Comparative perceptions of counselor behavior: A replication and extension. *Journal of Counseling Psychology, 24,* 464–471.

Lafferty, P., Beutler, L. E., & Crago, M. (1989). Differences between more and less effective psychotherapists: A study of select therapist variables. *Journal of Consulting and Clinical Psychology, 57,* 76–80.

Libby, G. W. (1974/1975). Source of referral, type of program, and the initial teacher-pupil relationship in selected resource programs for the child with emotional difficulties. *Dissertation Abstracts International, 35-A*, 5172.

Lietaer, G. (1974). Nederlandstalige revisie van Barrett-Lennard's Relationship Inventory: Een factoranalytische benadering van de student-ouderrelatie. *Nederlands Tijdschrift voor de Psychologie, 29*, 191–212.

Lietaer, G. (1976). Nederlandstalige revisie van Barrett-Lennard's Relationship Inventory voor individueel-terapentische relaties. *Psychologica Belgica, 16*, 73–94.

Lietaer, G. (1984). Unconditional positive regard: A controversial basic attitude in client-centered therapy. In R. F. Levant & J. M. Shlien (Eds.), *Client-centered therapy and the person-centered approach: New directions in theory, research and practice* (pp. 41–58). New York: Praeger.

Lietaer, G. (1993). Authenticity, congruence and transparency. In D. Brazier (Ed.), *Beyond Carl Rogers* (pp. 17–46). London: Constable.

Lietaer, G. (2001). Being genuine as a therapist: Congruence and transparency. In Wyatt, G. (Ed.), *Rogers' therapeutic conditions: Evolution, theory and practice. Vol 1: Congruence* (pp. 36–54). Ross-on-Wye: PCCS Books.

Linville, P. W. (1987). Self-complexity as a cognitive buffer against stress-related illness and depression. *Journal of Personality and Social Psychology, 52*(4), 663–676.

Lipkin, S. (1954). Client's feelings and attitudes in relation to the outcome of client-centered therapy. *Psychological Monographs, 68*(1), Whole No. 372.

Luber, R. F., & Wells, R. A. (1977). Structured short-term multiple family therapy: An educational approach. *International Journal of Group Psychotherapy, 27*, 43–58.

Madrid, M. (1993). Psychological type among nurses' and patients' perception of received empathy. (Doctoral dissertation). New York University, *University Microfilms 9333912*.

Marci, C. D., Ham, J., Moran, E., & Orr, S. P. (2007). Physiologic correlates of perceived therapist empathy and social-emotional process during psychotherapy. *Journal of Nervous & Mental Disease, 195*(2), 103–111.

Marques-Teixeira, J., Pires de Carvalho, M. M., Moreira, A. M., and Pinho, C. (1996). "Group effect?" Implementation of the Portuguese translation of the Barrett-Lennard Inventory on five group types. In R. Hutterer, G. Pawlowsky, P. F. Schmid, & R. Stipsits (Eds.), *Client-centered and experiential psychotherapy: A paradigm in motion* (pp. 585–598). Frankfurt am Main: Peter Lang.

Mason, J., & Blumberg, A. (1969). Perceived educational value of the classroom and teacher-pupil interpersonal relationships. *Journal of Secondary Education, 44*, 135–139.

McKitrick, D. S., & Gelso, C. J. (1978). Initial client expectancies in time-limited counseling. *Journal of Counseling Psychology, 25*, 246–249.

McNeill, P. (2014). Duet for life: Is alexithymia a key note in couples' empathy, emotional connection, relationship dissatisfaction, and therapy outcomes? (Unpublished doctoral dissertation). Edith Cowan University, Western Australia.

Mearns, D. (1999). Person-centred therapy with configurations of self. *Counselling*, May, 125–130.

Melchior, W. C. (1981). The effects of counselor and observer gender, empathy level and voice inflection upon observers' perceptions and evaluations of counselors' communication. *Dissertation Abstracts International, 41*, 3013-A.

Messina, I., Palmieri, A., Sambin, M., Roland, J., Voci, A., & Calvo, V. (2013). Somatic underpinnings of perceived empathy: The importance of psychotherapy training. *Psychotherapy Research, 23*(2), 169–177.

Moon, K., Rice, B., & Schneider , C. (2001). Stanley W. Standal and the need for positive regard. In J. D. Bozarth & P. Wilkins (Eds.), *Rogers' therapeutic conditions: Evolution, theory and practice. Vol. 3: Unconditional positive regard* (pp. 19–34). Ross-on-Wye: PCCS Books.

Mozak, H. (1950). *Evaluation in psychotherapy: A study of some current measures* (Unpublished doctoral dissertation). University of Chicago.

Murphy, K. C. & Strong, S. R. (1972). Some effects of similarity self-disclosure. *Journal of Counselling Psychology, 19*, 121–124.

Myers, S. A. (1995). *Contextualizing empathy: A relational study* (Doctoral dissertation). Harvard University, Cambridge, MA.

O'Connor, P. (1989). Service in nursing: Correlates of patient satisfaction. *Dissertation Abstracts International, 50-B*, 4985.

O'Donohue, W., & Fisher, J. E. (2009). *General principles and empirically supported techniques of cognitive behavior therapy*. Hoboken, NJ: Wiley.

Persaud, S. D. (2002). *Nursing graduates' perceptions of caring relationships with nursing faculty* (Unpublished Master of Science thesis). D'Youville College. New York.

Prouty, G. (1994). *Theoretical evolutions in person-centered/experiential therapy: Applications to schizophrenic and retarded psychoses*. Westport, CT: Praeger.

Purton, C. (1998). Unconditional positive regard and its spiritual implications. In B. Thorne and E. Lambers (Eds.), *Person-centred therapy: A European perspective* (pp. 23–37). London: Sage.

Quick, E., & Jacob, T. (1973). Marital disturbance in relation to role theory and relationship theory. *Journal of Abnormal Psychology, 82*, 309–316.

Quinn, O. (1950). *Psychotherapists' expressions as an index to the quality of early therapeutic relationships established by representatives of the nondirective, Adlerian, and psychoanalytic schools* (Unpublished doctoral dissertation). University of Chicago.

Rank, O. (1936/1945). *Will therapy* and *Truth and reality* (single volume ed.). New York: Knopf.

Ranney, E. C. (1995). *The relationship between childhood sexual abuse and empathy levels in late adolescent and adult women* (Unpublished doctoral dissertation). St Louis University, St Louis, MO.

Raskin, N. J. (1948). The development of non-directive psychotherapy. *Journal of Consulting Psychology, 12*, 92–110.

Raskin, N. J. (1949). An analysis of the six parallel studies of the therapeutic process. *Journal of Consulting Psychology, 13*, 206–219.

Rimm, D. C., & Cunningham, H. M. (1985). Behavior therapies. In S. J Lynn & J. P. Garske. *Contemporary psychotherapies: Models and methods* (pp. 221–259). Columbus, OH: Merrill (Bell & Howell).

Riso, L. P., Pieter, L du T., Stein, D. J., & Young, J. E. (2007). *Cognitive schemas and core beliefs in psychological problems: A scientist-practitioner guide*. Washington, DC: American Psychological Association.

Rodríguez Irizarry, A. M. (1993). *Los estilos de comunicacion verbales y no verbales del consejero y la percepcion de empatia del cliente* [Verbal and nonverbal communication styles and the perception of empathy] (Unpublished doctoral dissertation). University of Puerto Rico.

Rogers, C. R. (1939). *The clinical treatment of the problem child*. Boston, MA: Houghton Mifflin.

Rogers, C. R. (1942). *Counseling and psychotherapy: Newer concepts in practice*. Boston, MA: Houghton Mifflin.

Rogers, C. R. (1946). Significant aspects of client-centered therapy. *American Psychologist, 1*, 415–422.

Rogers, C. R. (1949). The attitude and orientation of the counselor in client-centered therapy. *Journal of Consulting Psychology, 13*, 82–94.

Rogers, C. R. (1951). *Client-centered therapy*. Boston, MA: Houghton Mifflin.

Rogers, C. R. (1953). Some directions and end points in therapy. In O. H. Mowrer (Ed.), *Psychotherapy: Theory and research* (pp. 44–68). New York: Ronald.

Rogers, C. R. (1954). The case of Mrs. Oak: A research analysis. In C. R. Rogers & R. F. Dymond (Eds.), *Psychotherapy and personality change* (pp. 259–348). Chicago: University of Chicago Press.

Rogers, C. R. (1956). Client-centered therapy: A current view. In F. Fromm-Reichmann and J. L. Moreno (Eds.), *Progress in Psychotherapy, Volume 1* (pp. 199–209). New York: Grune & Stratton.

Rogers, C. R. (1957). The necessary and sufficient conditions of therapeutic personality change. *Journal of Consulting Psychology, 21*, 95–103.

Rogers, C. R. (1958). A process conception of psychotherapy. *American Psychologist, 13*, 142–149.

Rogers, C. R. (1959a). A theory of therapy, personality, and interpersonal relationships as developed in the client-centered framework. In S. Koch (Ed.), *Psychology: A study of a science. Vol. 3: Formulations of the person and social context* (pp. 184–256). New York: McGraw-Hill.

Rogers, C. R. (1959b). A tentative scale for the measurement of process in psychotherapy. In E. A. Rubinstein & M. B. Parloff (Eds.), *Research in psychotherapy* (pp. 96–107). Washington, DC: American Psychological Association.

Rogers, C. R. (1961). A theory of psychotherapy with schizophrenics and a proposal for its empirical investigation. In J. G. Dawson, H. K. Stone, & N. P. Dellis (Eds.), *Psychotherapy with schizophrenics* (pp. 3–19). Baton Rouge: Louisiana State University Press.

Rogers, C. R. (1975). Empathic: An unappreciated way of being. *The Counselling Psychologist, 5*(2), 2–11.

Rogers, C. R., & Dymond, R. F. (Eds.). (1954). *Psychotherapy and personality change*. Chicago: University of Chicago Press.

Rogers, C. R. with Gendlin, E. T., Kiesler, T. J., & Truax, C. B. (Eds.). (1967). *The therapeutic relationship and its impact: A study of psychotherapy with schizophrenics*. Madison: University of Wisconsin Press.

Rosen, H. H. (1961). *Dimensions of the perceived parent-relationship as related to juvenile delinquency* (Unpublished master's thesis). Auburn University, Alabama.

Salvio, M., Beutler, L. E., Wood, J. M., & Engle, D. (1992). The strength of the therapeutic alliance in three treatments for depression. *Psychotherapy Research, 2*(1), 31–36.

Scheuer, A. L. (1969). A study of the relationship between personal attributes and effectiveness in teachers of the emotionally disturbed and socially maladjusted in a residential school setting (Doctoral dissertation). Columbia University. *University Microfilms*, No. 70-12,568.

Scheuer, A. L. (1971). The relationship between personal attributes and effectiveness in teachers of the emotionally disturbed. *Exceptional Children, 38*, 723–731.

Seay, T. A., & Altekruse, M. K. (1979). Verbal and nonverbal behavior in judgements of facilitative conditions. *Journal of Counseling Psychology, 26*, 108–119.

Seeman, J. (1989). Toward a model of positive health. *American Psychologist, 44*, 1099–1109.

Seeman, J. (2001). On congruence: A human system paradigm. In G. Wyatt (Ed.), *Rogers' therapeutic conditions: Evolution, theory and practice. Vol. 1: Congruence* (pp. 200–212). Ross-on-Wye: PCCS Books.

Simmons, J., Roberge, L., Kenrick, S. B., & Richards, B. (1995). The interpersonal relationship in clinical practice: The Barrett-Lennard Relationship Inventory as an assessment instrument. *Evaluation and the Health Professions, 18*(1), 103–112.

Skinner, B. F. (1953). *Science and human behaviour.* New York: Free Press.

Skinner, B. F. (1974). *About behaviorism.* New York: Knopf.

Smetko, J. A. (1982/1983). Student perceived facilitation as a correlate of academic achievement, academic self-concept and self-concept among inner city seventh and eighth graders. *Dissertation Abstracts International, 43*, 1902-A. *University Microfilms,* No. DA8226021.

Snelbecker, G. E. (1967). Influence of therapeutic techniques on college students' perceptions of therapists. *Journal of Consulting Psychology, 31*, 614–618.

Soldwisch, S. S. (1990). *An examination of the association between caring in nursing and Erikson's epigenetic theory* (Doctoral dissertation). University of Wisconsin-Madison (UMI no. 9024792).

Solomon, L. N., Berzon, B., & Weedman, C. (1968). The programmed group: A new rehabilitation resource. *International Journal of Group Psychotherapy, 18*, 199–219.

Spence, S. A. (1988/1989). The presence of and relationships between helping elements and task steps in post-observation supervisory conferences. *Dissertation Abstracts International, 49-A*, 2887–2888.

Spotts, J. E. (1965/1966). Some effects of exposure to a psychotherapy rating task in teachers of emotionally disturbed adolescents. *Dissertation Abstracts, 26*, 5553B.

Standal, S. (1954). *The need for positive regard: A contribution to client-centered theory* (Unpublished doctoral dissertation). University of Chicago.

Standal, S. W., & Van der Veen, F. (1957) Length of therapy in relation to counselor estimates of personal integration and other case variables. *Journal of Consulting Psychology, 21*, 1–9.

Stephenson, W. (1953). *The study of behavior: Q-technique and its methodology.* Chicago: University of Chicago Press.

Stephenson, W. (1980). Newton's fifth rule and Q methodology: Application to educational psychology. *American Psychologist, 35*, 882–889.

Sundaram, D. K. (1977). Psychological adjustment as a function of interpersonal relationships: A field study. *Dissertation Abstracts International, 37*, 5380–5381B.

Taft, J. (1933). *The dynamics of therapy in a controlled relationship.* New York: Macmillan.

Taylor, J. A. (1953). A personality scale of manifest anxiety. *Journal of Abnormal and Social Psychology, 48*, 285–290.

Thompson, J. M. (1967/1968). The relationship between Carl Rogers' helping relationship concept and teacher behavior. *Dissertation Abstracts, 28*, 2524–2525A. University Microfilms, No. 68-15.

Thompson, J. M. (1969). The effect of pupil characteristics upon pupil perception of the teacher. *Psychology in the Schools, 6*(2), 206–211.

Thornton, B. M. (1960). *Dimensions of perceived relationship as related to marital adjustment* (Unpublished master's thesis). Auburn University, Alabama.

Tolan, J. (2003). *Skills in person-centred counselling and psychotherapy.* London: Sage.

Tosi, D. J. (1970). Dogmatism within the client-counselor dyad. *Journal of Counseling Psychology, 17*, 284–288.

Townsend, M. E. (1988). *Self-disclosure and psychological adjustment: Towards an understanding* (Unpublished bachelor's thesis). Monash University, Melbourne.

Van der Veen, F. (1961). The perception by clients and by judges of the conditions offered by the therapist in the therapy relationship. *Wisconsin Psychiatric Institute Bulletin, 1* (10e).

Van der Veen F. (1970). Client perception of therapist conditions as a factor in psychotherapy. In J. T. Hart and T. M. Tomlinson (Eds.), *New directions in client-centered therapy* (pp. 214–222). Boston, MA: Houghton Mifflin.

Van der Veen, F. and Novak, A. L. (1971). Perceived parental attitudes and family concepts of disturbed adolescents, normal siblings and normal controls. *Family Process, 10*, 327–343.

Van Kampen, K. L. (2011). *Contextual variability in sense of self: a thematic analysis of individuals' experiences whilst completing the Contextual Selves Inventory* (Unpublished bachelor's thesis). Murdoch University, Perth.

VanSteenwegan, A. (1979). Residentiële partnerrelatie-therapie: Een evaluatie-onderzoek. *Tijdschrift voor Psychiatrie, 21*, 426–440.

VanSteenwegan, A. (1982). Intensive psycho-educational couple therapy: Therapeutic program and outcome research results. *Cahiers des Sciences Familiales et Sexologiques,* No. 5. De L'Universite Catholique de Louvain.

Vargas, M. J. (1954). Changes in self-awareness during client-centered therapy. In C. R. Rogers & R. F. Dymond (Eds.), Psychotherapy and personality change (pp. 145–166). Chicago: University of Chicago Press.

Verwaaijen, A. A. G. (1990). Therapist behaviour in the treatment of families with adolescent girls at risk of placement (Unpublished doctoral dissertation), Catholic University, Nijmegen, Netherlands.

Walker, A. M., Rablen, R. A., & Rogers, C. R. (1960). Development of a scale to measure process changes in psychotherapy. *Journal of Clinical Psychology, 16*(1), 79–85.

Walker, B. S., & Little, D. F. (1969). Factor analysis of the Barrett-Lennard Relationship Inventory. *Journal of Counseling Psychology, 16,* 516–521.

Wampler, K. S., & Powell, G. S. (1982). The Barrett-Lennard Relationship Inventory as a measure of marital satisfaction. *Family Relations, 31,* 139–145.

Wampler, K. S., & Sprenkle, D. H. (1980). The Minnesota Couple Communication Program: A follow-up study. *Journal of Marriage and the Family, 42,* 577–584.

Wargo, D. G., & Meek, V. C. (1970/1971) The Relationship Inventory as a measure of milieu perception in rehabilitation centre students. *Rehabilitation Counseling Bulletin, 14,* 42–48.

Watts, P. S. (1989). *Utilisation of the Relationship Inventory: The development and evaluation of a computer form, and its application to couple relationships* (Unpublished master's thesis). Murdoch University, Perth.

Wedding, D., & Corsini, R. J. (Eds.). (2001). *Case studies in psychotherapy* (third edition). Illinois: Peacock Publishers.

Weir, N. L. (2011). *Stability within the variability of a contextual self* (Unpublished Bachelor of Psychology thesis). Murdoch University, Perth.

Wells, R. A., Figurel, J. A., & McNamee, P. (1975). Group facilitative training with married couples. In A. S. Gurman and D. G. Rice (Eds.), *Couples in conflict: New directions in marital therapy.* New York: Jason Aronson.

Weston, T. (2011). *The clinical effectiveness of the person-centred psychotherapies: Impact of the therapeutic relationship* (Unpublished doctoral dissertation). University of East Anglia.

Wiebe, B. (1975). Self-disclosure and perceived relationships of Mennonite adolescents in senior high school. *Dissertation Abstracts International, 35,* 6472A. University Microfilms No. 75–9105.

Wilkins, P. (2000). Unconditional positive regard reconsidered. *British Journal of Guidance and Counselling, 28*(1), 23–36.

Withers, L. E., & Wantz, R. A. (1993). The influence of belief systems on subjects' perceptions of empathy, warmth, and genuineness. *Psychotherapy, 30,* 608–615.

Wolpe, J. (1973). *The practice of behavior therapy.* Oxford: Pergamon.

Zec, C. (2011). Multiple selves and the ideal: Variability in the self-concept and its implications for female self-esteem (Unpublished bachelor's thesis). Murdoch University, Perth.

Zuroff, D. C., & Blatt, S. J. (2006). The therapeutic relationship in the brief treatment of depression: Contributions to clinical improvement and enhanced adaptive capacities. *Journal of Consulting and Clinical Psychology, 74,* 130–140.

Zuroff, D. C., Blatt, S. J., Kelly, A. C., Leybman, M. J., & Wampbold, B. E. (2010). Between-therapist and within-therapist differences in the quality of the therapeutic relationship: Effects on maladjustment and self-critical perfectionism. *Journal of Clinical Psychology, 66,* 681–697.

Index*

---

*See References for a full listing of the names of authors and investigators cited in this book.